China
and the New World Order

How Entrepreneurship, Globalization, and Borderless Business Are Reshaping China and the World

by

George Zhibin Gu

author of *China's Global Reach* and *Made in China*

Foreword

Fast-Moving China and Global Development

by

William Ratliff

Fultus™ Books

China and the New World Order

How Entrepreneurship, Globalization, and Borderless Business Are Reshaping China and the World

by

George Zhibin Gu

ISBN 1-59682-107-8

Published by Fultus Corporation

Corporate Web Site: *http://www.fultus.com*
Fultus eLibrary: *http://elibrary.fultus.com*
Online Book Superstore: *http://store.fultus.com*
Writer Web Site *http://writers.fultus.com/gu/*

Table of Contents

Foreword.
Fast-Moving China and Global Development

by William Ratliff

China has traveled light years during the past three decades. After Mao Zedong died in 1976 and the Chinese people step by step became freer to cultivate their entrepreneurial inclinations to improve their lives, China has seemed to be a film spinning ahead in fast-forward. Images flash before the eyes, but before you can really focus they have been replaced by others and yet others.

Vast Changes in China

On his last visit to China in 2003, Cuba's dictator Fidel Castro blinked and openly wondered where he had landed, things were so different from his previous trip several years earlier. But others too have found the images of the changing China a challenge to assimilate and interpret. Outsiders often look toward the Middle Kingdom and ask, what is going on? What does it all mean? Is all of this good for the Chinese people, and for the rest of us?

The China Deng Xiaoping took over in the late 1970s was staggering and moribund at home and a pariah worldwide in the wake of the nation-devouring recriminations and outrages of the Cultural Revolution. Whether from conviction or panic to preserve the discredited Communist Party, or both, Deng opened the door to some truly revolutionary economic change, and the spin-off over time has gone far beyond the economic field.

One critical step in his campaign occurred in 1980 when he created several Special Economic Zones (SEZs), which are geographically confined laboratory-cities for experimenting with market-oriented economic reforms as well as engagement with the outside world. The most important of these SEZs was down south, just across the border from the then-British-controlled Hong Kong, a place Nobel laureate economist Milton Friedman has often called the freest market in the world. The name of the overnight city that sprang up was Shenzhen.

No tiny region on earth has ever attracted so much foreign direct investment in such a short time as Shenzhen, over U.S.$60 billion. Never has any city in so short a time attracted so many people who were not just fleeing hard times in rural regions but actually all fired up to succeed.

The city has grown an average of about 27% annually since it became a SEZ, and many of the 12 million who now live there have prospered. Many others, often in their teens and twenties, have worked very long hours under miserable conditions and barely survived, though they usually earned a little more than they ever had back home in their villages. Thus Shenzhen is China writ small, though conditions are at very different stages throughout the vast country.

George Zhibin Gu was one of over 12 million Chinese to move to Shenzhen, the epicenter of change. He was born in Xian, the heartland of vast expanses of Chinese history and governments, and got his university training in Nanjing and the United States. He proceeded to move into the most anti-Maoist of all professions, namely investment banking and business consulting.

A Unique Guide

No one I know of has come so close to capturing the spirit and meaning of an explosively changing China as Gu. When you read about Shenzhen and the other topics of this book, ranging from bank and stock market reform to new Chinese multinationals on the world stage to the need for a federation of the mainland and Taiwan, you are as good as parachuting into Chinese cities, businesses, sweatshops, and policy discussions. You become immersed in the tiny but persistent realities of individual and group successes and failures, in the battles over reform, money, and power, and you feel the elation and frustration of the Chinese people in their widely varying human conditions.

You also encounter the global issues raised by China's rise that affect people worldwide almost as much as they do the Chinese themselves. Even people around the world who can hardly find China on the map know that the civilization has a very long history and ancient traditions. Many know that it has not done well in recent decades, even centuries, but that things are changing.

An old joke used to be that the only poor Chinese in the world were the Chinese who lived in China because there government repression sapped them of the will and opportunity to really better their lives and thus the conditions and prospects of the country. This is no longer true, though many remain poor. Today, upward mobility is becoming a reality inside the nation.

But the outside world has more direct experience with the overseas Chinese. Chinese who moved or escaped abroad, whether to Hong Kong or Singapore, to the United States or Panama, were often highly successful in small and large businesses and other professions demanding a dedication to education, hard work, and raising one's status in life. Throughout the English-speaking world today, and in some respects this includes China itself, we find Chinese students working 18-hour days and excelling in every field they enter.

Key Challenges Ahead

Despite China's astonishing and continuous progress from the end of the Mao era to today, major challenges remain. Gu often focuses on bureaucracies, which, as he asserts, essentially frame China's politics, society, business, and economy.

China has relied on bureaucracies for millennia, and Mao picked up where the earlier emperors had left off. He created the largest bureaucracy in the history of humankind and one that took control of every aspect of every person's life everywhere in the country. And though during the Cultural Revolution Mao and the Gang of Four killed hundreds of thousands and demolished much of what the Communist government up to then had created, the bureaucracy, in modified form, persists in power to this day.

Gu argues that even though government leaders have permitted great change, which originally flowed from the initiative of some peasants and others shortly after Mao's death, this bureaucracy is the chief impediment to completing the revolution. It seeks to retain power, setting up one of the ironies of the Mao legacy.

The Great Helmsman used to urge people to strive tirelessly to overcome seemingly insurmountable odds by referring to the ancient Chinese fable of the Foolish Old Man Who Removed the Mountains.

Now the mountain that stands in the way of completing the current and real revolution in China, Gu argues, is above all the corrupt and self-serving bureaucracy. Though the government has allowed economic reforms, it still tries to be both "player" and "referee" in the marketplace.

Seen through the lenses of Chinese history, truly revolutionary change is indeed under way throughout the country, but it can be completed only through a drastic curtailment of the continuing power of the government over so many aspects of national and daily life. The change now must come through ever-greater individual private initiative, an increasingly open society, and international involvement.

Over the past quarter century China has awakened and, as Napoleon warned, it is and will continue shaking the world. But is this a good thing for China, and for the world?

Gu argues that this phenomenal growth of China, this awakening, is not something for the world to fear, but rather an opportunity and also a challenge. He argues that progress in the modern world is not patented by the currently developed countries, but available to all peoples who are willing and able to work hard for it. The developed world itself will benefit from the advancement of the late developers.

If you want to immerse yourself in the awakening of modern China, take George Gu with you as your guide. With him along you are not leaping dizzily into the frames of the fast-forwarding story, for you have an experienced and articulate guide who fills in facts and at least as importantly adds insights into what is happening, why it matters, and what it feels like to be there in the middle of it all.

I have traveled extensively in China for many years and I relive many things that I have seen and heard and felt over the decades in every page of Gu's book. And I learn a lot that is new to me too.

William Ratliff
Fellow and Curator
Hoover Institution
Stanford University

Acknowledgments

I am very grateful to the following media outlets for providing highly valuable forums: *Asia Times, Beijing Review, The Seoul Times, Financial Sense, Gurus Online,* World Association of International Studies, *Publico Daily, Expresso Weekly, Money Week, Online Opinion, Asia Venture Capital Journal, Centro Atlantico Magazine,* and *Sinomania,* among others.

I must express my sincere appreciation and gratitude to all the editors, especially David Lenard of *Asia Times,* Professor Ronald Hilton of Stanford University and World Association of International Studies, and Jorge Nascimento Rodrigues of *Gurus Online,* for encouragement and help. I must further thank all the people I interviewed for this book.

I am most grateful to Professor William Ratliff of the Hoover Institution and Stanford University for his encouragement as well as the Foreword. I also thank Professor Joyce Sexton of Madison, Wisconsin, for editorial help.

My deep appreciation also goes to my wife, Chen Liang, who sacrificed for many years as this and two other books were produced.

Introduction.
A New World Order in the Making?

Is a new world order in the making? The answer: yes. Up to now, only about 20% of the world's people have attained solid development, growth, and modernity. Now the rest are catching up at an unprecedented speed. This sudden surge in so many late developers suggests a brave new world in the making.

What has promoted this new life? It is entrepreneurial work above all. For a long time, the United States has been a haven for entrepreneurs; today, entrepreneurs are emerging everywhere. China alone has some 40 million entrepreneurs. Never before has the world seen so vast an army of entrepreneurs in pursuit of prosperity at the same time.

Equally significant, record-breaking flows of capital, humans, goods, ideas, and technology are in place. Things are happening with a much greater speed and scale.

One other basic change is that the late-emerging nations like China, India, Vietnam, and Mexico have increasingly become manufacturing and business centers, though on the low end at this time. Increasingly, the developed world, as in the United States and Western Europe, is becoming a service and high-tech economy while the developing world focuses more on manufacturing.

In fact, the world has entered a new era, that of a convergence of global civilizations. All nations increasingly rely on one another in countless ways. Despite all the worries and conflicts, this trend will only strengthen. In short, from very divergent movements in the past, the world now embraces a convergent movement for the first time in human history.

The Residence of Fortunes

One great puzzle of all time is this: Fortunes never stay in one place for long. Rather, different regions have moved ahead at different times. Europe was in poverty for thousands of years while China enjoyed an advanced life characterized by abundant goodies, technological progress, and prosperity.

For ages, a typical Chinese had more material things to enjoy in life than his or her European counterpart. The great Chinese cities far exceeded European cities in comfort and prosperity. The vast volumes of Chinese poetry, philosophy, and writing on the arts of living had no equal in the world until recent times. Some 500 years ago, European farmers used wooden sticks to plow the land while Chinese farmers employed steel tools as well as fertilizers.

When Marco Polo (1254-1324) came to China, he was amazed by the riches of the East, though China was at relatively a low point at the time. Even very simple things such as the fact that the Chinese had chairs, tables, and plenty of meat to eat impressed Polo in no small way, as such things were uncommon in the old Europe. His fantastic tales about a prosperous East stirred up the poor Europeans like thunder. Two centuries later, men like Columbus sailed off to get to the riches of the East.

This great European openness and sense of discovery turned fortunes toward the West for centuries. The industrial revolution produced more wealth than ever before. As a result, the global production map was altered in favor of the West.

By the 19th century, the British islands dominated global politics and commerce, with the biggest and best industries as well as maritime fleets that explored the world. Traditional farming societies like China and India had little advantage in competition with this new power. As a result, these nations simply chose to close their doors to fend off Western expansionists.

In turn, for the last 100 years or so, the United States has had the biggest influence. The United States has become a haven for upward mobility as well as a vast middle class. Its enormous wealth has become the marvel of the world.

Is the wind of fortune changing now? No one can truly foretell the future, but the quick upward movement in numerous late-developing nations is indicative of a major shift in the making. Above all, this fast-expanding pie offers the world unprecedented opportunities.

Several Key Changes

Huge changes are happening, within a vastly expanded sphere for all people and nations. We can identify four in particular.

First, wealth making through industrialization and commercialization has become a universal thing. For a long time, products made in the United Kingdom, the United States, and Germany dominated global markets. Today, products made in China, Mexico, Vietnam, and Indonesia, among other developing nations, are increasingly flooding the world, changing the global production map again.

Behind this changing map, interestingly, many poor nations have rapidly taken on active roles in the global economy. But their biggest weapon remains low-cost labor, which provides a working platform for cooperation and sharing between the rich and poor nations.

Today, most developing nations are extremely limited in resources and strengths. Hence, for them, this cost gap is a survival gap. In fact, other than cheap labor and hard work, they have few advantages. However, it turns out that low labor cost and hard work do make a difference.

For now, manufacturing activities, especially in the low end of the value chains, increasingly shift to the poor nations, while the developed nations focus more and more on a service and high-tech-oriented economy. This giant change, though only beginning, will impact the future world economy even more.

Second, all regional markets are connected to each other. Interdependence is opening up the old national boundaries dramatically. Most profoundly, the flows of capital, technology, goods, and people have reached a new level. Moving from survival of the fittest to rational collaboration and sharing, life on the earth will never be the same again.

Third, wealth making has gained a record-high status. Consequently, old ideology is lost to the new economic waves. This is a truly golden age for capitalists anywhere, who can reach all corners of the world for the first time in human history.

Multinationals are gaining unprecedented power in shaping global life. Their share of trade approaches 50% and is still on the rise. Actually, they are warmly courted by all nations, rich or poor. Courting them has become a high art for all governments. The new picture is this: Incentives move the world—not politics, not ideology, not empty words.

Fourth, hundreds of millions of ordinary people everywhere have joined the entrepreneurial army. Starting a business is no longer for the privileged few as in the past, especially in the developing nations. Furthermore, individual private initiatives are undermining state domination especially in many less developed nations. This is hugely significant especially given that traditional bureaucratic powers in many developing nations have been strong and abusive.

Above all, such changes have happened within a short time, which is possible only in an increasingly globalized world. Naturally, more consequences will follow.

Interdependence and Beyond

The sudden surge in late developers is bound to create ripple effects. Since well over 5 billion people are involved, development in these countries will be much more influential than ever before.

But this new growth for most late developers started from extremely low levels. As a result, achieving full development, growth, and modernity will take a long time. At present, China and many other late developers are still bogged down by countless mighty problems, which make transitions very painful to say the least.

The Role of the Developed World

Still, there is no way to overestimate the role of the developed world in what is happening. After all, the existing world order is centered on the developed nations. They collectively control most wealth and the biggest markets. As the pie expands, the few rich nations are the biggest beneficiaries. What is more, they continue to act as an engine of growth as well as a catalyst for change. Without doubt, the developed nations will continue to exert the biggest influences as time passes.

All things considered, the late developers should continue to learn from the developed countries, whose experiences and lessons are relevant in countless ways. After all, development is a human issue. In many ways, what is happening inside the developing nations simply follows the growth trails of the developed world.

For a long time, the idea of learning from the early developers did not get enough attention or even was rejected. Now, more people realize that development experiences are of universal value; this represents a basic change. It is this new spirit of learning that has directly promoted quick growth in many late developers. China is one example of making progress through learning.

Challenges

Challenges are plentiful as well. The vast development gaps remain a key challenge. New conflicts emerge everywhere. As one example, trade friction has increased sharply even though record-breaking trade has brought unprecedented opportunities and prosperity. To handle trade disputes, nationalistic protectionist measures are still widely used, and there is still a strong Cold War mentality.

Furthermore, the vast economic gaps have produced more adverse consequences. In particular, some extremists wish to address their woes by employing violence. The terrorist acts in New York City and London took place largely in this environment, showing, among other things, the urgent need to close development gaps.

Only after the underdeveloped nations gain reasonable growth and prosperity will the world walk out of the old traps of poverty and conflict. As a Chinese saying goes, "The way to protect the rich to the fullest is to help the poor gain a better life." Indeed, with a more progressive mindset, the developed world would be able to make more contributions to global development in the next stage.

Despite all the imperfections, the convergent movement of global civilizations cannot be reversed. A new world power balance will have to replace the old one. Furthermore, this new world order will emerge gradually and most likely indirectly. This is so simply because military conflicts in the old style will no longer do nations any good. Indeed, as more developing nations achieve progress, life on this planet will be more peaceful and rational.

China's New Lessons

China is moving, finally! The most significant change is that the nation's new development has taken place in an open, globalized world. By now, China has become a new global theater. As if overnight, this ancient land has taken on numerous new roles — as the biggest frontier market and a manufacturing hub, as well as a top trading nation and a top destination for foreign capital.

What is behind all the changes? To me, three new lessons are highly relevant.

First Lesson

China's first new lesson is that a truly meaningful development must depend on individual private initiative and entrepreneurial work, not government officialdom at all. China's new growth comes directly from a new entrepreneurial force, which makes a stunning contrast to the frozen life of the Mao era.

In the old days, the bureaucratic power had completely penetrated into all aspects of life. It totally controlled all businesses and all organizations. Furthermore, it arranged all people's lives according to its own needs. Even marriage or travel required official approvals. China's society and people suffocated in all sorts of ways (see Ch. 13 and 14).

This bureaucratic crusade destroyed human flourishing for decades. What is behind this bureaucratic wilderness? By its nature, China's self-appointed bureaucracy stands against the society and people. Squeezing has been its very purpose of existence.

For a long time, the bureaucratic aim was to get all the fish in the pond. To get the job done, it chose to pump out the water. Naturally, the dry pond failed to provide more fish. This greed led to vast destructions of all good things in life.

But one thing could not be destroyed — the entrepreneurial spirit. After 1978 a new environment emerged. The creative spirit immediately blossomed, which has led to vast changes in the nation and beyond.

By now there are some 40 million Chinese entrepreneurs. This private sector employs about 25% of the urban workforce and contributes about one third of the nation's economic output. Its further growth is all needed in order for China to escape the traps that kept the nation and people in the mud for long.

Second Lesson

The second lesson is that rational development must take place in an open society, the more open the better. Openness is the biggest enemy of bureaucratic power, but it does people and society all good. Above all, an open society frees people from all sorts of man-made barriers. Under openness, people can change their lives through their own efforts. In this era, upward mobility has gradually become possible. All this leads to a meaningful and productive society.

In the Mao era, China lived in a tightly closed society in which wild bureaucratic power squeezed hard on people. People had no rights to travel or to select a profession or place of residence, not to mention political rights. In this closed society, serving the bureaucracy was the only way of life. Poverty was the only consequence. In fact, tens of millions of people starved to death, not to mention about vast killings, which was a daily event in the Mao era.

In this era, an ever-increasing openness has changed countless things. Popular desires for prosperity have quickly proliferated. In an increasingly open environment, people's power is on the rise. Today, the Chinese people are much more productive, happier, and more confident than in the Mao era. Interestingly, in this new environment, a large burdensome population is turning into a creative and productive force. Though this development is still at a very early stage, it is bound to grow.

Development through openness is nothing new in world history. Old Europe was stuck in the mud for thousands of years under a rigid, closed society dominated by church-state. Upward mobility was impossible: Serfs remained serfs and aristocrats remained aristocrats. All this changed as openness was gradually embraced. Through this openness, and the resultant free flow of people, capital, and goods, Europe was able to decisively move away from the Dark Ages. After all the struggles, old Europe transformed itself into a progressive place.

Japan offers another kind of example. In the past half century or so, Japan has had huge outward economic expansion around the globe, but has kept its society and economy closed. The latter has backfired in the past two decades or so. As a result, Japan has lost much of its competitive edge. Today Japan is struggling toward more openness, which is badly needed in order for it to land on the growth path again.

Third Lesson

The third lesson is that a rational, sustainable development must involve the entire world. Evidently, nations with greater international participation see faster and healthier development, as is shown by China and India today. Without outside involvement, the water in the pond is dead and little happens. What is more, no sustainable development can take place without global involvement.

The United States is the biggest example of progress through global participation. Fundamentally, world involvement is behind the U.S. strength. For well over a century, the United States has outperformed the rest. This outstanding performance has relied on the entire world, which has supplied much of the requisite capital, labor, talent, natural resources, and technology.

Moreover, the United States remains the biggest destination for foreign direct investment now. In particular, foreign nations now hold many trillions of assets and debts in the United States. Increasingly the late-developing nations bring fresh capital into the U.S. market.

For example, China alone has some $300 billion invested in the U.S. debt and general market. This foreign capital is partly behind the prosperous lifestyle in the United States. Being an open society for the US attracts huge outside investments. If less foreign capital went into the United States, there would be vast negative effects.

Furthermore, the prosperity of the United States has relied on global markets. Today, the United States has the biggest crowd of multinationals, which have had the biggest influence around the world as a group. As a result, the U.S. economy has long led all others.

Today, China is just beginning to follow this path. An ever-increasingly open land is attracting more and more global talent, professional skills, capital, and goods. This foreign involvement is a necessity for China's development.

By early 2006, more than $640 billion in foreign direct capital had arrived in the nation. More than 560,000 overseas companies are established, which has helped to make China a top trading nation as well as a leading manufacturing center. In the Mao era, China's trade was next to nothing, but as of 2005 it had reached $1.42 trillion. What a difference!

Moreover, over 24 million Chinese work for overseas employers today. This massive foreign presence has impacted Chinese life in all sorts of ways. By now, the old state sector has been reduced to one-third of market share, while the domestic private sector and the overseas sector each take about another third. The foreign share is growing the fastest today and will very likely reach 50% of China's economy within a decade.

Furthermore, development feeds on development. A fast-developing China is attracting more international involvement. In turn, this helps to make China more open and dynamic. One can say that the new China is being transformed into a *Global China*. In short, the Chinese market, society, and life are already part of global life in spirit and practice.

In many ways, today's China is already more open than Japan. This greater openness will carry China forward positively. Though the reform started in business and economic areas, it now extends to political, institutional, and social areas as well. With this openness, the Chinese people are able to quickly walk out the deadly bureaucratic traps. Moreover, the nation is becoming a full and equal member in the global community, for the first time in history.

Restoring Old Wealth?

Some people take the view that China's new growth is a way to restore its old wealth. But what is happening goes well beyond restoring old wealth. True, China was one of the richest nations in the world for thousands of years, but the nation now aims to go beyond the past way of life completely. There are many reasons.

First, old China was an agrarian society, but now it is being transformed into a modern commercial and industrial nation. This means that China has stepped into a new sphere.

Second, whereas China's old life was self-contained and mostly independent of other nations, its development today is taking place in a global context. Hence, becoming an equal and full member of the global community is the top desire for the Chinese. Fully embracing global development is a basic goal.

Third, old China was always ruled by a self-appointed, ruthlessly overextended government. As a self-appointed body, it must constantly squeeze on the society and people. This squeezing role reached a new height in the Mao era.

Even today, this bureaucratic squeezing continues, which causes hellish problems still. As such, a new, modern China must completely get rid of this untamed bureaucratic power. Replacing this traditional bureaucracy by modern law and institutions is a must for China to become a modern nation.

In all these ways, China is leaving the old way of life and embracing a completely new one. And it is happening in an open, globalized context.

This Small Book

This book examines China's new lessons and their implications for the world. The aim is to identify the key factors that will promote more positive changes for China and for peoples everywhere.

Despite all the changes, China's fundamental weakness is still the overextended, self-appointed bureaucracy, which is inherently self-serving. Moreover, countless government officials employ the unchallenged state power to enrich themselves. In the past five years alone, some 200,000 corrupt officials have been arrested. Unlimited bureaucratic power is the mother of corruption.

To abolish this massive bureaucracy remains the number one task for the Chinese civilization. To move ahead, China must rebuild its government, society, and economy completely. So far, China has taken the very first step, the most significant one, in this brave new direction. Getting the job done remains a might task.

When I wrote this book, I had two convictions. The first was that studying China's new development in relation to global development might help one better understand our changing world as well as opportunities and challenges in the new century. The second conviction was that the lessons from China are universally meaningful, for they concern people's lives as well as development issues. Above all, development is a global issue that affects lives everywhere.

This book consists of 26 chapters, which are organized into eight parts:

I. China's New Role in the World
II. The Yuan, Trade, and Investment
III. China's Fast-Changing Society, Politics, and Economy
IV. China's Banking, Insurance, and Stock Market Reforms
V. Chinese Multinationals vs. Global giants
VI. The Taiwan Issue: Current Affairs and Trends
VII. India Versus China: Moving Ahead at the Same Time; and
VIII. The Japan-China Issue: Evolving Relations in Light of History

Many materials contained here were originally published by various newspapers and magazines. Here I have added new materials to make the discussion more specifically relevant to the overall aim of the book.

Part I.
China's New Role in the World

SUMMARY

China's development in this era started at an extremely low level, basically from a general poverty, but its growth rate has set a new world record. This quick surge has become possible under an increasingly open environment. In short, it has directly involved the entire world.

But is a developing China a good or bad thing for the world? To some worried minds, it is a disaster in the making. If this is true, why does the outside world keep putting more money into China and why are more outsiders rushing in? The reality is that a fast-developing China is nothing but good for the world.

Another truth is that without the outside involvement, China could not have developed in this era. A booming regional development can hardly exist in isolation. Furthermore, our world has stepped into a new era of increased ties and sharing in addition to competition. All this is positive as far as global development is concerned.

Today, there remain huge unsettled issues. China's people have two basic goals. First, they desire to create a completely modern and law-based society. This new society will enable the common people to pursue their interests and happiness through their own efforts.

Second, they wish China to become a full, true, and equal member of the global community. To most Chinese, China can only and deeply wish to share its progress with the entire world. Already vast interactions and exchanges are occurring, which can only increase as time passes.

Chapter 1.

China's Social Changes vs. the Tourism Explosion

Lately, Beijing residents have become reluctant to bring visiting friends to tour the six-century-old Forbidden City. The reason is simple: the crowds. The world's biggest royal palace complex, filled with Ming and Qing Dynasty imperial treasures in some 1,000 rooms, is one of China's obligatory tourist destinations, and the visitor numbers increase every year.

All over China, this story is repeated for other attractions: The golden age of Chinese tourism has arrived—out of nowhere seemingly. This sudden surge in tourism is a sharp turn of fortune.

China is now one of the top four global tourist nations. In 2005, inbound tourists reached 120 million, a new record. This huge surge in tourism is a sea change; in 1978, the number of overseas tourists was only 230,000.

Unexpected Outcomes

In the 1970s, China was beginning to open its door, and this soon impacted Chinese life in important ways. The sudden appearance of foreign tourists interested the typical Chinese immensely. Back then, foreign tourists were often surprised to find themselves being treated like pandas. They were followed by large crowds of extremely friendly but very inquisitive locals. China's isolation had been painfully long, and the Chinese were naturally highly curious about foreigners. But that age is long gone.

Nowadays, foreign tourists can be found in every corner of the country, with the biggest crowds in major cities like Shanghai, Xian, Harbin, Dalian, Hangzhou, Chongqing, Nanjing, and Guangzhou. Overseas travelers are also visible in major scenic spots like the Yellow Mountain in Anhui province; Mount Emei in Sichuan province; Guilin, the lake-filled city in Guangxi Autonomous Region; Mount Hua in Shaanxi province; and Mount Lu in Jiangxi. Even remote, mountainous Tibet has become a hot tourist spot.

As one of the world's oldest civilizations, China has historical tourist attractions that are second to none. For culturally inclined tourists, a saying goes, "To see 25 years of Chinese history, go to Shenzhen; for 150 years, Shanghai; for 500 years, Beijing; and for 5,000 years, Xian."

The country is projected by industry experts to become the number-one tourist country worldwide within only a few years. The industry's numbers are already formidable: Total tourist income for 2005 reached $96 billion, an amazing change considering that China's tourism sector hardly existed 30 years ago. The sector now employs over 7 million people directly and over 33 million people indirectly.

But the real implications are much broader and deeper. Through travel, China's openness has increased immensely. This in turn leads to a more relaxed society and greater personal freedom for the typical Chinese.

From Overseas to Domestic Tourism

The most spectacular change of recent years has been a shift from foreign to domestic tourism. In 2005, overseas tourists contributed over $29.3 billion to the Chinese economy. But their contribution was far outweighed by that of domestic Chinese tourists, who contributed $66.7 billion.

Today, China is already the world's biggest domestic tourism market in terms of number of tourists. Also helpful is that fact that China's urban holiday days have been extended to about 113 days annually, so people have plenty of leisure time.[1]

Most Chinese tourists go to local scenic spots. But well-to-do Chinese are increasingly willing to travel anywhere within China and beyond. Foreign travel, restricted or unaffordable for decades, has become irresistible for tens of millions of Chinese. Most — over 90% in 2005 — visit other Asian nations.

The attractions of the entire outside world are immense to the Chinese. More and more Chinese tourists are visiting Europe, Australia, North America, Africa, and the rest of the world. The Chinese are as curious as anyone else. They are eager to see as many places as possible. As one Chinese travel executive said, "Countless Chinese would rush to see the moon at once if it became commercially possible."

Overall, mass tourism is a relatively new phenomenon in China and has emerged only since 1978. Its popularity has both taken advantage of, and helped to bring about, the greater openness and vibrancy in Chinese society. Hence, the greatest impacts are on the vast economic-social changes.

The Bad Old Days

In the Mao era, travel as a commercial activity was almost nonexistent, due to enormous bureaucratic barriers. Travel was restricted, just as choices were restricted in other areas like employment, residency, and fashion. The government managed the lives of people according to its own needs, and whatever citizens wanted to do, including travel, required official approvals. The general situation was that the more people wanted to do, the more the government stood in the way. This vast restrictiveness produced a perfect bureaucratic society (see Part III).

Restrictions on travel have existed throughout China's history, but the Communist government pushed them to an extreme. Its control was so exhaustive and complete that Chinese people lost their choices over all aspects of life. Instead, their lives were completely arranged by the government in any way it saw fit.

Commercial tourism was basically impossible in this environment. Aspiring tourists first needed to obtain approval from their employers. Merely having the money to travel was not enough.

Because the food supply was controlled by the government, there was a constant food shortage, along with shortages of cooking oil, soaps, tea, and all other essential products, for several decades; each citizen was allowed a fixed amount with government-issued ration coupons, and these coupons could be used only in certain areas.

People who traveled from one city to another within the same province first had to get special coupons for food in the destination city, besides paying for transportation and accommodation. Traveling outside a province required different food coupons.

Those classified as farmers faced even greater hurdles, because farmers were completely banned from travel in general. Even patients seeking better medical treatment in major cities often ran into problems. Since medical services in rural regions are backward in general, this caused vast miseries.

Restrictive measures were innumerable even for those who were allowed to travel. For example, checking into a hotel required an employer's introduction letter. Even this could not get you a room in the top hotels, which were reserved for high-ranking bureaucrats.

By government design, freedom went with your bureaucratic ranking. All citizens, including poets, teachers, dancers, farmers, business executives, and even monks, as well as all organizations, were given a bureaucratic ranking by the government. The higher your ranking was, the greater your entitlement to freedom.

Under this system, only high-ranking government officials had exclusive entitlement to the top hotels and resorts, among countless other benefits. Even the top manager at a small company was not allowed to stay at a nice hotel or take a first-class train, because the company's bureaucratic ranking, hence his or her own ranking, was not high enough.

Ironically, most good-quality hotels and resorts were underused during the Maoist period. Even if there were not enough qualified officials requesting accommodation, the hotels were not allowed to sell the rooms to other people. Such hotels and resorts were heavily guarded and were off-limits to low-ranking officials, not only commoners.

There were additional restrictions. For example, travelers who stayed in a city for a few days had to register at the local police station. Those who wanted to stay longer than originally specified had to obtain new permission.

It was under this general environment that Chinese people lived for several decades. In short, traveling was troublesome for urban Chinese, if not impossible. For rural Chinese, it was simply a nightmare.

Such travel rules were gradually lifted in the reform era. For example, by 1991, the government stopped requiring domestic travelers to show their bureaucratic ranking to take a first-class train. But there were massive socioeconomic forces behind the rule changes.

What Caused the Tourism Boom?

Many factors have contributed to the tourism boom, which has happened more by accident than by design. But these factors have produced a new reality nonetheless.

First, the economic expansion has helped fundamentally. For example, Shenzhen, a Special Economic Zone (SEZ) since 1980, has built countless new factories, requiring millions of workers, which attracted tens of millions of inland Chinese. Most of them were first-time travelers. These workers became accustomed to travel and familiar with the tourism infrastructure during their journeys between Shenzhen and their home provinces, which ultimately promoted the travel industry.

Because more than 200 million rural Chinese have migrated to urban China in the past three decades, the magnitude of this effect has been large. Citizens wish to improve their lives fast, so they rush anywhere for opportunities. Hence, travel has become a necessity for a better life, pushing forward the travel business in no small way.[2]

Second, the private sector has come to life, and as a by-product, tens of millions of businesspeople have needed to travel. In particular, small rural businesspeople preferred to set up shops in major cities. The huge numbers of such people, and their adroitness at exploiting holes in the old system, made it essentially impossible to control their movements, further boosting domestic travel.

This new game is reminiscent of an old Chinese saying: "The devil reaches an inch higher, but the Tao [hero] goes a foot higher. So the devil is defeated."

In this era, even the government has no way to contain this massive movement regardless of how hard it tries. The government has devised clever new tactics in order to benefit from people's wish to travel. This means countless new demands, all with fees attached, all aiming to squeeze travelers.

But these bureaucratic schemes cannot stop the businesspeople. An art of living of the businesspeople is to play with this bureaucratic power, and even turn it to their advantage. So far, private businesspeople have been winning in their own ways. This is evident by the fact that millions of private shops exist in the cities.

Third, the ever-increasing foreign involvement has helped tremendously. For one thing, foreign companies are given special privileges. They can hire all sorts of people from anywhere in the country. Over 24 million Chinese now work for overseas employers, and these employees are allowed to travel anywhere. This further pushed aside the old travel restrictions.

In addition, of course, more and more overseas tourists have come to China, setting new records every year. They always get preferential treatment from the service providers as well as the government, which has created an overall improvement in China's tourist industry. In fact, most top hotels and services were designed to meet the needs of the foreigners.

Fourth, the expanding economy has given rise to income increases for average citizens. As a result, more and more Chinese have gained the financial resources to travel. Also, this increased income has expanded the lifestyle of citizens.

Seeing places is a popular desire. Now well-to-do Chinese spend more and more money on travel, entertainment, education, and information. The travel industry has become a top beneficiary of this new lifestyle. A few years ago, the collective contribution of Chinese people to tourism revenues surpassed that of foreign tourists, and as time goes by, their predominance in the sector will only become greater.

Fifth, rapidly improving infrastructure as well as service quality have helped. Only 20 years ago, traveling by air was uncommon, but today it is extremely common. There are daily flights to most sizable Chinese cities. A complete chain of tourism services now exists, ranging from tour services to hotels to a full menu of transportation options, that did not exist as recently as the 1980s.

Whereas in the past, travel by train was the most popular, travel by airplane or bus has taken away tens of millions of people from rail. The rail passenger rate has dropped to about 60% from the previous rate of 90% or higher. This new competition has further boosted improvement in travel.

Sixth, tourism has become an enormous source of income for local government bodies, especially in inland areas like Xian, which have world-class attractions but a relatively narrow economic base. This has caused these areas to compete with one another to attract even more tourists. Huge promotional boards are now everywhere: "Welcome!" This regional competition has further lifted the old barriers. In the end, it is clear that government barriers harm the government itself.

Even Beijing has employed the tourist industry for its own ends, and numerous policies favorable to the industry have gradually emerged. One very significant change came in 1999, when domestic tourism was already a major force in economic growth. The shortage-ridden economy had changed into an economy characterized by chronic oversupply. In particular, large numbers of state companies were in trouble. This demanded both greater consumption and a cut in production; one of numerous measures introduced to deal with the situation was an extension of holidays.

As a result, Labor Day and National Anniversary Day were both extended from one day to a full week (the so-called Golden Week). The Golden Week holidays have further fueled the travel industry, though they have also created major problems with congestion because so many people travel at the same time.

In 2000, during the Labor Day break, I traveled to the seaside city of Xiamen in Fujian province, but failed to find a hotel room—the city was completely filled with vacationers. As a result, I moved on to a nearby port city, Quanzhou, which fortunately turned out to be a very nice alternative. The city is one of the cleanest places inside China.

Signs of a Changing Industry

The Chinese tourist industry has seen many changes, especially in the past decade. For example, travel companies are no longer exclusively state companies, though the biggest names remain state brands, like China Travel, China International Travel, and China Youth Travel.

Countless private travel companies have emerged, though most are small compared to their state counterparts. Many state travel companies have changed from within; they have become shareholding companies and are even listed on the stock market. Internet travel companies now exist as well—for example, eLong, a private firm that is already listed on NASDAQ.

Many government resorts have gradually become commercially oriented; most realize that there is more business potential in serving ordinary travelers and businesses than in limiting themselves to their traditional client base of government officials.

This new attitude in the official world was born in the new commercial waves that have swept all China. In this era, the government officials have refocused their attention to economic issues in general. Whatever could advance their private interests would become possible. As a result, collecting fees from the traveling public serves as a vast incentive.

Many private businesspeople now employ these government resorts to entertain clients and host promotional shows. Having the privilege that used to belong exclusively to a few officials is a popular desire today.

I encountered an interesting example of this phenomenon recently in the popular hot spring resort town of Chonghua, located in a rural area near Guangzhou. The biggest hot spring resort there, Guangdong Hot Spring Hotel, was formerly reserved exclusively for top officials. It is bigger than the next five biggest resorts put together. But it was off-limits for the average Chinese for decades.

Lately, the resort has become accessible to the general public. Naturally, the management tries to woo consumers. Its way of getting results is to publicize its privileged history. Its promotional window displayed many old photos of leaders of the Mao period, like Zhou Enlai, who visited there.

The only foreign face was that of former U.S. president Richard Nixon, who visited in the spring of 1976.

The resort is now open to anyone who has money to spend. During my visit, two Chinese companies from Guangzhou had rented the entire place for the purpose of entertaining their distributors and clients.

Directly across the small river is a new resort owned by a private businessman from Guangdong province. Though much smaller and less scenic than the government resort, this new contender is cleverly designed, with two dozen pools named "rose," "ginseng," "coffee," "wine," and so on according to what is mixed into the water. This resort is doing better than the government resort, according to locals.

The International Rush

Naturally, the Chinese tourism boom has attracted interest from around the world. All major global players such as Hilton, Marriott, Holiday Inn, Shangri-la, Sheraton, and ANA are established in China, and their hotels can now be found in leading cities.

Many Chinese-owned hotels and resorts hire these international brands as contract operators. The idea is to take advantage of customers' familiarity with the brand, which increases the success rate of a new hotel. Chinese hotel operators are also eager to learn from their international counterparts. After all, business traveling is rather new to China. Learning through direct interaction is the quickest way to progress.

There are tremendous opportunities for the global operators in this area. Often the Chinese government units put enormous capital into building nice hotels, but they don't really know to get clients, especially from overseas. This forces them to link up with overseas operators. The first five-star hotel in China, the state-owned White Swan Hotel in Guangzhou, has been run by an overseas management team since its start in 1983.

This outsourcing model has become popular in China's hotel business and has led to fast improvement in the quality of service for business travelers, contributing to the general improvement in the tourist industry. It allows global hotel brands to make more money in China without committing substantial investments as China's tourist boom continues. More and more international travel operators are rushing into China. In March 2006, for example, Holiday Inn signed a deal to manage six Chinese hotels.

Not limited to hotel operations, opportunities are fast emerging for foreign tourism companies in general. This is partly due to China's participation in the World Trade Organization (WTO) accord. By the end of 2006, foreign travel operators will be allowed full access to conduct their business within China.

Actually, this is already occurring, as numerous international travel operators are rushing over to set up their shops in top cities. They have no problems getting Chinese clients. Chinese travelers often prefer to do business with established international brands in the hope of getting quality services.

Government Adds to Tourists' Woes

Despite these positive changes, there is plenty of room for improvement, especially for the political establishment. Government units still have a tendency to see tourists as a resource to be exploited rather than as clients to serve.

For example, the municipal governments of both Tianjin and Shanghai charge a fee of $2.50 to $3.00 for inbound cars with out-of-city plates. Recently, in a well-publicized case, a Chinese lawyer who had to pay the fee went to court to try to get his money back, but his claim was denied in court, a disappointment for the Chinese public.

Internal movement controls left over from a more restrictive era also continue to impede tourism. A good example is the fence surrounding the SEZ of Shenzhen, intended to prevent peasants from entering the zone without permission. The government also wished to squeeze domestic travelers.

The construction of the fence was one of the first acts undertaken by the government after the SEZ was established in 1980. The cost was 130 million yuan (equivalent to over U.S.$260 million today in terms of purchasing power), which was nearly the total amount of the income contributed by Guangdong province to the central government that year.

Passing through the fence required a special permit costing 30 yuan, about a month's salary for a typical urban worker and three months' earnings for a typical rural worker at the time. The fee was paid by hundreds of millions of Chinese visitors, providing a very high return on the government's investment. (Access has been free for overseas travelers since day one.) How many more Chinese visitors might have come without the annoyance of the permit and fee will never be known.

For the last couple of years, the restriction has been relaxed somewhat. Though the fence is still guarded by soldiers, the fee was reduced to 2 yuan in 2004 and dropped completely by 2005, though paperwork is still needed. Also, very significantly, instead of applying for a permit in one's home residency town, the traveler can now do so at the gate. Behind this change was a new level of social protest.

Another act on the part of Shenzhen's government was to build several top hotels and resorts exclusively for senior government officials, especially from Beijing, though the city had hundreds of star hotels already. Why?

The reason was simple: The city officials wanted to please their superiors, who after all controlled their jobs and promotions. Besides, the hundreds of millions of dollars used for these sites was *nobody's money*. Therefore there was every incentive to use it. Even today, these hotels and resorts are not open to the public. At the same time, the city officials have little interest in building schools and training centers for migrants, which would not advance their interests with the top officials.

I once asked a government official why the authorities created so many hurdles for people. He replied: "Well, it is just the way for the government to provide effective management for the interest of society. For example, if you don't stop rural people from seeking employment in the cities, very soon all cities would be filled with rural migrants."

But the reality is that at least 200 million rural Chinese already work in the cities and are among the biggest contributors to China's progress. The official's comment was, "It could become very chaotic if the government controlled movements less."

The real problem is that all the obvious government intrusions are presented as modern management. A greater truth may be this: If 900 million rural Chinese could control the actions of the government, China's wealth would increase sharply.

The worst aspect of a self-appointed government is that it can intrude upon people freely. An old Chinese saying goes, "The government officials can burn people's houses freely, but people are not even allowed to use candles." Unchecked government power remains China's key weakness.

The Future of Chinese Tourism

Despite such obstacles, the interests of Chinese tourists have been promoted by their increasing popularity within the international tourism industry, which covets their free-spending ways, and foreign governments, which see big profit potential in attracting more Chinese travelers.

The results of this trend are already evident: In 2005, over 31 million overseas trips were made by Chinese holding private passports, a 50-fold jump from 20 years ago. One can safely predict that the number of outbound Chinese tourists may reach 100 million within the next decade.

Another trend is in view as well: Many business groups and government institutions from countless nations come to China to attract Chinese tourists. They put on splendid shows in many major cities, often to enthusiastic audiences. Competition to attract Chinese tourists has become a new international art.

Behind this courting is the ever-increasing spending by Chinese travelers. They are especially fond of buying famous brands and luxury goods that are often not available or are more expensive at home. The average travel spending per person can reach up to $5,500 per trip, which has put Chinese tourists on the top spenders list.[3]

The impact of the tourist boom goes well beyond the travel industry. For example, the increasing awareness of what *good service* is, by itself, will have a substantial impact on the quality of life in China.

And the internationalization of hotels has fed the internationalization of other industries, as foreign investors staying in the hotels exert their influence beyond the hotel doors. These effects will only grow in the future as the benefits of tourism continue to sink in year after year.

But the greatest impacts of this booming tourism are social. That hundreds of millions of people are suddenly able to travel is no small thing for this ancient land. This change is bound to affect life in China and beyond in countless ways.

Finally, a fast-expanding economy is giving rise to a hugely expanded sphere of personal freedom, and this is helping to lead toward a more liberal and open society along with economic advancement.

Chapter 2.

Whose 21st Century?

China's sudden emergence on the global stage is causing great debate. To some, its development will mean Chinese domination of the 21st century. A new world power, many historians claim, alters the world's power balance, often leading to new conflicts.

Is a prosperous China good news or a disaster in the making? The truth is that a rising China will benefit the entire world, not just China.

In reality, the old assertion that a rising national fortune causes global chaos belongs to the past, not the future. Why must the development of a poor nation like China bring chaos and harm to the world?

In truth, China's development is giving rise to a creative and productive era, a better world through ever-increasing sharing and common responsibility for all members. That is why all nations have been playing a part in China's development.

At the same time, China's new openness is helping the Chinese people to gain a new life based on individual private initiative. This new environment is enabling people to get out of the bureaucratic cage of the old era. The increased power of the people is in turn helping to lay a new foundation for world progress and peace.

China's Growth Benefits the World

Above all, China's expanding economy is creating a new engine of growth. Today, China is the biggest frontier market and a top trading nation as well as a global economic center. This provides numerous direct benefits to the outside world.

First, consumers can get cheaper products than ever before. China now produces a vast range of the cheapest products, meaning new choices for global consumers. To be sure, they are saving countless money. Why should anyone pay $200 for a microwave oven when one can pay $50? How many people want to shop for the most expensive products? Maybe 1%. But most of us can get by without a Rolex. That's how Wal-Mart has attained more than $310 billion in annual sales. In this regard, China is playing the right role, and global consumers are making huge savings.

But the benefits to the Chinese laborers are rather limited. Many of them work for 10 hours or more per day, six or seven days a week, but earn only $100, or less, per month. There are few additional benefits for them in general.[1]

Being a world factory means countless sweatshops in operation, involving over 150 million low-paid men and women, and even children. Lifting their living standard is by no means easy. These jobs are often backbreaking. Furthermore, workplace abuses are common. In particular, salaries can easily be stolen by employers. Behind the flood of made-in-China products, the toll on these hardworking Chinese is extremely high.

Second, all sorts of new opportunities are emerging as China's economy expands. The world is economically connected as never before. This produces more wealth for the world as a whole. In fact, most finished products require shared work involving numerous nations. No single nation can dominate in this endeavor. This presents a new direction for all.

This interdependence brings vast benefits to China's trading partners and participants. Indeed, there is no other way a country can have so many trading partners. Benefits are immediate.

A television set is made in China. But the chips are from Europe, Japan, and the United States; metals and raw materials come from Latin America, Africa, and Australia; and other components come from a number of developing nations.

Furthermore, multinationals make more profits than the Chinese manufacturers. For every DVD (digital video disc) made in China, the foreign technology patent holders charge at least $5. How much do the Chinese manufacturers make? Fifty cents. Chinese businesspeople say they make less money producing DVDs than selling vegetables on the street corner (see Part V).[2]

Indeed, global multinationals have enormous benefits to gain by selling products made in China. This has become a way for them to increase profits sharply. Wal-Mart purchased goods worth about $18 billion from China in 2004. But more than 5,000 Chinese suppliers combined could make less than 5% of Wal-Mart's profits.

A rising Chinese economy is also adding new wealth to the world. China's developing economy means, first of all, a rising domestic consumption. This translates into sharply increased selling to China. In 2005, international players sold $658 billion worth of goods to China; in 1978, the nation's total trade was only $21.1 billion. The trade growth has added wealth around the globe. This Chinese buying spree could double within five years.

In China's stores, foreign brands are innumerable. When a consumer wants a washing machine, he or she is confronted with vast choices: Sharp, LG, Siemens, Electrolux, Hitachi, and Whirlpool, among others.

These foreign brands have all become household names. This is of course after the consumer has decided on which store to go to in the first place: Makro, Jusco, Carrefour, Wal-Mart, Metro, or Tesco, among others. There are more than 300 overseas retailers in China now.[3] They are following each other's tails closely and adding new stores in a hurry. More international retailers are on their way. Booming Chinese retail means a gold mine for them. What is more, buying such high-ticket items is on a cash basis, as credit is relatively new in China.

As China buys more products from the international markets, ripple effects occur. For example, there are signs that Japan could finally be coming out of its long economic slump. This is significantly aided by Japan's ever-increasing exports to China. In fact, in the past few years, 50% or more of Japan's increased exports have been to China. Further help comes from the presence of countless Japanese multinationals inside China, with cheap Chinese labor reducing their costs of making products for the global markets (see Part VIII).

Without China, Motorola, Samsung, and Nokia would be 20% smaller. Indeed, China has saved these companies' fortunes. They are grateful to the 400 million-plus Chinese mobile users (as of early 2006). According to their projections, this market will jump to 500 million by 2007. How can any telecom player avoid China?

A Better World

Benefits are hardly limited to these things. The new convergence of civilizations will promote a far better era for all peoples everywhere.

Mutual benefits have brought all nations closer to each other as never before. Besides increased interdependence between the developed and developing nations, there is ever-increasing trade and cooperation among developing nations. In particular, a booming China helps to bring more developing nations into the global development orbit. This is evident in the sharply increasing economic interactions among the developing nations in Asia, Latin America, and Africa, among others.

In the new economically connected world, sharing is more important than war—cold or hot. But the real problem is that world politics lags behind. The Cold War ideology is still very much alive. It continues to block the road leading to more global sharing, common wealth, and joint responsibilities.

The resurgence of a Cold War mentality still looms. This alternative is terrible for all nations and people. It could block healthy development for the world economy and community.

One could ask, if China stuck with general poverty, would the rest of the world benefit? But still, a quickly growing Chinese economy causes concerns and even worries among some people.

Is our world entering a new era? Definitely yes. Increasing global cooperation and exchange is the new reality. Many nations are adding to the total wealth in a new way. What is more, no nation can dominate the global community in the traditional fashion. In short, the 21st century belongs to everyone. China can only share its progress with the world, and deeply wishes to do so.

This new reality is a dramatic departure from the past. The old national expansions led to constant bloodshed. Europe's previous global reach, for example, led to dozens of colonies and the suffering of countless people. In countless ways, Europe's development and modernity came from the sacrifices of the underdeveloped nations.

As another example, the rise of Japan and that of Germany in the recent past led to bloody wars. Both nations relied on ideologies aimed at building world supremacy through military conquest. The result was huge disasters for humankind, not just themselves.

But a developing China makes a strong contrast. Through economic expansion, the nation is becoming more and more open; there is more and more international involvement; and the rising living standard promotes a more liberalized and freer society, which in turn attracts greater outside participation in China's development. Finally, a fast development has led to positive chain reactions, which has happened in a globalized world.

Already, impressive progress is visible to all. As one example, China had over 123 million Internet users as of mid 2006. Though free expression is still seriously restricted, the Chinese Web, where free expression blossoms, is a different story. Seeking fuller personal expression has become a new passion, especially for youth. This Internet world promotes openness in all sorts of ways.

Also, to meet market demands, more and more media outlets are also trying hard to report on this changing reality, a thing that was nonexistent in the Mao era.

This enlarged sphere of personal freedom can only grow as the nation's economy continues to expand. More and more personal choices in such matters as expression, travel, employment, and residency are in turn helping China to become a true participant in global life.

This fast-changing China offers unprecedented opportunities for the whole world. Furthermore, it is under this increasingly positive environment that Chinese people have become more productive and creative, which directly promotes China's convergence with life in the outside world.

Chapter 3.
Go East, Young Man!

Regardless of how one feels about globalization, it has unquestionably led to an unprecedented level of international interaction as national economies have become increasingly interwoven. And as the world's biggest frontier market, China has become a top destination for foreigners: Expatriates in China now number in the millions. More and more international professionals are rushing to work and live in China.

These latter-day Marco Polos come from anywhere and everywhere. They generally value their China experiences highly: Being in a rapidly developing society such as China can expand their horizons in many ways.

Equally significant, they act as bridges between China and the world. At the same time, the Chinese public is, by and large, delighted to have them here. The Chinese people are well aware that China has departed from its past isolation and entered a new era, and the expatriate presence reflects the giant step China has taken in joining the global community.

Overall, openness is the top driving force for China's progress. Having so many foreign workers is a great blessing both for China and for the world.

From Here, There, and Everywhere

It is becoming easier and easier to find foreign professionals and their firms in Chinese cities. They cover all sorts of businesses, from manufacturing to trade and retail to education and culture.

One case is the import-export business of a Syrian consumer products merchant. A veteran China player, he has maintained an office in Shenzhen, Guangdong province, for several years. His business model is straightforward: He buys made-in-China products and ships them back to the Middle East. He finds that Chinese products are cheap and their quality is fast improving. He has said that China has "a fast-growing market in the Middle East" and that "selling Chinese products has better profit margins than selling other products."

Other foreign nationals are experienced professionals from around the globe. One of these is an Englishman who previously worked as a marketing and media specialist for British Airways and several other companies in Europe and Australia. About two years ago, he landed in Shanghai. Now he works for a foreign chamber of commerce in the city. He finds his new environment "stimulating and fun . . . filled with daily interactions with local Chinese."

There is also a large contingent of foreign entrepreneurs who have found plenty of work to do in China. They cover all sorts of sectors, ranging from high-tech to media, education, and manufacturing.

One U.S. native exemplifies this group. After graduating from a top U.S. college, he worked as an investment banker for a Wall Street firm for some 10 years. A year ago, he started new ventures of his own in Beijing while remaining a consultant to the investment firm. He has given lectures on investment at two top Chinese schools.

Another project for this expatriate is a new Web site, which is somewhat like a Yellow Pages for the city; local businesses and organizations can use it to announce their events. The site also provides some news coverage and analysis on China. He wants to bring the best possible information on China back to other Americans.

His team members come from Canada, the United States, Australia, and China. They have all found Beijing a perfect place for their ambitions. They hope to make a lasting mark on the city with their Web site.

Another business consultant is an Australian native who has been in China for some 20 years. He has traveled to more Chinese cities than most Chinese and now divides his time among Australia, China, and the rest of Asia.

In fact, this author has run into many foreign professionals who are eager to start a new business in China. Foreign businesspeople are given numerous privileges by China's government. The idea of setting up a small business is becoming very popular among foreign professionals in China, to say nothing of the countless shops run by global multinationals.

Culture Shocks

I well remember my culture shock after moving to the United States in 1981 — at the independent lifestyle of Americans and the absolute need for a car, for example, even among 80-year-olds. Visiting the United Kingdom, I was amazed to see afternoon tea conducted like a religious ceremony. What is surprising to foreign nationals about living in China today?

A Frenchman, now working as a writer and editor for a U.S. magazine based in Shanghai, has been struck by the openness of the

Chinese. He feels that Chinese people are much more open-minded than Westerners think, especially the older generation, who are often said to be conservative. He finds the Chinese warmhearted and readily able to show their feelings—not afraid to cry, in sadness or happiness.

Some foreign professionals are surprised by the new economic freedom of Chinese businesspeople—the relative ease with which they can start a business and the relatively low tax rates.

China's friendly environment was a surprise to the Syrian trader: "Though there are always bad guys around anywhere, the Chinese people are very friendly in general," he said.

Shanghai has one of the largest crowds of foreign nationals, numbering in the hundreds of thousands. For many of them, living in Shanghai has been eye-opening. The aforementioned Englishman said, "Every day is unique, and something new and interesting is always going on in this dynamic, fast-moving city."

Living in the heart of a Chinese community makes foreigners feel closer to the Chinese way of life and gives them a clearer understanding of the culture. The speed with which urban China is expanding also surprises many newcomers. The face of the nation seems to change year after year.

To many foreign professionals, living in China means the ability to enjoy some of the best things in life. Some appreciate a full menu of Chinese food and the low prices, while others most enjoy the vast diversity of Chinese culture.

On dealing with the Chinese, the Australian consultant said, "Chinese people are very helpful and if they like you, they give you 110% of their efforts."

Many expatriates prefer inland regions to the coast, though there are far more foreign professionals on the coast at this time. Among their favorite places, they may mention Sichuan, Henan, Shaanxi, and Henan.

Suggestions for the Outside World

Living and working inside China, foreign nationals have learned a great deal about the country and are eager to pass on their knowledge and experiences to others. But they also stress the difficulty of becoming and remaining an expert on China given the extremely rapid pace of change.

The Frenchman said, "Many foreign countries see China as a virgin land, a land of huge opportunities, but to do business or to get a company running as a foreigner is the trickiest task. There are 1.3 billion people here, but one forgets that 70% of the population are from the countryside and don't have much money to spend."

What is his suggestion for foreign businesspeople? "There is always a Chinese businessman smarter than you; you need to make friends with the right people."

Thus many foreign businesspeople feel a need to understand China's market from the inside out. They believe that foreign businesspeople should spend enough time on the ground to get real experiences. To many foreign businesspeople,

Also, China is a great place to source products, but they have to be very selective about choosing suppliers and then ensure that the suppliers adhere to product specifications. On the investment side, the Australian consultant cautions that foreign investors need to have a realistic business plan as well as find the right managers. Otherwise, things can go terribly wrong. In this regard, nothing can substitute for first-hand experience.

But there have been failures. For example, some foreign businesspeople have no idea how to adapt to China's market environment. They do not put enough time and effort into understanding the market. Instead, they simply want to apply their established concept in a new arena. This naturally leads to problems.

Many foreign businesspeople appreciate the significance of the right partnerships. As one said, "Finding the right partners is the way to success. Otherwise, life can become a mess." But many overseas businesspeople agree that vast opportunities are everywhere in China today. Hence it is important for foreign investors to grasp their chances. The key is to grow with an expanding market for the long run. This is behind the success stories of many international operations in China.

Observing Changes

The enormous scope of change in China is evident to its foreign residents, along with the imperfections. Most expatriates are well aware of the transitional pains China is going through. Many are willing to express their opinions in this area as well. One of China's biggest challenges is the fast-expanding gap between the rich and poor. In the eyes of many foreign professionals, China's wealth disparity is getting very serious, demanding quick action in order to ensure social stability. Hence, they suggest that China needs to be more resourceful in some areas of life and business.

The Englishman said, "Obviously, more government funds must be plowed into helping the poor people and educating the population, especially in the countryside."

All in all, China's development has yet to catch up with that of Japan or the nations of North America and Europe. Many foreign professionals are well aware of the need for China's sustained growth.

One European professional commented, "Living in China is okay, especially in Shanghai, although the country doesn't offer the same comfortable services as in Europe or the United States for things like social insurance, health care, pensions, and many other aspects of a quality life."

Nonetheless, many expatriates hold out hope regarding China's continued overall development. They point out the need to address environmental issues—China must focus more effort on solving its huge environmental problems and on energy conservation. In addition, as noted by the Englishman, "Countless people still people drink contaminated water. Once such deep-seated problems are solved, China will move to a higher stage of development."

Despite all the challenges, many expatriates agree that China's openness is creating vast opportunities. They also wish to have more foreign nationals join them, and believe strongly that their involvement can make a difference in China's development.

More and more foreign professionals are coming to China these days. They are more prepared to tap into the new opportunities over here. Their presence shows how small the world has become. As expatriates in China pursue their own goals, as they disperse into every corner of the country, they have become a vital catalyst for change.

Chapter 4.

Everyone in the Same Boat

Throughout history, unequal development has been the norm: There has never been a time when different nations did not have radically different levels of development. But the economic forces causing a convergence of development levels have never been so powerful as they are today.

The countries moving ahead most quickly, including India, China, Egypt, Brazil, and Russia, are often called *late-developing nations*. Along with their obvious huge challenges, these countries have advantages unique to their status as late developers. Many have leapfrogged over transitional stages of development by adopting advanced technologies. This new reality has promoted accelerated growth in unexpected places.

Changes in the Later Developers

For example, China has jumped directly to ATM cards, bypassing the checkbook stage. Since the ineffective legal and banking systems cannot support the wide use of checkbooks, ATM technology has nicely covered up the holes. As a result, both ATM and credit cards are widely used now.

Another example is the adoption of mobile phones before conventional landlines: China now has more handsets than wired phones, over 400 million versus some 360 million as of early 2006. This is a direct result of developing late.

China's rapid development has generated vast interest around the globe. Any nation that can consume 100 million hamburgers, sodas, and chocolate bars a day is sure to attract interest from McDonald's, Coke, and Nestle. As the Chinese saying goes, "It is easier to share good fortune than misery."

Today, foreign investors are racing into China and benefiting hugely from the expanding pie. But they are contributing more than capital, products, and services. These foreign "wolves" are causing the domestic "sheep" to run faster. Lenovo, the Chinese PC maker that recently acquired IBM's legendary PC unit, is only one of the new domestic competitors produced by the "wolves" (see Part V).

India provides more examples of this phenomenon. Indian railroads may be third-world quality, but its "IT army" is world-class and has become a powerful link between India and the global economy. The Indian biotechnology industry is also on the move.

Islamic states, Latin American countries, and the ex-Soviet states are examples of countries facing underdevelopment, but with plentiful natural resources. Rising commodity prices recently have been a boon for these nations. Resource revenues, particularly for oil and minerals, have boosted their economies more than any conceivable aid program ever could. The resource windfall has opened the door to sustainable development for these countries — if they are wise enough to enter it.

Today, the late-developing states, especially China and India, have become new global theaters. By being open and pragmatic, they can better employ their best resources and energy for development. The vast entrepreneurial armies in the two Asian megastates are the best creations of the new openness, which has decisively helped both nations to participate effectively in global development.

These new entrepreneurs are vast in number, limitless in their capacity for hard work, and boundless in their aspirations. Indeed, it is not too much to say that they represent the best hope for a better society. The recent history of both countries shows convincingly that what most impoverished nations really need is more entrepreneurs and less bureaucratic interference. If the number of government bureaucrats can be halved and the number of entrepreneurs doubled, the potential gains to humanity are staggering.

Challenges for Later Developers

The flip side of the coin, of course, is a set of common problems faced by the late-developing economies. These formidable obstacles include

1. weak financial markets and regulatory structures;
2. growing income inequality, which threatens social stability;
3. lack of an independent legal system; and
4. overextended government power and resultant corruption.

In all this, there is no shortcut as far as building modern institutional and legal systems is concerned. Today, many developed nations have yet to find ways to escape from old traps.

The ups and downs of China's stock market are a good example. The Chinese market has existed for only about 14 years, but it has already involved more than 73 million investors. Foreign institutional investors are interested, too, although they have been allowed market access only since the spring of 2003.

Some 40 overseas financial players—including HSBC, Citibank, Deutsche Bank, UBS, and Nomura—are now investing in Chinese stocks. Even Bill Gates's family trust fund has bought into China. Overall, up to $10 billion of foreign money has been injected into the infant stock market, which now has 1,400 listings with a market value of some U.S.$500 billion (see Part IV).

But the stock market has also shown frightening volatility, caused many naive investors to lose their shirts, and at this writing stood at a six-year low, having deflated even more dramatically than the notoriously overinvested NASDAQ in the United States. It is seriously affected by widespread abuses and built-in flaws and is populated by many Chinese Enrons and WorldComs. As a result, investor interest in the Chinese stock markets has cooled so much that reforming the stock market has become a major priority for the government.

Why did China fall into this trap? One might think that, as a late developer, China would have learned the hard lessons from older markets elsewhere. True, every nation with financial markets has seen great crashes. But the Chinese, instead of learning from past mistakes, are reliving them. It seems that folly knows no nationality and that *the madness of crowds* is universal.

But the Chinese are not alone. In India, certain statements of the New Congress Government caused a panicky sell-off, reducing the stock market's value by more than 20% in just two days in 2004. Although dramatic new reform policies have now pushed the index to an all-time high, what turmoil Indian politicians have created for investors!

Russia and Latin America have faced similar problems—wild currency fluctuations have caused all sorts of damage.

The potential instability in the late developers casts new light on the current clamor to revalue the Chinese currency. To some people, strengthening the yuan might provide temporary relief for developed countries facing a trade deficit with China. But it could backfire as well.

In addition, China's trouble-prone legal and financial system, with its chronic corruption, means that a free exchange of the yuan now might seriously destabilize the country. Eventually, there is no doubt that China must free its currency and have a free flow of capital, but to take that step now without rooting out corruption first would create more problems than it would solve.

Although the late developers' recent progress has attracted much attention from the outside world, in actuality they have made only small steps toward prosperity, a fact that is often missed.

In the case of China, it may have over 25 million cars on the road, legions of millionaires, and even a few billionaires; but its gross domestic product (GDP) per person is still only around U.S.$1,700, and the average manufacturing job pays only around U.S.$115 per month. Economic development remains very much at the early stages. Lifting the standard of living for 1.3 billion people is no small task.

For now, China is going through a very painful transition from a bureaucratic society to a multilayered one. To insiders, China stands uncertainly between a failed old bureaucratic system and a new one that is being introduced very slowly. Moving to the next stage will not be straightforward. It will be more like the evolution of an aquatic creature into an animal that can live on land.

It would not surprise the Chinese if it took a couple of generations, or even more, to build a functional market economy and modern legal framework — fair to all, and free from bureaucratic meddling.

Of essential significance, creating well-defined property ownership demands complete abolition of the old, overextended bureaucratic power. In short, China needs to rebuild its society, economy, and government completely. How big is this task? Indeed, it requires nothing less than a true revolution, which has never happened in China's long history. This accomplishment will be no less significant than the ending of the West's church-state power, which dominated European life for thousands of years.

At present, there are just too many barriers to overcome. At the same time, countless people depend on the old system; in 2004 alone, 43,757 government officials were found guilty of corruption.[1] Knowing the depths of these problems is a necessity for understanding the tremendous struggle China is going through. Although exaggerating the problems may be harmful, minimizing them could be equally damaging.

With the increasingly open society brought about by globalization, China has gained a vast new platform for resolving its institutional problems. This in itself means a breakthrough for China. With openness, many once-tough problems can be seen in a new light.

The Role of the Developed World

The developed world, which is hardly problem free itself, has a great influence on the prospects of the late developers. Indeed, increasingly, the developed world risks losing its historic role as one key engine of global growth.

The well-known problems with the anemic Japanese economy pose a direct threat to global health. What are the possible root causes of the

Japanese mess? They stem directly from the tightly closed, exclusive Japanese society.

This closed Japanese system is most effective in fending off foreign interests. As a result, selling to Japan takes more than pricing, quality, and competitiveness. For example, your beef may be five times cheaper than Japanese beef, but the Japanese have invented numerous barriers against your entry. Further, there are complete closed business formations among business groups. These tightly closed organizations buy products and services from each other even if there are better and more competitive alternate products and services.

Yet Japan is most vulnerable to the woes within. Protectionism is a very ancient practice based on a tribe mentality, but today it has backfired against Japan's own interest. As a result, Japan has paid massively in the past two decades. Backing out of this mess is easier said than done. Hence, more than likely, the Japanese economic problems will not go away until the society and market become truly open (see Part VIII).

Even Europe has many lessons to learn. Indeed, Asia's entrepreneurial life has far exceeded that in Europe recently. Europe has sought to increase government power as a way to handle social and economic issues. An unemployment rate of over 10% in most European nations fails to point in a more entrepreneurial direction.[2]

Instead, much of Europe has tried to increase government power to address social woes. Consequently, the number of civil servants in Europe has risen sharply. For example, in Britain, the number of civil servants has increased fourfold over the past century. This has a significant drawback: A bigger and bigger government has overshadowed the entrepreneurial component. What is more, many dislocated Europeans have depended on government programs for their existence, thus creating a negative movement.

Indeed, to many Asians, much of Europe has made itself a welfare state. This provides a strong contrast to the entrepreneurial trend in the rest of the world, especially in Asia. Private initiative in China has created a lesson that should be relevant to Europe.

Furthermore, there is great uncertainty currently over the weakening dollar. What is really troublesome is not the dollar's declining value per se, but the underlying conditions. The United States has become the biggest debt issuer ever. Spending beyond one's means would spell trouble for anyone, and the United States will ultimately be no exception. There is a great need for the United States to put its fiscal house in order. Failure to do so risks reduced long-term borrowing power, an economic downturn, or both. To express these concerns is not scaremongering. The U.S. savings rate is flat, but spending keeps rising. At the same time, the U.S. government keeps borrowing from the outside world, with total borrowing now exceeding U.S.$1 trillion. Even some U.S. writers forecast a potential economic doomsday if current trends continue too long.[3]

One way out is faster development in the emerging economies, which will give rise to more consumption in these countries. In this regard, the high-speed growth in India and China, among other developing nations, is very positive. China's trade with the outside was next to nothing in the past, but China is now one of the top three trading nations, exceeding 7% of global share. India, Russia, Brazil, and many other emerging nations have been sharply increasing their consumption of late.

One thing is clear: Developed nations and the late developers are more than ever in the same boat. Hence, creating a new world order is apparently needed. The interests of all nations are tied together closely. Only with a new order can we hope to enter a new brave era and gain broader benefits for all.

Chapter 5.

Power and Limits of Later Developers

China's sudden economic surge has caught the world by surprise. A new player on the global stage is bound to get noticed. However, China and the world must learn how to coexist with each other. The following interview focuses on this issue.

But China is not the only nation that is embracing global development. The quick advancement of so many late developers will inevitably have vast effects on global life. One reasonable conclusion may be this: A new world order will emerge gradually and most likely indirectly, simply because a fast-expanding pie creates vast opportunities for all parties.

Leader or Follower?

Question from Jorge Nascimento Rodrigues: Does the full engagement of China with the world mean Daguo Xintai (*mentality of global power*) or Heping Jueqi (*peaceful rise*)? Does China have a "mission" as a global power as the Portuguese, the Dutch, the British, and the United States had in the past 650 years?

Answer from George Zhibin Gu: Strangely enough, the outside world feels the effects more than the Chinese. Most Chinese are more concerned about improving living standards and gaining new opportunities. They are little aware of China's future role on the global stage. More often than not, they are shocked when foreign visitors say that the 21st century will be Chinese.

That said, there is a common feeling that a fast-developing China will reverse history in one sense only: The Chinese will be treated as equals in the global community. For some 200 years, they have been treated as inferiors. This is changing for the better. The Chinese are proud that their creative efforts are beginning to be recognized by the world. But China is not ready, or really willing, to play a more significant role on the global stage. Maybe the reason is that China has suffered terribly in the past for thinking itself the center, which happened in a very closed society.

Today, most Chinese would prefer to be following the leader. That is a safe play, and a better alternative; it will help the Chinese learn from the rest of the world, especially the developed societies. This learning is only good for China, as well as urgently needed. China's quick development is largely the result of this serious learning. Additionally, learning feeds on itself. So the Chinese love to learn from everyone else.

Historical lessons on national rises and falls are plentiful. Even the various European nations have learned their lessons from the recent past. Being a teacher can become burdensome if one stops learning. And being a world leader can also invite unwanted troubles. Who can offer solutions to all the world problems all the time? This is something the United States has yet to learn.

Question: Do you think that the 21st century will be a truly "Asian century"?

Answer: Asia could provide global leadership in a different way. Asians have countless merits: They have strong family ties, they love education, and they are willing to work hard. Their greatest strength may be that they face tough situations with a smile and harder work. If the West suffered similar woes, it could soon collapse. As Asians attain more economic progress, the rest of the world will become more willing to learn from them. This will reverse recent historical trends. In this way alone will the 21st century be Asian.

I think the 21st century will belong to the world, not just Asia or China. Sharing and common wealth will become more significant than ever before, and more nations will benefit. This is a trend that can only grow, for the world is already tightly linked by business and economy.

A car produced in Detroit has an engine made in Europe and wheels made in Asia — with raw materials coming from Latin America, Africa, and Australia. This entails a sharing of work, and the benefits go beyond any single country.

At the next level, China's and India's strength lies in their low cost structure. But the developed nations can easily tap into these markets. In fact, they benefit more than anyone else. Also, for consumers in the developed nations, they can enjoy the cheapest products. Such benefits increase sharply as these late developers move forward.

This new century presents a grand platform for the convergence of global civilizations. This aspect is underestimated especially by the developed nations, but it is truly the brightest development for humankind.

A New Power Balance

Question: Can China become a global challenger to the U.S. hegemony? Or will its takeoff as a global economic challenger be like that of the Japanese of the 1980s?

Answer: The emergence of both China and India, among other late developers, will certainly impact the global power balance, but perhaps in a different way—gradually and indirectly. One basic reason is that India and China have more than 36% of the world's population. If their income doubles in the next 10 years, the rest of world will feel it. In addition, their development is taking place in an open, global context. That is even more meaningful for the outside world.

How about the U.S. hegemony? The U.S. government will become more willing one way or another to engage in consultation and dialog with India, China, and others. Even if the U.S. government is not willing to be more directly open, it will be more aware of the others' existence. Thus a new power balance will emerge gradually and most likely indirectly. More significant, the future may not see a repetition of the bloody rivalries of the past. History shows that such rivalry may produce no winners. Slowly but surely, the mind-set of the world is evolving, which may be viewed as a natural development.

As far as the U.S. government is concerned, it is also learning how to act like a leader. There are no real teachers. The leader bears most of the weight of its own mistakes, which can become too burdensome to handle. This has happened again and again in human history. The great powers in the past have all been pulled down more by their own weight than anything else. Should the future be any different?

Question: What more can be said about global development in this new era?

Answer: The world has gone through a sharp divergence in development in the last 600 years or so and now is embracing a profound convergence. This should be the foundation for a new world order. The key is to share development experiences, resources, and strengths with each other. Indeed, the development experiences of the West are extremely relevant and important for the late developers to learn from. At the same time, the early developers should share more of their resources with the rest of the world. These two elements are key to global development in the next stage.

China's Careful International Work

Question: Will China be able to build, even if slowly, a sustainable coalition against the incumbent power—which the new Russia did not do after the 1980s? Can strategic agreements among various countries (like those in 2004 among Brazil, Venezuela, South Africa, Iran, the Gulf Council) change the world balance?

Answer: Though economically the world is more connected,

political rivalry is still intense, as the Cold War mentality still looms large. The old political mentality must change to meet the changing realities. Otherwise, this Cold War mentality will produce world disarray. The old world order divided the rich and the poor, West and East, and the developed and developing world. The bottom line was that the few rich nations made the rules. Obviously, this old framework is a problem in the context of the changing realities.

Today, China is learning fast and is being very careful not to let the old world politics interfere with its economic development and growth. This will become a long-term strategy as well as a dominant mentality. At the same time, China is highly conscious of international concerns. Above all, the new China is eager and willing to learn. The fact that China has gone beyond the old mentality has given China's development its global character.

Question: Do you think China in the first half of the 21st century can surpass the United States in pure economic terms, as reports from Goldman Sachs suggest?

Answer: It is not very meaningful to say that China will surpass the United States at any given time. Nonetheless, China's growth is real, despite all the imperfections. This conclusion has more to do with the massive population size and their desires for a better life than with the economic realities. The current Chinese growth started at such a low level that after a 500% increase in the GDP over the past three decades, its development level is still very low. Many regions within China are only beginning to develop. Also, the state sector has yet to start true reform. There is still vast room for improvement, especially in the political institutional aspects, which are fundamental for China's sustained growth.

There may be a more meaningful way to look at this issue. For example, if one in every five Chinese uses one more roll of Kodak film a year, that business will be twice the size it is in the United States. The mobile phone business in China is already more than twice the size it is in the United States.

But no, China will remain a low-income nation for a long time to come. A direct comparison may be less meaningful in part because these two nations have such different cost structures. Even so, China will enjoy a prosperous life if its income per capita reaches 20% that of the United States due chiefly to a low cost structure. The situation may be similar for India and many other developing nations in Africa, Latin America, and elsewhere.

Very significantly, the new lesson from China is that a burdensome large population can be turned into a productive and creative force if a fair and rational platform is created. In this context, both India and China are moving forward brilliantly.

Question: Must China enter into a G-something club of world powers? Some think tanks proposed that China enter a G4 with the United States, the European Union, and Japan.

Answer: It is highly positive for the outside world to be more open. But let us not expect too much regarding benefits from such memberships. Even so, gaining access shows the increased international interest in a growing China. Leaving behind the old world mentality requires efforts from everyone. But China's ties with the outside world have reached a new record, mostly because of the fresh opportunities that come from the fast-expanding Chinese pie.

Question: Are North Korea and Taiwan really volatile issues for Chinese strategy, compromising the possibility of a "peaceful rising"?

Answer: For China, the Taiwan issue is most urgent. It is complex because it involves significant U.S. interests. But it is more than a political issue. Economically, Taiwan is well connected to mainland China. One highly feasible approach is not to let the water boil too much and wait for future generations to create solutions. The only problem for now is that politicians on both sides are impatient. This is made worse by outside troublemakers.

But there is a bright alternative for a peaceful resolution: a federation for the mainland and Taiwan. This could become a win-win alternative for both China and the world (see Part VI).

The North Korea issue is easier. China is willing to play its part in finding a resolution. Even so, one should not expect smooth sailing on this issue. It still poses a great challenge.

Question: Is the Chinese diaspora around the globe positive for China's development, as the Indian diaspora (what the Indian strategists call the "bollystan") has been?

Answer: So far, overseas Chinese have been the largest group of investtors in China. Also, they add value by playing a bridge role between China and the outside world. But their power is best displayed by their vast numbers. They mostly focus on low-end businesses. For example, Hong Kong businesspeople are the biggest investment group in China. But they focus on toys, clothes, and household products mostly.

Individually, the global multinationals are more influential in China as a group. They are the leader in information technology (IT), pharmaceutical, retail, energy, auto, and other capital-intensive businesses. Most Chinese professionals want to work for these multinationals. At present, more than 24 million Chinese work for overseas employers.

Expanding Chinese Manufacturing Power

Question: Will China be the world factory of the 21st century? Or can it be more than that, with a global positioning in offshoring business processes and other services, including R&D and innovation?

Answer: In this era, China has been able to build a manufacturing hub for the world. This hub has emerged in a natural, even accidental, way but is now reaching a rational level. It is bound to expand in all directions. It is being upgraded and is moving toward R&D, financial, and services. This process is unavoidable and also may take less time than one might have thought. International multinationals play a large role. By early 2006, more than 900 sizable R&D centers were in operation in China, all owned by foreign parties or joint ventures.

At the same time, Chinese companies are trying hard to move up in the value chain. For example, China's retail chain business is vibrant, though only about 14 years old. By now, retail business takes about 30% of market share. Within the next decade, it will take at least 60%.

A better Chinese economy will have to come from innovation. This is not restricted to technological issues. To me, it has to do more with leadership and organizations as well as governance and accountability.

Question: What you mean by the management revolution?

Answer: There is huge room for innovation in all these things. Otherwise, R&D would not make business sense. In general, China Inc. is still weak in terms of building professional organizations and effective management. Professional management is new to the nation. In the West, CEOs may work for five different companies during their career. In China, they can work only for one. It takes time to build modern professional organizations. In today's China, the biggest foe, the bureaucratic power, remains strong in the business sphere and is the biggest roadblock to real progress.

Also, every sector is overcrowded now. For example, China has over 100 DVD makers and 100 carmakers. They face deadly competition. To move ahead, there must be consolidations. But rational consolidations demand a professional environment. Otherwise, mergers and acquisitions will not work.

Now in the face of lethal market competition, China is beginning to embrace merger activities. Indeed, if China's electronics and home-appliances makers, now numbering about 1,300, were reduced to half a dozen, the resulting companies would be the biggest in the world. This may take a couple of decades to materialize. The problem is how to turn both the state sector and private sector companies into professional organizations so that meaningful mergers can function properly.

It is a basic reality that there are no small issues where China is concerned. Turning China from a government-centered economy into a modern economy requires creating the entire package with all the right components. The great thing is that in an increasingly open environment, the deep institutional issues can be resolved much more easily. Both the challenges and the opportunities are impressive.

Question: Can you give an example?

Answer: One salient example involves the big-four state banks. Despite an economic boom, they have been faltering. There is an urgent need to clean up the banking house. But this is hardly only a banking or business issue. The entire political-economic framework must be reformed. In short, these four banks must be turned into independent professional organizations with well-defined ownership and professional management. They will have to serve market needs rather than government. Today, more badly needed actions are being taken in this direction.

Question: What is exactly behind the banking mess?

Answer: These banks have no true owners, so they have been subject to bureaucratic power for six decades straight. In fact, this bureaucratic power has preyed on the banks since day one.

Question: Is the foreign buying into these banks the right direction?

Answer: Absolutely yes. Otherwise, these banks would be trapped in the bureaucratic swamp forever. It is interesting that so many foreign banking giants and investors are jumping into these banks (see Part IV).

Curtailing Bureaucratic Power

Question: You wrote in your book, *China's Global Reach*, that China is like an old man wearing baby clothes. Is the major obstacle to China's growth still the bureaucratic power?

Answer: Uncontained bureaucratic power has been the ultimate and lasting problem for China. In my book, I state that this bureaucratic problem is like a cancer that has spread all over the body. China's bureaucratic power has been expanding for at least 2,200 years, from the Qin Dynasty to the Mao era, or even much longer than that. This bureaucratic power has been able to contain all private initiative effectively and completely. China has always had a vibrant private sector, but it has failed to create a modern market economy and true private ownership (see Chapters 13 and 14).

Since 1978, though, China's bureaucratic power has been on the decline. This has resulted in the sharp rise of the private sector. It is this private sector that is most responsible for a booming economy. What a contrast! And the contrast is even more meaningful when one considers that China has the same soil, land, and people as always. But people are happier, more prosperous, and more productive than in the Mao era.

Question: The pragmatic approach of Sun Yat-Sen in the 1910s and of the late Deng Xiaoping in the 1980s is not sufficient for a path of political and social change?

Answer: Throughout the long search for a better nation in the past 200 years or so, China has not really had the opportunity to resolve the basic issues of untamed bureaucratic power from the root causes. Instead, there have been many shortcuts. Socialism was nothing but a shortcut in China in the past half century (though many outsiders argue that China has not had a true socialism).

Using socialism as a cover, government power reached the lowest grassroots levels. The society and people were trapped for decades and the economy went dead. But the government bureaucrats benefited greatly. Their power expanded in all possible ways and eventually reached the household and individual levels. No citizens were left independent, not even monks. All citizens were made servants to the government. This had never happened before in China's entire history.

The old dynastic governments had small official bodies. One hundred years ago, the government had only some 20,000 officials, with some 500,000 supporting staff, administrating over this vast nation (400 million at the time). In the Communist era, the bureaucratic body bulged to well over 45 million. But this vast official body is needed for complete control over the society and people (see Ch. 13 and 14).

Under this wild bureaucratic expansion, China experienced the biggest man-made tragedies ever. They included the people's commune, the Great Leap Forward, and the Cultural Revolution, among many other disasters. In short, vast bureaucratic power forced the entire society, the economy, and the population to serve its own needs. Even today, China's highest and most formidable goal is to contain this untamed bureaucratic power (see Part III).

Question: What could be the biggest driving force in accomplishing this?

Answer: Three things. First, private initiatives. Second, an open society. And third, international involvement. China's new growth and development has taken place exactly under these three new elements.

Chinese Multinationals and Partnerships

Question: Is the IBM-Lenovo agreement a signal of a new era for Chinese multinationals? Is this a different path from the Japanese strategy of the 1980s that you reported so clearly in your book *China's Global Reach*?

Answer: Chinese companies have made enormous progress, especially in manufacturing. But they have made limited progress with brands, intellectual property, and distribution networks, especially in the outside world. Moreover, their profits are tiny due to intense home competition and low-value-added manufacturing business. As a result, there is no way for the Chinese to follow the Japanese model for international expansion. Japanese businesses made healthy profits at home before they went outside, which happened when the domestic Japanese market was closed to outside competition. But Chinese businesses make tiny profits at home. So instead, they must seek active partnerships with the outside world. This is a realistic way for the Chinese. Some interesting progress is already visible in this context. For example, TCL bought Thomson's distressed TV unit and Alcatel's distressed mobile phone assets. Then came the high-profile deal for IBM-Lenovo.

Question: Why did IBM do it?

Answer: It not only dumped a low-profit business, but also gained a growing partner that is beginning to tap into the outside world. Also, through this partnership, IBM hopes to cross-sell more products to China. For Lenovo, becoming a global player is a dream come true. China as a dumping ground for low-value business could turn into a trend. This new type of strategic alliance will become more popular. In this way, the best resources from both worlds can be better utilized (see Part V).

Question: What are the main economic clusters that are changing the international specialization profile of China?

Answer: China is on everyone's map. An effective channel is being built and expanded. More international companies will add programs to get more from China, both as a factory and as a market. China needs to become more than a mere manufacturing hub or, more precisely, a world assembly center. Urgent needs include better banking, more effective financial systems and services, and higher-level intellectual work.

For a long time, China has been known as a cheap labor hub. Now international businesses realize that there is a vast pool of intellectual talent in China. Oracle and HP need to pay only $1,000 monthly to get a top Chinese engineer. In this respect, India is far ahead of China. Indian IT companies are already leading global players.

Question: What's your main advice for foreign investors, particularly from Europe?

Answer: There are great success stories of European companies in China. They include names like Glaxo Wellcome, AstroZeneca, Nestle, Nokia, Siemens, Unilever, Philips, BP, IKEA, Bayer, Carrefour, H&Q, Makro, HSBC, and Volkswagen, among many others. Siemens has 30,000 Chinese employees and 45 factories in China now. Carrefour can make more profits in China than anywhere else. It now has 78 megastores and is adding more. As to Unilever, China is already its profit haven. But Unilever must compete with P&G and many other brands.

Question: How did these companies succeed?

Answer: Well, all happy players are the same, while the unhappy ones have their own stories. The successful ones have done all the right things in China. They have long-term commitment, well-organized and flexible organizations, realistic strategies, and, most significantly, leadership. Localized management is also significant. No shortcuts. The bottom line? Grow with China. My book offers more than a dozen case studies, including both successes and failures.

A Tale of a New Society

Question: What are the main "growth engines" in China?

Answer: Domestic consumption is certainly major. As one example, by early 2006, China had over 400 million mobile phone users. So far, international suppliers have made more profits by selling their chips, components, equipment, and raw materials to the growing Chinese manufacturers. But services, especially financial, education, medical, logistics, and retail, are badly needed. In short, China needs everything, and anything can be profitable if done right.

Question: Can we consider that a middle class is booming in China?

Answer: Urban centers are the hubs of great wealth. So 50 top Chinese cities possibly take 60% or more of the wealth in the nation. Most urban residents in the big cities are already middle class in one way or another; among this group, businesspeople, teachers, civil servants, and professionals are the core. Rural income growth is less impressive. Today, an average rural person earns less than one-third what an urban person does.

However, more than 200 million rural migrant workers are effectively narrowing the gap, all on their own initiative. Many make profits in cities through very hard work. They then open their own shops in their hometowns or elsewhere. By now, they are running millions of small businesses such as retail outlets and beauty shops. This is a very significant factor in promoting overall development. Finally, a vast flow of people, ideas, and goods has become a new mandate, which lays the foundation for quick development for the nation.

Question: Probably in less than a decade, China will have more cybernauts and customers (for a market economy) than the United States. What will be the major consequences?

Answer: There will be more international flavors, above all. China will be more open, diverse, and mature, but more competitive as well. China will be become a *Global China*.

This makes a strong contrast to what is happening inside Japan, where things are still largely a Japanese play. China's theater will have countless international actors. In many sectors, such as auto, film, beauty products, drugs, retail, and IT, the foreign businesses are also the leading players. In short, China is becoming a global theater. A grand lesson from China is this: No nation can truly develop without making itself open to the world. This lesson should be universally relevant.

A Personal Story

Question: What impressed you most in the period after the fall of the Gang of Four?

Answer: It was an age of wonder and hope. The most impressive thing in 1978 was that colleges reopened. Some of us, much fewer than 1% of youth, could go to college (today, this number is much bigger, as there are 23 millions students in colleges). Before then, for some 11 years, urban high school graduates were sent to work in rural regions. Suddenly, some of us could get a college education. Immediately, things changed completely for the better. Schoolteachers became important and kids took books seriously. Some kids who failed to enter college took their own lives.

It was also a time of eye-opening and questioning. In the late 1970s, the old bureaucratic society suddenly became restless, having gone through many bitter experiences. All Chinese became interested in things outside China, anything and everything. This made a fundamental difference in the general atmosphere of the era.

All Chinese were eager to know what was in the outside world. Chinese newspapers were busy reporting on events elsewhere. There were debates on street corners on the pros and cons of the outside world. Criticism of the developed world would invite immediate attacks from all sides, though people knew next to nothing about other places. The national passion was turning in a completely new direction.

Looking back, one sees that most of the information about the outside world was not very precise or accurate — but this did not matter, as all Chinese were hungry for such information. (This is somewhat like the situation with the ongoing international media coverage on China. It is often inaccurate and somewhat imaginative, but international audiences devour it nonetheless.) The Chinese had been completely tied to a life of profound isolation. Each and every citizen wanted a new life somehow.

So many of us developed a mentality that everything in the West was great and everything at home was bad. The changing national passion had vast impacts on the policy making of the time. That was when China began to open up. The feeling was highly intense, and many of us vaguely sensed that bigger things were on the horizon. Yet we did not quite know what they might be.

Question: In your book you say that you consider yourself and the generation born in the 1960s a lucky generation. Why?

Answer: This generation is a lucky group indeed. They entered the era of reform at the right age. They had more opportunities than their elders. They were young enough to get more out of life. Today in China's fast-changing society they can increasingly focus on things that interest them. Many high-profile businessmen today are in this age group.

Question: Do you think this lucky generation is today the anchor for the changes needed?

Answer: This generation has done the right job. They have performed a leadership role for the last two decades. They have helped to create a new competitive economy. But the future belongs to the younger generations for sure. They are more open, their tastes are more international, their desires boundless. They are more egoistic and entrepreneurial and are better informed and educated. They will lead China into the next stage.

Furthermore, breaking away from the old bureaucratic life demands huge physical and mental strength, something the outside world is unfamiliar with. Positive institutional changes always demand a decisive public voice as well as massive private action. Hence, the Chinese youth will have to play a bigger transitional role, but this should be easier than in the 1980s. Back then, even little institutional changes demanded great effort. Today, changes are so dramatic that that the effect may be to create a new generation in less than 10 years.

Part II.

The Yuan, Trade, and Investment

SUMMARY

Within a very short time, from nowhere seemingly, China has leaped forward, becoming a top manufacturing center and a top trading nation. In 2005 alone, China manufactured 80 million TV sets, 300 million mobile handsets, and 70 million air-conditioning units. These things were unimaginable in the Mao era. What was behind all this?

A basic fact is this: China's quick development is tied to the outside world. The international involvement has many dimensions. First, the outside world had invested more than $640 billion in the Chinese market by early 2006. Second, overseas investors created over a half-million companies in this frontier market. Third, through their direct involvement, China's economy is now directly linked to the global markets. These overseas businesses are responsible for the majority of China's exports. In 2005 alone, nearly 60% of exports from China came through foreign-funded enterprises inside the nation.

This expanding manufacturing power is altering the global production map, and the changing reality also causes trade frictions of all sorts. Different nations have different interests. Reaching common ground is burdensome, to say the least. But there is no alternative and no shortcut. The economic interdependence demands rational thinking and actions.

Among the trade issues, the yuan's exchange rate stands out. Some people feel that a rising yuan offers an immediate solution to the trade imbalance as well as advantages to the world. But will a rising yuan resolve the deeper issues? Are there any other options?

Chapter 6.

China's Competitiveness vs. a Rising Yuan

China's surprise revaluation of the yuan on July 21, 2005, has raised many questions and issues. As a result, both inside and outside of China, there has been a great deal of commentary on how different sectors of China's economy stand to gain, or lose, from the policy change.

But the most important question is how the stronger yuan will affect China's competitiveness over the long term. A serious analysis shows that the revaluation could boost China's general competitiveness. And the entire world may benefit from a more competitive Chinese economy.

China's most basic economic challenge for the next generation will be to move from a low-value-added, investment-driven economy to a high-value-added, efficiency-driven one. The stronger yuan and the outside world will both play a significant role in causing this shift.

Business Chains: China's Hidden Strength

China's vast underpaid labor force is widely regarded as the foundation of the nation's competitiveness. But cheap labor is not the key ingredient in the recipe. True, the average manufacturing job in China pays only $115 per month. But many other developing nations, such as India and Indonesia, have a large supply of inexpensive labor — yet China has pulled ahead of them, and other developing nations, as a top business and investment center. Why?

What has made the biggest difference is that China has built a set of complete business chains, especially in the manufacturing sector. The term *business chain* encompasses all the phases a product goes through before it reaches the customer, from raw material to parts manufacturing, assembly, marketing, the provision of technology and capital, and so on. To a far greater extent than competing countries, China has successfully achieved critical mass for its business chains: Increasingly, all the required elements are present within the country.

Very significantly, China's business chains increasingly connect final products directly with global markets and buyers: In 2005 alone, Dell purchased about $16 billion worth of products made in China. General Electric (GE) reached over $5 billion in outsourcing plus over $5 billion additional sales in 2005, and Philips did over $10 billion of China business in 2005.

A dominating reason for the localization of business chains inside China is the domestic consumption explosion. For example, prior to 1990, hardly any homes had air-conditioning. Today air-conditioning is very popular; China produced 80 million units in 2005 alone. This rising consumption has become a magnet for international capitalists. Without it, attracting foreign investment would be very difficult.

Obviously, global multinationals want immediate transactions and quick profits. Naturally, they invest mostly in those markets where consumption rises quickly. All business leaders today are under enormous pressures to produce quick results. Their eyes are tightly fixed especially on markets that offer immediate benefits. Therefore, rising consumption has made China a top destination for global capital.

This Chinese consumption growth has had no equal in the world. In 2005 alone, China manufactured around 300 million mobile phones, some 100 million of which were sold to Chinese customers, helping to make China the world's biggest mobile phone market with over 400 million subscribers as of early 2006.

Furthermore, with such an exploding market, international telecom players have little choice but to compete in China if they intend to win in the world marketplace. Nokia's global leadership in 2004 was helped in no small measure by its $6.9 billion in business from China. This foreign rush has further expanded the business chains.

The great advantage of complete business chains is that all manufacturers, Chinese or international, can make products in one place—China. In fact, regions like Guangdong and Shanghai have highly concentrated business chains that provide the best services for all sorts of businesses. This high degree of efficiency exists only in very few markets around the globe. It has been decisive in helping to make China a new business center.

All participants have gained vast opportunities in the process. With countless players in the same market, improvements occur daily. Making any end-product is supported by a self-sufficient business chain inside China. This has huge global dimensions, naturally.

In one extreme case, Geely Group, a private, fast-growing Chinese firm, which has been manufacturing cars since 1998, has been able to sell over 100,000 cars to some 30 developing nations in Southeast Asia, Eastern Europe, and Africa. This quick growth is attributable to the fact that there are already thousands of auto parts makers inside the nation. In 2005, China's auto export exceeded import for the very first time. This was certainly helped by Geely Group.

In essence, Geely Group is no more than an assembler of parts made by Chinese manufacturers. However, it has been able to produce the cheapest cars in the world: Geelys sell for as little as U.S.$3,800, a price point that has created a market not only in China, but also in many developing nations. Improbably, the company is even planning to team up with the Hong Kong government for a new plant in Hong Kong, which aims to sell sedans to the global markets.

High Concentration of Business Chains

An even more significant factor in making China a new manufacturing center is the high concentration of same-business chains in one location, be it a city or province or a multi-province region.

For example, Guangdong has more than a half-dozen new industrial towns that focus on consumer electronics, home appliances, toys, and clothes. In the province of Zhejiang, many new industrial towns focus on shoes, small appliances, and clothes. Manufacturing in these locations gives one all the advantages in terms of parts suppliers, distribution, and logistics. Such advantages are rare on a global basis.

Under this environment, it is small wonder that this Chinese manufacturing center is able to supply the world with more than 50% of its shoes, garments, and mobile handsets as well as 70% of its microwave ovens, DVDs, and watches, among other things. Only in a globalized world could this have taken place and in such a short time. But it has involved innumerable businesses from around the world.

Foreign Multinationals vs. Business Chains

China's complete business chains have helped the country's enterprises to exhibit the international economy's key virtues: efficiency, convenience, competitiveness, and low cost. A small increase in the value of the yuan exchange rate can hardly harm these ever-growing business chains. The latest trend is for foreign multinationals to set up research and development centers within China; IBM, Sony, Philips, Microsoft, Siemens, Intel, and LG, among others, have set up more than 800 of them.

These centers have extensive functions. They are responsible for making not only products localized to cater to Chinese demand, but in many cases, next-generation products for the global markets. Countless businesses from the developing world have also rushed into China, advancing the business chains even further.

The business chains are bound to expand even more because all their participants, whether foreign or Chinese, have huge vested interests in their continued progress. The general trend has several elements. One is a wider connection between Chinese business chains and the global marketplace. By now, more and more international players are rushing in to participate. These foreign players are key in connecting China's economy to the global economy.

Second, more improvement is taking place in terms of quality, accountability, and efficiency. In particular, huge efforts are directed toward expanding the logistics and technological standards. This helps to make China's business center more relevant and attractive to all.

Third, global management standards are being adopted more and more by Chinese players. The ever-increasing interactions between Chinese businesses and their foreign counterparts are playing a part. Learning by doing is an important secret to the progress of the Chinese companies and is powerful in promoting more ties between China and the outside world.

A booming Chinese economy is the key attraction of this manufacturing center, which has made it a new profit generator for multinationals. This trend will certainly continue. As long as China remains politically stable and has a fast-growing consumption as well as a friendly business environment, foreign investors and multinationals will continue to treat China as a priority. This foreign rush has naturally led to greater competition in the Chinese marketplace.

This new center has already altered the global economic map. Different nations are now trying to take advantage of the opportunities China offers to boost their own long-term development. But some are doing better than others. Japan Inc., in spite of recent Japan-China tensions that have somewhat cooled Japan Inc.'s ardor, is arguably doing better than U.S. Inc. in this regard.

The auto industry is an example. Both Japanese and American automakers have sought to reduce costs by shifting production to lower-cost countries; U.S. firms have mostly gone to Mexico, while Japanese firms have used China. But the scale of Japan's investment in China is greater; and, partly because of the larger scale of the market in China as compared to Mexico, the potential gains to Japanese firms are greater. Japanese automakers are now considering selling their Chinese-made cars to international markets.

The Challenges of the Strong Yuan

At the same time, the yuan's appreciation will undeniably take a toll on Chinese exporters, in particular textile and consumer products makers, whose profit margins were already low, usually below 5%. So they must try hard to move up in the value chain or possibly be forced out. At the same time, they are more vulnerable to potential punitive measures imposed by foreign governments, which would have more adverse consequences on their health.

All in all, domestically the stronger yuan raises tough issues. But there are more fundamental issues China must resolve. One of the most pressing is overcapacity, especially in the manufacturing sector. China Inc. has enormous challenges ahead, but these challenges go well with a rising yuan.

Indeed, the overcapacity issue is worsened by two factors. First, there are simply too many players in most sectors. In air-conditioner manufacturing, for example, there are more than 50 companies now, although this is actually an improvement from the 400 that existed in 2000. Though the market is still growing fast, many of these companies are no longer profitable.

One example is Kelon, which has been the Chinese market leader in making cooling products and which trades on both the Hong Kong and Shenzhen stock exchanges. It has been showing serious losses lately, chiefly due to the overinvestment in the sector. As a result, its controlling shares have recently changed hands.

But achieving rational consolidation is very difficult at this time because most of these companies are still controlled by the government. Consolidation is clearly necessary and would be much easier if political interests could be completely separated from the business world. Fundamentally, China must resolve the institutional barriers imposed by a traditional bureaucracy. To move away from the government-dominated economy and society is a most urgent necessity, with few if any alternatives or shortcuts (see Ch.13 and 14).

Another difficult issue is that most Chinese manufacturers don't have sufficient intellectual property and cutting-edge technology. Instead, they must pay high prices to buy technology from the outside world. This problem is a significant contributor to the poor profitability of many Chinese manufacturers. For example, in 2005, China produced some 80 million TV sets, but most Chinese TV makers lost money.

This slow intellectual development has everything to do with government domination. The state companies are not innovative, but they still control some 70% of the nation's business assets. Today, the state sector shares only about 20% in Chinese R&D, while the private sector takes about 80%. For example, in the frontier city Shenzhen, some 90% of R&D is carried out by mostly small private companies as now.[1]

In general, to most Chinese manufacturers, a rising yuan will produce both good and bad effects. On the minus side, their already low profit margins are further eroded by loss of the competitive advantage provided by the weak yuan when they sell to Wal-Mart and other international buyers. As the yuan continues to rise, regardless of how slowly, they are the first to feel the pain.

On the plus side, throwing away the undervalued-currency crutch could force them to become more competitive. This means that China Inc. would have no choice but to focus more on innovation, intellectual development, and rational consolidation, among other beneficial measures. In the long term, this pressure should make China Inc. perform better.

In particular, a stronger yuan will force greater reform in the state sector. This sector faces more and more problems than it can handle in any rational way. The only option is to privatize the entire sector. The sooner this is achieved, the better for the overall economic performance of the nation. Otherwise, the sector faces a death sentence from cruel market competition in general and the continuing bureaucratic manipulations in particular.

China has come a long way to reach this stage of development, despite all the imperfections. Above all, China has successfully integrated its economy with the global economy. Though there remain huge trade, political, and economic issues for China and the outside world to work on, everyone has directly benefited from the Chinese expansion. The small but decisive increase in the yuan's value shows, above all, that China is committed to playing its part in the maintenance of a stable, growing global economy.

Chapter 7.
Where to Invest Your Money?

Capital always chases after growth; and with the world's economic center of gravity increasingly shifting to new frontier markets from Latin America to Africa, Eastern Europe, and especially Asia, capital is flowing into these "emerging markets" as well. When it comes to experts on emerging markets, it is hard to find a more prominent one than Mark Mobius, president of Templeton Emerging Markets Fund since 1987.

A Traveler and Emerging-Market Veteran

In international investment circles, it is said that if you are in a new emerging market anywhere in the world, you can expect to bump into Mark Mobius. After getting his PhD in economics and political science from the Massachusetts Institute of Technology in 1964, Mobius began to work in Asia as an investment professional. He has been mostly based in greater China (Hong Kong and Taiwan) for the past four decades, though constantly circling the globe like a pilot. Traveling more than 200 days a year, he spends more time on the road looking for opportunities than almost any of his competitors.

His many activities besides investment research have included writing three books, which focus on investment pros and cons and global capital markets. Highly regarded as a lead manager for the Franklin Templeton Emerging Markets Fund, he has also served as joint chairman of the World Bank and on the Organization for Economic Cooperation and Development (OECD) Global Corporate Governance Forum's Investor Responsibility Taskforce, among other public posts.

The Franklin Templeton funds have had a truly global reach and have invested more than $20 billion in Chinese stocks alone. When asked what was the biggest surprise about his China experience, Mobius said, "The speed at which China's development is now taking place, and also how the transformation has been so dramatic between the Mao era and now. When I was visiting China in the 1970s the situation was clearly different from what it is now. That is quite amazing."

As one who has been through the ups and downs of world capital markets for decades, what advice does Mobius give on global investments? "Take the long view—like the Chinese do," he said. And what is his biggest concern about today's China? "The longevity of the bureaucracy, and the resultant corruption, as well as pollution."

For now, the quick development of nations such as China, India, Mexico, Brazil, and Hungary is impacting the world in no small way. With the global economy expanding as never before, international trade and investment are adding new wealth to the world. But there are tremendous new challenges, such as increasing trade frictions. People say that change brings both challenge and opportunity. This writer talked to Mark Mobius about some of the difficulties confronting the world.

Interview

Question from George Zhibin Gu: So many investment opportunities are emerging everywhere today. For the next 10 years, where do the biggest opportunities lie around in the globe?

Answer from Mark Mobius: Emerging markets have the biggest opportunities for the next 10 years. The reasons for this are clear: Those countries are growing the fastest, they include countries like China and India with very large populations whose per capita income is growing, and capital markets in those countries are now undergoing rapid development.

Question: Nowadays, the buzzwords are China and India. But these two huge nations have had rather different paths in the current growth period. How do you see their development stories?

Answer: Of course their cultures are different, but China and India do not differ markedly in the sources of growth and prosperity. As these countries privatize their moribund state enterprises and as they continue to liberalize their economies, allowing private enterprise to flourish, there will be continued rapid economic growth for both nations.

Chinese Investment

Question: China has experienced rapid growth in this era of globalization. Which industries or regions of China do you regard as especially promising?

Answer: Almost all regions in China are attractive investment candidates, although at the present time the east of the country is the most developed. The sectors with the greatest prospects are the consumer products and services sectors. There is a growing demand for consumer goods and services such as clothing, electronics, overseas travel, et cetera.

Question: China's institutional and financial reforms seem to have picked up steam lately. As a result, several very interesting developments are going on simultaneously. First, China is inviting foreign banks and investors to buy into state banks. The Bank of America, Citibank, HSBC, Temasek, and the Royal Bank of Scotland, among others, have spent billions on these new ventures. Is this a good move for China? Is it also a good move for the international parties? What kind of long-term impact on global development will there be if China is successful in reforming these troubled state banks through getting foreign partners and listing them on overseas stock markets?

Answer: This is a good idea for both China and the foreign investors. China receives not only new capital with which to recapitalize its banks, but it also receives know-how and experience from foreign investors. With the entry of the foreign investor banks, Chinese banks will learn about new management and financial methods used in other parts of the world. Long-term reform of the banking system in China will have a very beneficial impact on the Chinese economy, since the banks will become more effective in lending money to viable enterprises.

Question: Another major financial reform is the complete flotation of shares trading in the domestic stock market. Do you see this as a positive development?

Answer: Yes. That is a positive development since the flotation of those shares will broaden the market and possibly bring new investors into the market.

Question: More than ever before, international investors are eager to invest in China's domestic stock market. But so far, only about 40 foreign institutional investors have been allowed to enter the market with a capital allowance up to $10 billion. Do you see this as a step in the right direction? What advice would you give to the Chinese government on this?

Answer: Yes, the participation of foreign institutional investors is positive, but it is important to move faster and allow a wider range of foreign investors.

Question: So many international fund management companies and investment banks are setting up shop in China through joint ventures. Is this a positive move for all participating parties? What more should be done? Should the Chinese government allow foreign parties to establish independent branches in the future?

Answer: Yes, that is a positive move, as it allows those companies to benefit from China's growing financial services needs. At the same time, they bring extensive knowledge and experience into China's market, allowing both parties to benefit.

Question: Over the past 10 years, Chinese businesses have tried their best to adopt international professional standards. Do you see any progress with these efforts? What is the biggest area of improvement that you think Chinese companies should work on over the next decade?

Answer: Yes, China has made good efforts in this area. With greater international exposure, China knows that it needs to improve its standards in order to compete globally. Chinese companies need to be more transparent and have independent management teams and independent board members who are focused on creating shareholder value.

Japan

Question: By now, Japan has had four consecutive growth quarters, finally. We see that Japan Inc. has been moving away, though painfully and slowly, from traditional, tightly closed business formations and cross-holdings among banks and their corporate clients. Also, plenty of consolidations have taken place lately, especially in the banking sector.

Furthermore, Sony and some other Japanese multinationals are opening the doors wider for international professionals to hold senior management positions. But still, many people wonder if this Japanese economic recovery is sustainable. Do you see any risks for Japan's recovery to be short-lived again?

Answer: Japan's recovery is well on track. Key drivers include consumer expenditure and corporate investment. The implementation of key reforms could further support growth and ensure that recovery is not derailed.

The Yuan Versus Global Development

Question: Global investments and world trade have expanded to record levels. But uncertainties and worries are emerging. In particular, the U.S. faces two hard realities: rising debt and a widening trade gap. Furthermore, this U.S. trade deficit comes from various sources—oil-supplying nations as well as Japan and China, among others. What do you propose to alter this picture?

Answer: The U.S. needs to increase its savings and investments, and cut federal expenditures and use the money it now has in the budget more wisely. Another factor would be an adjustment of currency values, with those values moving more in line with the competitive realities.

Question: Some Americans feel that making the Chinese yuan go up farther would help the U.S. trade balance. What do you think about this opinion? If the yuan should continue to go up, how much should it be? Would a strengthening yuan help to stabilize the U.S. and global trade picture? Some people feel that what is sold at Wal-Mart stores is mostly products that are no longer manufactured in the U.S. Therefore, regardless of where these products are made, the U.S. must import them anyway. What do you think?

Answer: A small revaluation of the yuan, which we have recently seen, will actually make the trade picture worse, since many products now sold in the U.S. are made in China and only China. A small U.S. dollar increase in prices will make those goods more expensive for the U.S. to import with no real alternative sources. Thus the value of imports by the U.S. from China will increase, making the trade balance worse.

The overwhelming fact is that China's labor costs are much lower than those in the U.S. Thus even if the yuan is revalued, the impact would not be large enough to seal the gap between wages in the two countries. Moreover, China also imports raw materials from neighboring countries, assembles products, and exports them to the U.S. Thus a general revaluation of regional currencies would be more helpful than just the yuan.

Question: Protectionist voices have become very loud in the U.S. and Europe recently. In case new protectionist measures kicked in, what would happen to the U.S., European, and global economy and financial markets?

Answer: The U.S. is no longer as important to global economies as it was historically. We now have the enlarged EU trade bloc, Latin America, Africa, Asian economic powerhouses China and India, and so on. Emerging markets are not only dealing with developed markets such as the U.S., but also with each other, and thus the dependence on the U.S. is lower now.

For example, Taiwan and South Korea are now exporting more to China than to the U.S. I expect this trend to continue. Nevertheless, the U.S. and Europe are important "engines" for the global economy, and a significant protectionist movement could have a big impact.

Chapter 8.

Behind a Rising Yuan

The ever-increasing Chinese export to the global markets has brought new concerns and conflicts. Many outsiders feel that the weak yuan has played its trick. Therefore, strengthening the yuan is one key way to alter the global trade picture. Will it work? Not likely. The following dialogue with Portugal's *Expresso Weekly* partly focuses on this issue.

Behind the Strengthening of the Yuan

Question from **Expresso Weekly:** Was the recent revaluation a political decision, or a true step in the monetary management of the yuan in the new global situation?

Answer: Yes and no. Yes, in a way it was a political decision, which has essentially involved the world, especially the developed nations. It shows that a developing China has become deeply connected to the global economy: Business affairs inside China cause chain reactions around the globe. International concerns have increasingly affected Chinese politics. Even at home, it took a long time to make this move. But no, it was not a purely political move because the issue involves many economic factors, which are as significant as the political ones.

Question: Is the Chinese economy cooling?

Answer: No easy answer for that. To gain a better understanding, let us widen our view somewhat. China's economy has been running like a racecar in the last three decades, with a record-making annualized growth of around 9.6%. This phenomenal growth has involved the entire world most directly. For example, within China, overseas-funded enterprises contributed around one third of China's total industrial output as now. Their share could reach 50% within a decade.

Furthermore, about 60% of China's export in 2005 was carried out by these overseas-funded enterprises. What is more, China's international trade is up to 65% of its GDP, reflecting a heavy dependence on international trade. These facts suggest that China's economy is very much tied to global markets. So, if the world economy continues to expand, China will benefit.

On the domestic level, China's development has been uneven, to say the least. One feature is that it has relied heavily on investment. In particular, the manufacturing sector has made huge progress. This kind of growth produces numerous weaknesses as well.

First, China's current growth started at an extremely low level — meeting the basic needs of a shortage-ridden economy. Now it has a surplus economy. Naturally, this makes high-rate growth very tricky. So China stands at another crossroads today.

Second, the quality of development is not high. In fact, one could say that the quality is very low and even troublesome. There are huge serious issues to be resolved. These include mismanagement and redundancies as well as an absence of modern corporate governance and professional management. Also, China Inc. has been very slow in moving to the higher-value-added, efficiency-driven sphere. These issues demand solutions before the nation reaches the next stage of development. In particular, the banking and financial systems are still having difficulties because of their ties to the bureaucratic world.

This slow political reform is the third negative factor, the one that is the most damaging to China's health. Above all, the government bureaucracy is not a service provider at all. Instead, it works to advance its own limitless interests and consequently has created countless barriers. But it is next to impossible to turn such a self-appointed, overextended bureaucracy into a modern service provider without huge struggles.

Question: What is really behind this bureaucratic problem?

Answer: So far, the reform has barely touched the basics of the old political structure. As a result, bureaucratic power remains the major barrier to resolution of economic and business issues from the root causes.

Question: Why so?

Answer: Because everything was built around the government, all economic, business, and social problems became political problems. This dominating bureaucratic power has eliminated all modern things such as true owners, right legal protection, and true professional standard, as well as true modern, merit based organizations and institutions. What is more, this untamed, self-appointed bureaucratic power remains the fundamental illness of China today (see Part III).

So, given these facts, one could say that an annualized growth of 9.6% for the past three decades should have been beyond imagination. At the same time, it would not be a bad thing if China's economy slowed down a bit. Indeed, it would be great for China to slow down so that the crucial issues, especially the political ones, could be truly addressed.

For now, one should not focus too much on the economic data. Instead, it is time to focus on resolving the deeper issues. Future growth must come from innovation with respect to institutional, legal, and government issues. In short, China's continued progress necessitates moving beyond the construction of factories, shops, and roads. After a fundamental change in the basic political-economic system, it would be much easier for China to address economic and business woes.

For example, income growth is impressive, but there is huge room for improvement, especially in rural regions. So far, China's development is more an urban affair. Rural development remains very slow and backward. Now the rural income is less than one third of the urban income. But 57% of Chinese remain rural bound. True rural development demands true political reform so that farmers are free of endless bureaucratic ropes.

Once this huge problem is resolved, rural income could easily double. If rural income doubles, China's economic size could easily double or triple. So, the next stage development must include rural development, which has been largely neglected until recently.

Question: Why was the readjustment only 2.1%, not 3% to 5%, as Goldman Sachs and the speculators anticipated?

Answer: It was a tough decision on the economic side. Indeed, most Chinese exporters have a profit margin less than 5%. Many textile, toy, and consumer products exporters will suffer a lot even with a 2.1% readjustment. But by August 2006, the yuan had appreciated to about 3.5%. It appears that it will continue to appreciate. All this will affect many Chinese business groups.

Question: Will even so small a revaluation affect the Chinese export machine? What clusters can be affected?

Answer: In general, the impact could become positive in the long run. The low profits for China Inc. prompt it to try to move up in the value chains. To achieve that, companies will increasingly need to do rational consolidation, technological innovation, and organization building. So, the era for easy money is receding, helped by upward movement of the yuan.

Chinese Multinationals

Question: With a stronger yuan, will Chinese companies soon begin to buy many more foreign assets?

Answer: A go-global strategy for China Inc. will accelerate certainly, but the rising yuan is not the crucial factor. The really crucial factor is that China has an overcapacity in most sectors, manufacturing in particular. So Chinese companies must increase their efforts to find new markets on the outside. Expansion strategies will involve many things, and buying assets is only one of them. I think creating extensive partnerships and joint ventures could become a top priority.

True, China Inc. is interested in buying international assets — distributions, established brands, technology, and natural resources. But in general the Chinese companies are very, very weak financially. Furthermore, they don't have a strong home base yet. Without a strong home base, they have enormous difficulties going global in a big way.

How were Japanese and South Korean multinationals able to expand effectively around the globe? Above all, they had strong home bases that enabled them to make healthy profits at home. This happened when these markets were largely closed to outside competitors. But most Chinese companies don't have that luxury, mainly because China's domestic market is very open and there are countless foreign players inside. This is fundamentally different from the situation in Japan and South Korea. In addition, it will take a long time for the Chinese to establish a strong home base.

Question: Is a stronger yuan of help to Chinese tech start-ups going IPO abroad?

Answer: From a Chinese perspective, it makes little difference. From an international perspective, Chinese assets could become more attractive, so that more foreign investments will rush into China. One should expect thousands of Chinese companies to be listed in overseas stock markets within a decade. So far, Hong Kong, New York, and Singapore are the top choices. To be sure, most Chinese companies wish to get listed in other places, especially Europe. But this requires more efforts from both sides.

Question: Does a stronger yuan mean less costly inputs (mainly energy and raw material commodities, denominated in dollars)? What will be the consequences?

Answer: China's expanding economy, especially the expanding manufacturing sector, demands ever-increasing oil and raw materials. At this time, for example, the supply of oil in many leading cities is insufficient. Even some gas stations in Guangdong are short on gas at times. But there is a hidden factor: China's low-level production creates a huge waste of energy and raw materials.

For example, for every $100 of production, China consumes about 4.4 times the energy that Japan does. The need to move to an efficiency-driven economy is huge and has become a pressing issue. But improvement will not occur immediately. This having been said, one must notice the huge efforts taken by China in this new direction. It is possible that improvement could take place sooner than previously expected. The driving force is survival itself.

International Impacts

Question: Will a stronger yuan mean less appetite for U.S. bonds and less financing of the U.S. budget deficit?

Answer: Interestingly, China has invested more money in the U.S. than the U.S. has in China up to now. Reportedly, China holds some $250 billion of U.S. government bonds today. For the foreseeable future, China will hold serious amounts of U.S. debts. But the increased yuan value is only a small issue for the future.

The bigger concern is the declining dollar and especially what is behind it—the erosion of the U.S. economic power. This is manifested by two basic facts: huge debts and the trade deficit. In short, the U.S. takes in more than it outputs. The risks of a further-declining dollar are apparent to all. However, an even bigger potential disaster in the making could be a nationalistic protectionist movement. This would cause huge adverse ripple effects around the world.

But the bottom line is that both nations have enormous benefits to share with each other. For example, 53% of shoes in the global markets were made in China as of 2004. But the global players such as Nike and Adidas and their distribution partners derive more benefits than the Chinese. Their shoes are made in China at a cost of around $20 per pair, but global consumers pay some $100 or more. The huge profits go to the brand holders, distributors, and retailers, and only $2 goes to the Chinese manufacturers.

Question: With a yuan pegged to a basket of currencies, including the euro, what can the Europeans expect from Chinese business partners?

Answer: The economic ties between China and Europe are strengthening rapidly. There seems to be a better understanding between them. This has helped to build strong economic ties. For example, China's total trade with the EU had surpassed that with Japan and the U.S. as of 2004. One can expect this trend to continue. Furthermore, more members of Europe Inc. will come to China. At the same time, expect more Chinese investment in Europe.

Interestingly, so far, China Inc.'s European ventures have focused on Eastern Europe more than Western Europe. The reason is simple: The cost in Eastern Europe is much less. The general picture is that China Inc. intends to use Eastern Europe as a base to better explore the opportunities in the rest of Europe. China Inc. is sharply increasing its investment in Latin America, Africa, and Southeast Asia for similar reasons. For the Western European markets, China Inc. prefers to create as many partnerships as possible, which may be a more effective as well as a very realistic way to get results.

In general, China Inc. hopes to gain better technology, brands, and distribution from Europe. But so far, Europe Inc. is more active in China than China Inc. is in Europe. This is changing, though very slowly. In particular, Chinese companies want to hire Western managers both inside China and beyond. I think hiring more European professionals will make sense for the Chinese.

Question: Some people claim that Chinese textile companies are trying to set up factories in other poor nations in order to avoid the frequent quotas and even bans from the U.S. and the EU. Is this true?

Answer: It may be true to some extent. In fact, most Chinese consumer products manufacturers, not just textile companies, are trying to expand overseas. There are many reasons. Avoiding quotas and trade bans is just one. The biggest reason is that there is a surplus in all manufactured goods inside China, which has been the case for the last 10 years or so.

To escape this surplus trap, the Chinese companies are forced to tap into overseas markets in all possible ways. But most Chinese manufacturers are financially too weak to set up extensive overseas operations. However, as trade fictions loom, such transfers will gain more popularity.

But China is not the only nation doing this sort of thing. Many nations such as the U.S., those in the EU, and Japan have done it. In the case of the U.S. and the EU, they have set up countless factories inside China just to avoid paying high tariffs, among other things.

In the case of Japan, its multinationals have set up operations around the world within a short time. Both Honda and Toyota have extensive U.S. operations in order to sell cars directly to the U.S. market. This is the Japanese way to avoid trade disputes with the U.S. So far, these overseas Japanese operations are much more successful than the Chinese. It will be a long time before China Inc. truly becomes internationalized in this context.

Chapter 9.

Beyond Textile Trade Wars

November 8, 2005, was a day to celebrate, sort of, for the exhausted trade negotiators from Washington, DC, and Beijing. After eight rounds of talks, they finally reached an agreement on future textile trade between the two nations, thus avoiding a potentially disastrous outcome.

The new agreement is somewhat parallel to the one reached between the EU and China in the late summer of 2005. Even with such agreements in hand, though, all trading partners are aware that there are more issues to be resolved.

The larger picture is this: Indeed, future challenges remain huge, but the underlying issue is the quickly changing world production and trade map. Low-end manufacturing activities are increasingly shifting to low-cost nations, with much of the developed world becoming more service and high-tech oriented. All this means a new world economic reality.

The bottom line: How can the developed and developing nations play the right roles in a changing global market? Any meaningful answer must focus on this new life.

Chinese Citizens' Confusion

On the streets of China, typical citizens are very confused about the endless trade disputes, especially lately. Most understand little about what is behind all these conflicts. Many feel that the matter should remain strictly between the buyers and sellers. But now, government bodies are working to put up barriers to business activities. This troubles the Chinese, especially when they hear that the developed world has a free market system.

Behind the textile and other consumer products are low-paid Chinese workers. Their working conditions are often shocking — similar to those that existed some 100 years ago in the West.

For sure, nobody in the developed world is interested in working in a sweatshop for 10 to 14 hours a day, six or seven days a week, for $50 to $100 per month. Such jobs are left to people living in poor nations such as India, China, and Vietnam. In today's China, low-paid workers may suffer workplace abuses; many of them may not even get paid for months or even years.

Changing Production Map

The larger picture is that the sharp rise in Chinese export is a natural consequence of the changed global production map. The United States and EU long ago stopped producing low-end textiles and garments, among other low-value-added items.

The United States and much of Europe are increasingly becoming service- and high-tech-oriented economies. The manufacturing work, especially in the low end of value chains, has increasingly shifted to the low-cost nations like China, Mexico, India, Indonesia, and Vietnam.

Furthermore, many Western multinationals outsource such production to these low-cost nations in order to increase profits. What is more, they may put their traditional price tag on these made-in-China/India/Mexico products and sell them in their established markets.

Trade frictions can backfire. For example, in the summer of 2005, due to trade frictions, at least 87 million garment pieces were stuck in numerous European ports. Losses were extensive for European companies, wholesalers, and retailers. In all this, the European consumers were the biggest losers and naturally wanted a quick resolution. Only then did the various EU members quickly reach an agreement with China to end the ban.

Similar realities were also behind the new textile agreement between Washington, DC, and Beijing. Neither nation could afford a trade war.

What have we learned from these events? At least one lesson: There are no true winners of trade wars. Because of the economic interdependence and cooperation that are a new reality in today's world, the trade game is different from that in the 19th century in which winners could take all.

Moreover, because of global interconnectedness, political measures alone can hardly resolve trade problems. Applying more rational and realistic thinking to this new reality, so that everyone wins, demands a completely new mind-set.

Increased Opportunity in China

Perhaps because China's development has proceeded so much faster than previously expected, understanding its full meaning is going to take more time and effort. But in the meantime, global businesspeople feel they cannot let opportunities slip by.

More and more foreign shops are being set up in all corners of China. Kentucky Fried Chicken celebrated the opening of its 1,500th outlet in China in late 2005. Both KFC and McDonald's could make more money in China than anywhere else in the world as time passes.

By mid-2006, McDonald's had more than 762 outlets in China. It is now expanding in a hurry. Its new China manager says that the company will add 100 more outlets a year and reach 1,000 outlets in total by 2008.[1] In addition, McDonald's has added drive-throughs that partner with Chinese gas stations. In this way, it intends to take a bigger share in this fast-growing market. But its success will invite more copycats, both Chinese and foreigners.

The giant entertainer Disney is another happy expansionist. Its new theme park in Hong Kong has turned out to be too small for the crowds of Chinese tourists. During the Chinese New Year in January 2006, mainland Chinese tourists overwhelmed the park. As a result, access had to be denied to thousands of visitors who had already paid, causing a public relations nightmare. The fact that it is not easy for mainlanders to get the permit to visit Hong Kong, which involves lengthy approvals and fees, made the situation worse.

This had never before happened in Disney's history, and not much could be done. Later, in an interview, a senior Disney executive said that he wept three times over the incident.[2] But the business prospects for Disney never looked better in this ancient land filled with people eager to get the best entertainment the world offers.

Upon Disney's initial success in Hong Kong, Disney is planning to enter the mainland. The only problem, seemingly, is where to put the next park—Shanghai, Beijing, or Xian? Regardless of the next Disney location, it will probably attract countless Chinese tourists, young and old.

Foreign success stories are everywhere inside China today. Unilever and P&G get credit for making Chinese women prettier, which translates to profits in the billions. Very soon, they will make more profits in China than anywhere else on earth.

The EU and the United States had surpassed Japan in total trade with China as of 2004. But some confrontational issues have emerged as well. Some parties feel that benefits are being taken from them and that actions are needed to reverse the trend.

In the case of the United States, there has been a sharply rising trade deficit with China. But a sound analysis would show that U.S. Inc. has huge opportunities to explore, which could promote the general health of the U.S. economy.

Certainly U.S. Inc. is the biggest and most powerful group in the world. But most sizable U.S. firms are far behind those in Japan, South Korea, and the EU in doing international business. Part of the reason is that the United States has about a $12 trillion market at home, the biggest market in the world. Venturing out takes extra effort, to say the least. So there is still huge room for the U.S Inc. to do more in other parts of the world, China included.

Education is one area in which the United States could do much more. Most Chinese students would love to go to a U.S. school. But for numerous reasons, only a few can travel to the United States. Hence, one good alternative would be for U.S. schools to set up campuses in China. In this respect, most U.S. schools are far behind the Canadian, Australian, and European schools.

For example, a top business school in China is the China Europe International Business School, an 11-year-old joint venture between China and the EU. Chinese college students, 23 million of them, really want more U.S. and international schools to come. With more international involvement, China's education would reach a new level, which would benefit all parties.

More business flows can significantly benefit the U.S. economy. Today, Chinese citizens have a strong desire to tour the outside world. But there are policy restrictions from Washington, DC. As a result, most Chinese tourists visit other regions. Once the United States opens the door wider to tourists, countless Chinese will rush in.

Medical service is another area of opportunity in China. The rising Chinese economy certainly could use help from the many advanced and well-managed hospitals in the developed world. So far, very few international medical organizations have come to China. Chinese consumers want more of them established over here.

And the list of potential new businesses is very long. The advantages for the United States and other developed countries would be huge. All that is needed is for them to become more active in grasping opportunities.

All things considered, more positive and creative thinking will allow more parties to take advantage of the expanding Chinese pie. The bottom line is that more economic exchange will help everyone.

Two Sides of a Coin

Today, the strongest desire on the part of Chinese citizens is to fully integrate their lives into global life, spiritually and practically. This has become the biggest driving force for all positive changes.

A poverty-stricken nation hardly interests anyone. A fast-developing country, on the other hand, may generate strong, but conflicting, reactions: immense interest along with worries and even fears. China has run into this difficulty. Taking China into the world club requires time and effort.

Despite all the uncertainties, economic ties between China and the outside world have been strengthening. Surely, business organizations have their own incentives to move capital, goods, technology, and people around the globe. This trend can only strengthen as time goes by.

A fundamental lesson about this era is that nations that actively participate in the globalized world have been able to make the most progress. China, even with its vast wounds of history, is able to move ahead quickly, which is a marvel in itself. But it also shows that being open to the world is a must in order to gain true development.

International multinationals are already among the biggest winners in China today. Their immense vested interests have helped to make China a top trading nation, a fast-growing market, and a global manufacturing center. Indeed, in 2005, nearly 60% of China's export was carried out by foreign-funded enterprises operating inside. With the outsourcing and joint ventures added, this international share in China's export could easily reach over 70%.

More significantly, if there is a $10 profit on the table, the multinationals will get $8. The developing nations must work hard to get the remaining $2. This will be the picture for a long time to come.

But still, the large issue about this fast-developing China remains. Tony Blair, the British prime minister, said in his 2005 trip to Beijing, "The emergence of China is a big thing. Everyone in the outside world needs time to think over it." This mentality is natural as well as positive. Furthermore, dumping the old world mentality is a must if more worldwide progress is to be made.

Chinese people can easily understand the difficulties in making a global transition from the old world order to a completely new one. This is the case because China has experienced dramatic changes in its relationship to the world in the last 200 years or so.

For example, in 1793, the Chinese emperor told the British delegation to Beijing, "China is a big nation with vast resources, self-contained and abundant in all things. There is little need for things from the outside world."[3] This mentality caused massive problems for China from that time on.

Yet, since then, the West took leaps and bounds while China had a long sleep. That is a great lesson for the world today, not just for China. For now, no one should expect smooth sailing into a truly open, brave new era. Interestingly, the most eager participants in a globalized world include many late-developing nations. This in itself is a profound departure from the past.

But leaving behind old ideologies based on racial and national lines cannot be straightforward or easy. Behind the existing order based on the developed world are great pride and prejudice. The worst prejudice is associated with national and racial matters, which can blind people to dealing realistically with changing realities.

Today, a new mindset is urgently needed. To move ahead for true global development, there is no alternative and no shortcut.

Part III.
China's Fast-Changing Society, Politics, and Economy

SUMMARY

To some outsiders, China is already a global power. But most Chinese hardly feel that way. Instead they feel that their nation still faces huge problems. They daily confront just too many man-made barriers, despite all the changes.

China's fundamental problem remains an overwhelming bureaucratic power. For at least 4,000 years, China's political body has been a self-appointed government. As such, this government serves itself above all and stands against the society and people. This was the case especially in the Mao era. In fact, in the Communist era, it reached an extreme.

Up to now, the universal rights of the Chinese government have never been truly challenged. The society and people are still too weak to confront bureaucratic power directly. This untamed bureaucratic power has produced a hugely twisted society, economy and market. In short, it has created a perfect bureaucratic society.

Furthermore, in this bureaucratic society, all the modern things such as true property ownership and independent legal system, as well as modern organizations and professionalism, are difficult to get established. In fact, even simple things like consumer rights have taken huge struggles to emerge. How about rights of taxpayers? They have yet to come to life. In short, China is going through great struggles toward a modern, law-based society, economy and nation.

Yet, among the vast changes in China today, one of the most visible is that people have much more personal freedom, including freedom in travel, employment, and residency. This expansion in freedom has also given rise to a rapidly growing private sector, which is in turn changing the nation in no small way. As a result, Chinese society is become more open and forward-looking.

The ever-increasing foreign involvement is another powerful factor in promoting progress. The vast foreign presence helps to create a more open, positive environment in general, which naturally benefits all parties. As time passes, even more international involvement will occur, with concomitant greater benefits.

Despite all the changes, China still lacks a modern political-economic system. An overwhelming Bureaucratic power continues to cause severe problems. Containing this bureaucratic power remains the biggest and most formidable task for the Chinese civilization. Now, however, China is at a crossroads. Dealing with the bureaucratic ills from the root causes has become a top agenda item.

This part of the book consists of five chapters. Chapters 10 through 12 are case studies, while chapters 13 and 14 deal with general political and institutional changes from a historical perspective.

Chapter 10.

Lessons From Shenzhen: China's New Powerhouse

The list of world cities with over 10 million residents isn't very long, and mostly contains familiar names like Tokyo, Lagos, Rio de Janeiro, and New York City. But of these megacities, which had a mere 20,000 residents only 26 years ago? The one and only answer would be Shenzhen, China.

Shenzhen, a SEZ located in south China's Guangdong province just north of Hong Kong, has become the economic locomotive of the region since it was founded 26 years ago as a kind of laboratory for market-oriented economic reforms. The city's annual growth rate, averaging about 27% since 1980, has no equal in the world.

The urban landscape left by the dizzying growth is awesome, with office towers, hotels, shopping centers, and apartments that can be compared only with what one sees in New York City or Tokyo. Yet all this has taken place within the last 26 years.

Observant visitors, after spending a bit of time in the city, might notice another odd fact: The average resident is in his or her twenties. By now, Shenzhen is the biggest migrant city in the nation. Vast new opportunities attract young Chinese from everywhere like a magnet. The dimensions are somewhat similar to those in the rush to the western United States in the 19th century, but larger.

But Shenzhen is not interesting just for itself: It reflects the fundamental changes China is going through and demonstrates how China's new participation in the global economy works. Because the boisterous SEZ suggests China's general direction, it offers tremendous lessons for Chinese and foreign observers alike. The most important is that an open society and private initiatives are most directly responsible for fast development.

The First Key to Success: Openness

On August 26, 1980, the central government granted Shenzhen privileges as a SEZ, placing it literally in a class of its own. The intention was to allow Shenzhen to become an experimental laboratory for dealing with the market economy and the outside world. SEZ status gave Shenzhen at least a decade's head start over *Shanghai* and other Chinese cities.

A key motive for this policy change was that, as absurd as it may seem from today's perspective, Guangdong province was considered somewhat backward: Shanghai had been the biggest income contributor to the central government for many decades; in 1980 its contribution was one sixth of the total. But Guangdong was a small contributor with less than 1% of share. In case anything went wrong with Guangdong, the political and economic risks for Beijing would be much smaller.

As such, Guangdong went one step ahead. Allowing Shanghai more economic autonomy came only 10 years later, beginning in 1990. As a result, this largest Chinese city suffered stagnation throughout the 1980s.

Given the realities Beijing faced back then, making Shenzhen a SEZ, along with three other small coastal cities in Guangdong and Fujian provinces, was a bold move on the part of Beijing. At the time, the central government was desperate to find ways to deal with its woes: China back then was more like North Korea today, with widespread hunger, general poverty, and increasing discontent following 30 years of bureaucratic abuses within a tightly closed society.

Back then, this policy change caused wide debate especially at the top. Deng Xiaoping stood very firm with this new experiment. He once told the Guangdong provincial leaders, "Have courage and find a bloody new path for us!"

After serious debate, new ideas surfaced in Beijing. Engaging the outside world was a new and key strategy and would become a vital one for national development. This produced huge unexpected consequences for China and beyond.

Huge Outside Investments

Initially, Shenzhen lacked capital and other resources, which meant it had to rely on outside help. This required becoming as open as possible to the entire world, creating a friendly business environment so that outside investors would have the incentive to inject their capital into the city. This strategy has worked well, to say the least.

Since 1980, Shenzhen has attracted well over $60 billion in foreign direct investment, becoming a global commercial center in the process. Though it is a key destination for overseas Chinese, especially from Hong Kong as well as *Taiwan*, it has also attracted investors from all over the world. At least 113 of the top 500 global multinationals maintain offices in the city today. In fact, it has become a must-be-in city for multinationals.

Many global giants have extensive operations in the city. IBM alone has set up eight companies in Shenzhen, and Japan's Sanyo Electric has 11 companies there. More and more multinationals are rushing in.

The current presence of multinationals was not easily obtained, however. Most of the early overseas investments were from neighboring Hong Kong, which did not hesitate to cross the border to pursue the vast opportunities in the SEZ. The multinationals came mostly after the mid-1990s; by then, Shenzhen was already a booming city, and the presence of global corporations simply accelerated the city's development.

Buying foreign brands has become part of daily life for Shenzhen residents. The major shopping districts are packed with foreign retailers like Wal-Mart, Carrefour, Jusco, and H&Q, with more on the way. Countless global brands, like P&G, Unilever, Mars, Coke, Nestle, Sony, LG, Nokia, Siemens, and Philips can be obtained in these stores; and the foreign vendors have found that Shenzhen, with its relatively affluent and brand-savvy population, is one of their most profitable markets.

The city is connected to the outside world in many ways. Tens of thousands of foreign nationals now live and work in Shenzhen. Countless businesspeople from Latin America, Africa, Australia, New Zealand, and the rest of Asia have come. In the local schools, hundreds of foreign nationals hold teaching posts.

Having foreign capitalists participate in Chinese development has obviously led to progress for Shenzhen and the rest of China. As a result, China has become more open and more dynamic. In many ways, China is actually more open now than even Japan, despite Japan's much longer experience of industrialization and modernization. In this context, Shenzhen leads China in openness as well as development.

Domestic Rush

But foreign investment is only a part of the total picture. The city has attracted substantial investment from other regions within China. There are countless businesses in Shenzhen originating from government units and companies all over China. Innumerable towers bear names like Sichuan, Henan, Shaanxi, Tibet, Shanghai, Jilin, and Jiangsu; the structures belong to enterprises controlled by various regional government units.

In addition, the central government ministries and companies also rushed into Shenzhen. For example, nearly all companies belonging to Beijing have set up shops in the city. This has further lifted the city's economic autonomy.

Fundamentally, granting special policy privileges to only one or two provinces has had vast impacts for the nation as a whole, both positive and negative. The positive aspect is that the new regional development is a departure from the traditional path dominated by the central leadership. Moreover, it has helped to promote greater competition and openness for all China.

At the same time, a basic built-in problem persists. Under the traditional system, different regions can hardly develop independently, even by relying on their own resources, as everything important is arranged by Beijing.

The Second Strategy: Entrepreneurship

The city's greatest strength is its entrepreneurs, who have flocked to the southern boomtown from all over China. Of roughly 200,000 registered companies in the SEZ, more than 160,000 are private. This private sector is entering its best and most productive time only now.

Key private companies include Huawei, already a global brand in the telecommunications equipment industry; "Everyone Happy Store" and "A Best Buy Store," leading Chinese franchise retailers that are competing head-on with foreign retail giants; and more than 800 small software companies that are now aspiring to expand beyond China's borders. The Chinese Internet instant messaging software company QQ.com, which has more than 500 million global users, was born in the city, set up by three young engineers.

For now, the private sector employs about half of the city's workforce and contributes about half its economic output. This heavy reliance on the private sector for prosperity has become a model for the rest of China to emulate.

In most inland regions, the private sector remains a small minority in terms of both employment and output. Many less developed cities and areas are still dominated by the state sector today. Government domination has continued to produce nothing but poverty. But many inland cities such as Xian, Wuhan, and *Chongqing* are now aiming to increase private sector involvement on their own initiative.

This type of regional competition, leading to regional emulation, is a major driving force in China's development today. Its significance in promoting a more liberalized economy and society is no less than that of the private sector. Through regional competition, a more progressive business environment has emerged.

Even some state sector companies in the city have moved ahead of the crowd, despite their imperfections. Among them are Ping An Insurance, the second biggest Chinese insurance player, already listed on the Hong Kong stock exchange with shareholders such as Morgan Stanley, HSBC, and Goldman Sachs; Merchant Bank, considered by many to be the best-run Chinese bank; and China Container Group, the world's biggest shipping container manufacturer.

Shenzhen has made itself a key business center for China and beyond. Some 22 local companies are in China's top 500; several of them will have a chance to join the global 500 club within a short time. The stock exchange in Shenzhen is as important as the one in Shanghai. The city is also a choice location for Chinese investment brokerages and fund management companies.

The city's high-tech sector has made huge progress, growing at an annual rate of 46.5% over the past two decades, reaching $39.5 billion in output in 2004. Shenzhen Inc. owns some 50,000 brands of its own creation. Most of these brands have emerged within the last 10 years, signaling that the local businesses have transitioned from short-term interests to a long-term approach. Though the local businesses as a group remain at the early stage of development, they could improve more rapidly as time passes.

Above all, the city is a major manufacturing center worldwide. In 2005, Shenzhen manufactured 11.44 million personal computers, 35.78 million mobile handsets, and 19.64 million TVs.[1] These products were made by both Chinese and foreign businesses. Many were shipped to international markets.

In addition, foreign banks such as HSBC, Citibank, and UBS have increasingly extensive operations in the city. More foreign banks are rushing over to set up shops.

But Shenzhen is also a haven for an estimated 350,000 small business owners, who are involved in every conceivable industry all over the city. Some have already become fairly affluent as they get ahead on their own initiative.

The city has set itself a higher goal, however: to become a high-value-added business center. This is actually a matter of economic survival, since rising land and labor costs are already forcing many low-value-added businesses to move to cheaper inland cities.

To achieve the high-value goal, the SEZ has encouraged the formation of R&D centers by both international and Chinese companies; and hundreds indeed have been or are being established. Last but not least, Shenzhen has become the number-one export city in China, reaching over $100 billion as of 2005.

Hong Kong has long been a good model for Shenzhen to emulate. But today, the winds of fortune have turned; Hong Kong is finding that it has a lot to learn from the city on its northern border. Ten years ago,

Hong Kong residents might have paid the bill after dining with Shenzhen friends. Now the Shenzhen residents are likely to compete to pay—a big change.

Today, Hong Kong no longer finds growth easy, with high salaries and land prices and with only the service and real estate sectors expanding. But Shenzhen has several growth engines: a fast-expanding manufacturing sector, high technology, and now (albeit at the beginning stage) R&D. Its room for further development is huge, especially in view of its dynamic, aspiring, and youthful workforce. It is no surprise that the city is fast catching up with Hong Kong.

The Rising Middle Class

So far, Shenzhen has created its own fairytale. But the most interesting aspect of Shenzhen's development may be the rising power of, and choices for, its citizens. Tens of millions of Chinese have tried their luck in this new frontier, and over 12 million now call it home. They have all come for opportunity. Some have gained enormous wealth, which has made the city even more attractive.

It is a city where the rich and poor coexist, somewhat as in New York City. This income gap is a new reality in the nation. The vast income gap, while remaining potentially disruptive, is not without one positive effect: The have-nots work hard as they seek to emulate the haves (who were often have-nots just a few years ago) whom they see all around them.

As a result of such social dynamics, a new middle class has come to life. The exact number depends, of course, on definitions; but one way to define middle class in China is given by the Chinese Central Academy for Social Science (the top Chinese social research institution in Beijing) as well as the central government statistics bureau: an annual family income of at least $7,246. By this yardstick, among Shenzhen's 12 million residents, roughly 5 to 6 million have joined the club.

The SEZ's middle class is just like that elsewhere in China: It consists chiefly of government employees, teachers, professionals, salespeople, and small business owners and managers. Certainly this middle class is the key consumption force in the city. More than 1.5 million cars are running on the already crowded streets. Equally impressive is that the city has some 15 million mobile phone subscribers, resulting from the fact that many people carry two handsets.

Admittedly, in absolute terms, people in Shenzhen's middle class have less than their counterparts in developed nations. But on a purchasing-power-parity basis, their lifestyle increasingly resembles that of the middle class in New York, Tokyo, Paris, or London. Many returning Chinese students have noted this, somewhat to their own surprise.

One factor behind the sharply rising middle class is China's low general labor cost: $1 in Shenzhen and elsewhere in China may be worth $3 or more, especially if you are purchasing labor-extensive services. For example, $1 or less can get you a basic haircut inside China; the same haircut may cost $8 or more in New York or London.

The Have-Nots

But life has never been the same for all economic classes of people. What about the less fortunate? They have participated much less in the city's rising fortunes. Of the several dozen residents I have interviewed, the lowest-paid workers make as little as $60 per month. The lowest-paid jobs are those of unskilled factory workers and retail clerks. Indeed, about half of the 12 million residents make $50 to $180 per month. Millions of rural migrants cannot really enjoy the rising fortunes of the city.

Furthermore, few extra benefits are provided with these low salaries. Increasing pay is very difficult overall chiefly because there are more job seekers than jobs. The recent small appreciation of the yuan may even prompt some companies to cut pay.

More often than not, the workload for these low-end workers is outrageously heavy. Millions of people work six days straight, and seven-day work weeks are not uncommon. These people often suffer workplace abuses even though they are the very backbone of the city's strength. The made-in-China products that flood the globe are mostly made by these workers.

Though their living and working conditions are improving, there is still a long way to go. In many ways, they are treated like second-class citizens — a term often used by the Chinese media. For example, the city has long denied the children of migrant workers the right to attend public school. Though the annual income for the local government reached $6.2 billion in 2005, hardly any money is spent for the benefit of low-paid residents.

Yet, to become a permanent city resident, with all the benefits this brings, is next to impossible. So far, the city has granted permanent resident status to only 1.8 million out of 12 million residents. Millions have worked in Shenzhen for years, even for decades, but find it enormously difficult to get permanent resident status. Even those born in the city are not entitled to permanent status. As a result, they must return to their family's hometown to get driver's licenses, marriage registrations, and travel documents, among many other official items. Missing any of the personal documents can produce a nightmare. There is no way to get help from the local government at all.

On the surface, the city has been trying to relax its residency policy, but progress has been extremely slow. For example, beginning in 2005, Shenzhen has granted permission to renew driver's licenses within the city, but there is a two-year residency requirement.

Furthermore, the city has lately widened the gate for migrants to obtain permanent resident status, but the new policy demands that applicants pay $24,700 in taxes over a period of three consecutive years. Millions of low-paid workers, who are still voiceless and defenseless, are naturally excluded as intended.

Despite all the changes, Shenzhen's low-paid workers have suffered all sorts of abuses. In particular, the city charges them as much as one month's salary for granting them *temporary* annual residency. This is in addition to the entrance permit costing $3.70 (see Ch. 1).

Failure to pay within 10 days of arrival can lead to additional problems, including fines, abuses, and even arrest. As a matter of fact, countless migrants are arrested each year for not paying the fees. Even after the fees are paid, abuses are widespread.

Several young women who work in the city told me stories about threats—how their dorms were kicked open and they were taken away by abusive officials at night.

One salesgirl said, "We were so terrified every night, as the officials could suddenly storm our dorm."

What would follow the intrusions?

"Over $120 in fines plus three months in forced labor. Several of my friends went through places like mines before they were sent home," she said.

This kind of "squeeze" has occurred everywhere inside China, not just in Shenzhen. Preying on the poor has involved little risk until recently. Within the last three years or so, social protests nationwide have helped to reduce the annual temporary residency fee to about $1.85 instead of the previous $45 or more—the typical rate in Shenzhen for many years.

This low fee has had one consequence: Tens of thousands of government officials have lost interest in storming poor workers' dorms at night. Nationwide, for many years, many million rural migrant workers were sent to prison each year. All sorts of physical and mental abuses took place. Countless victims could not even register their complaints.

Beyond abusive regulations, there are too many incentives for the various government officials to go after these defenseless people. The city of Shenzhen has been well known for squeezing the less fortunate. In this booming city, workers still lack adequate legal workplace protections, which puts them at the mercy of employers.

Very often, employees are not paid for months and even years. But getting help can be burdensome, if not impossible. Though the city government has been doing more lately to help the victims, their number is hardly decreasing, mainly because of weak legal enforcement.

A recently passed local law mandates fines of up to $6,112 for abuse by an employer with regard to pay. But even if the law were perfectly enforced, employers can save much more than this small fine by short-changing workers.

As in the rest of China, the city's court system is weak. Statistics show that only about 12.3% of all court orders can be executed.[2] With respect to those who commit abuses, the court system is rather powerless to do the right thing. This troublesome legal system has made the situation much worse. In short, between employees and employers, the employer is always the stronger—and the situation is not going to change anytime soon.

Worse still, government units often lead the way in refusing to pay workers properly. When this happens, the workers cannot fight back at all. Any sort of action on the part of unpaid workers can invite more serious trouble, a reality in Shenzhen as well as in the rest of China. But the stakes are very high.

For example, in the city's construction business alone, city government units illegally withheld more than $40 million from independent project contractors for a long time. Increased media exposure forced the local government to behave more rationally, and the city paid the overdue money by the end of 2005. But citywide, total unpaid wages and contract fees totaled nearly $400 million. [3]

For now, positive change seems to be occurring with respect to the interests of low-paid workers, made possible only by widespread protests and heavy media exposure. But the low-paid workers are still too weak to demand more serious changes on their own. This reality is not going to change in the near future.

One new development that has improved the lives of migrant workers in the city is the introduction of a health insurance program providing basic health coverage. Each month, workers pay about U.S.$0.50 in premiums, while employers contribute about $1. Though this program is new, it was already covering some 700,000 low-paid workers in the first six months of 2005. Further assistance like this would obviously be welcomed by the SEZ's legions of migrant workers.

Transforming Government Into a True Service Provider

The difficult environment for less privileged workers demands that the government take on a new and unfamiliar role as a modern service provider to the masses — a new concept for Shenzhen and for China as a whole.

Although the city's government has tried to adapt to its rapidly changing situation, there are still great challenges. One increasingly pressing issue concerns a true separation of government from the business world. China's tradition of government domination is still going strong in Shenzhen; being a reform frontier does not mean that the city has totally abandoned the framework in place since 1949.

What is the general trend in the city's bureaucratic world? Government offices may be eager to offload troublesome responsibilities, but none desire less power. All government offices — globally, not just in Shenzhen — have a vested interest in expanding power. Indeed, the bureaucratic interest groups are ingenious in figuring out ways to expand their scope at the expense of society, as is true everywhere (see Part VII).

And despite the city's newness, government power has already penetrated deeply into the business sphere. So far, residents have not been able even to raise their voices directly against this bureaucratic tide. The aim of the ongoing reform has been for the government to increase its power. This has created vast barriers to China's progress in general and the city's health in particular.

A key barrier to Shenzhen's progress is the governmental demands on the business community. Innumerable transactions that could be privately handled require official involvement. For example, permission is required to engage in international trade, hiring, and travel. As a result, building a hotel entails 105 governmental approvals.[4] Each has a fee attached.

Why are there so many government demands in China, India, Russia, and Brazil, among other developing nations with similar problems? Do these demands benefit society in each case? Hardly. But China and many other developing nations have yet to follow the example of the West in adopting modern institutional ways. The key point to is get bureaucratic power under control (see Ch. 13 and 14).

As it is, the Shenzhen business community feels that these government activities have more to do with vested bureaucratic interests than the greater good of society. Many official requirements are, in essence, tactics to increase bureaucratic power at the expense of the larger community.

Needless to say, the high cost of government requirements greatly increases opportunities for official corruption. Indeed, the whole system has created a prime environment for corruption. It is no wonder that a small government clerk in the city, Wang Jianye, squeezed literally millions of dollars from businesses, as they were required to get approval from his office for foreign currency exchanges.

Wang was later executed, but the contributing systemic flaws remain in place. On the surface, the local government talks a lot about controlling corruption, but the existing system encourages corruption.

Beset by changing realities, the rapid development of the private sector and the huge international presence, Shenzhen's government has quickened its efforts to improve its services, though making fundamental changes necessitates even more effort.

Regional competition within China has spurred things along, as has China's WTO entry. But, though the city's political power has been trying hard to cope with new realities in one way or another, becoming a modern service provider is still far in the future.

Knowing the troublesome consequences of the multiple approval demands, the city government has offered express services and privileges to a select group of some 300 local companies in both the private and state sectors. These businesses can get preferential treatment in international trade, hiring, bank financing, and travel, among other services.

But obviously, over the long term, such services need to be made available to the rest of the business community. Complete abolition of all unnecessary official barriers is the ultimate solution. As one local businessman said, "The only fair way is to abolish these bureaucratic tricks completely."

More Changes Ahead?

On the surface, impressive institutional changes are taking place. Three rounds of administrative reform have been promulgated in the last few years. Total administrative demands on the business community have been reduced to 239 items, from 1,091 items in the late 1990s.

More recently, 145 of 225 temporary government agencies were abolished. But the motive for this move was "not to let them create conflicts with the permanent government units," according to the local government, which has nothing to do to cut down government fat.

At the same time, the local business community still feels the need for further reform if Shenzhen is to compete with business centers like Hong Kong and Singapore. That is, the government must change its functional role to become a servant of the public rather than a mandarinate-like institution in which supplicants must appear to beg for favors. More importantly, the government must learn how to provide useful service to the society in order to survive in the long term.

But departing from old practices is not easy. One might think that, with so many temporary government agencies, together with hundreds of permanent offices, officialdom would at least have the manpower to effectively enforce existing laws. Regrettably, an examination of the local business environment shows that this has not been the case.

On the contrary, regulators have been unable to curtail abusive business practices. For example, the city has countless unlicensed businesses, including illegal retail outlets, restaurants, and even factories, medical clinics, and real estate projects. Their inferior products and services pose a serious threat to consumers, not to mention the damage their existence poses to the rule of law.

A recent reform effort has aimed at eliminating such abuses, but the task is formidable. Underlying the situation are partnerships between government officials and business owners, according to the local media. By July 2006, the city's government announced that it had shut down some 210,000 illegal businesses or projects.[5]

In addition, attacking abuses outside the government is much easier than taking on problems within. Corruption is a plague in the city. Thousands of local government officials, some of them high ranking, have been arrested for corruption.

In one case, the former top three government officials in the city's South Mountain (Nanshan) district—Party Chief Yu Dehai, Chief Administrator He Cuben, and People's Congress Chairman Peng Hu—squeezed millions from local businesspeople for many years. The Nanshan trio are now serving 8- to 12-year prison terms.

Such problems occur because government offices tightly control all sorts of business assets and their allocation. Also, of course, some businesspeople desire to partner with corrupt officials to take advantage of the officials' power. These officials, in effect, rent their offices for personal gain.

So far, the anti-corruption efforts have taken on a quality reminiscent of the "whack-a-mole" arcade game; as soon as one perpetrator is prosecuted, another appears somewhere else to take that person's place. As a result, the number of corruption cases has not decreased, and the public feels helpless about the situation. One professional Shenzhen investor noted that corruption is "widespread," saying, "It is really time to do something about this."

The city's government gives foreign businesspeople numerous special privileges. Naturally, the privileges granted to foreign companies have attracted resentment from local Chinese business owners. A common creative response is to register their companies in offshore locations so that they can also enjoy special privileges.

Can Shenzhen Get Out of the Bureaucratic Swamp?

Considering Shenzhen's youth and relatively relaxed ground rules, it is rather remarkable that the state sector there is as large as it has become: The state controls about half the business assets in the city. But the built-in flaws of government ownership make the sector a disaster waiting to happen.

In many cases, it has already happened: Out of some 90 publicly listed companies in the city, more than 28 are in financial distress. In one instance, a major industrial company, the Shenzhen Chemical Group, went de facto bankrupt as a result of chronic mismanagement. Consequently, the local government sold its controlling stake—for $1.20.

Government units don't want to sell their enterprises because they have a huge vested interest in them. But this makes effective supervision of state companies almost impossible and has already caused many disasters. In one case, former chairman and Party boss Lao Derong of Shenzhen Energy, a city-owned utility company, was arrested for stealing more than $7.2 million of investors' money during her reign in 1998-2003.

But this is hardly an isolated case. Cases like this have contributed greatly to the perception of many Chinese that long-term prosperity can be produced only by a fast-growing private sector. Despite foot-dragging by some, there is a significant trend to sell off state assets as a way of escaping from the corruption trap (but critics claim that it is more as a showcase). Recently, the city cashed out smartly by selling a badly performing retail bank, Shenzhen Development Bank, to U.S. venture capital firm Newbridge Capital.

The city has also sold minority stakes in several highly profitable public utility companies to overseas buyers. But critics say the city government needs a firmer commitment to completely withdraw from the business world. One local scholar noted, "The state sector assets have no true owners. Otherwise, how could corrupt officials steal them so freely?"

Everyone knows that power corrupts and absolute power corrupts absolutely. But not everyone is aware that *under an absolute power, there are no true owners of property at all*. Instead, bureaucratic power preys on ownerless property without limits. This is what confronts China's state sector in general and Shenzhen's public assets in particular.

In spite of these built-in problems, China's southern boomtown has made impressive progress. One wonders how much more progress it could make if the root cause of many of its most serious problems — abusive bureaucratic power — was addressed.

The city has bright and diligent people, as well as huge capital, but in order to meet its overall development goals, the government will have to evolve into a true modern service provider. Because Shenzhen is a bellwether for the rest of China in this respect, its success or lack of success in official reform will say a great deal about the possibility of success for similar initiatives elsewhere.

Chapter 11.

Hunan Province:

From Red State to "Supergirl" and "Super-Rice"

Since the spring of 2005, China has been consumed by a new media fad: the *supergirls*. An average Chinese girl, with talent in singing, dancing, or acting, can be elected a supergirl by TV media outlets. Once chosen, she will immediately become a national idol, thrust into the public limelight and showered with numerous commercial rewards.

This hero-like status used to be the exclusive right of powerful politicians, movie stars, and top athletes. In a society dominated completely by the government, ordinary people usually have little opportunity to display their talents and desires. But today, this is fast changing, as the Chinese public gives its highest regard to the supergirls—a sign of the coming of age of a mass commercial movement.

In fact, seeking more personal expression has become a new national passion. In this regard, Chinese youths are leading the way. The popularity of supergirls is indicative of this new mass movement.

Which part of China was behind this new social wave? Shanghai, the traditional show business center? Or booming Guangdong? Surprisingly, the answer is neither: Instead, the fad started in Changsha, in the central province of Hunan. The star-making TV station is Hunan TV, a rising media star itself. Once the cradle of the Communist revolution (think Mao Zedong), Hunan has now bravely embraced a new world—globalization. In fact, the words most frequently used in the local media include "internationalization," "going global," and "globalization."

Yet there are tremendous problems, fundamentally tied to the old establishment. In this reform era, Hunan has fallen behind coastal rivals such as Zhejiang, one of the most prosperous provinces now. Hunan is trying to catch up. To move forward, the province needs to push for greater reform in the state and public sectors, whose poor performance is a serious drag on development.

Visiting Hunan

Visitors to Changsha, the provincial capital of Hunan (which has 70 million people), see a burgeoning city in the making, with a fast-rising population of over 6.5 million. The streets are jammed with traffic, including countless cars, and hundreds of high-rises shine at night.

Tens of thousands of shops, cafes, and restaurants line both sides of all the streets. Familiar foreign brands, including KFC, Carrefour, Wal-Mart, and McDonald's, are prominent. Even in secondary cities like Xiangtan (Mao Zedong's hometown), KFC and McDonald's outlets are plentiful. Like many other parts of inland China, long considered laggards in China's economic reforms, Hunan has finally become part of the country's globalization.

Notwithstanding the somewhat pretentious prosperity reflected by the cars, high-rises, and neon lights, the Hunanese people are anything but complacent about the great challenges they confront. Among the several dozen local people this writer interviewed, none was satisfied with the general situation in Hunan. In fact, all say that Hunan has fallen seriously behind.

Indeed, in terms of economic development, this province, once considered advanced by Chinese standards, is backward compared to its southern neighbor Guangdong and also to Zhejiang, far to the east.

One local banker said, "In 1980, Hunan was much more advanced than Guangdong province. In fact, Hunan was about the same as Jiangsu, which has long been a leading economic province in China. But today, Hunan has pitifully fallen behind both Guangdong and Jiangsu."

Statistics back up the banker's observation. In terms of GDP per head, Jiangsu's is some four times greater than Hunan's. In terms of foreign direct investment, Hunan has received about only $4 billion so far, less than 10% of what Shenzhen alone—a single city in Guangdong—has obtained.

With respect to exports, Hunan shipped only $3.65 billion to overseas markets in 2004, a tiny fraction of what Guangdong or Jiangsu sent abroad. Overall, Hunan, which in the past was among the most important industrial and agricultural bases in China, has fallen into the minor leagues economically. This situation has surprised many Hunanese.

Indeed, prior to 1980, Guangdong did not have much manufacturing activity except for certain consumer products, but Hunan had a vast range of industries: rail cars, metals, construction machinery, precision equipment, and steel, as well as consumer products. But the central government policy has changed all that. Today, the picture is almost exactly the opposite.

This situation is considered shameful by many Hunanese, including retired prime minister Zhu Rongji, another Hunan native. According to one story, when Zhu was touring Hunan in the 1990s, a provincial leader proudly told him how much pork Hunan shipped to Guangdong, Hong Kong, and Macau. Zhu raised his voice:

"When you ship a truckload of pork to Guangdong, you only bring back a truckload of bottled water. What is the value created for Hunan? It is time to use your head instead of your mouth."

One reason for Hunan's problems is the capital outflow caused by the better business opportunities on the coast. Central government favors granted to Guangdong made a huge difference for its development, partly at the cost of inland regions like Hunan.

One Hunan business executive said, "This current underdevelopment for Hunan is seriously caused by the fact that Hunan companies have carried tens of billions in cash and invested it in Guangdong. This money has resulted partly in the high-rises in Shenzhen, Zhuhai, and Guangzhou, but the outflow was terrible for Hunan's development."

Under a centralized structure, Beijing makes all the policies. Lower government units are unable to pursue their interests independently because the central government holds the power over appointment of lower officials. Though allowing one province to move ahead at the expense of others seems irrational, China has taken this route over the ages.

The Millstone of the State

Many people in Hunan also blame the province's backwardness on the slowness of reform of its state sector and government structure. The reason is simple: It is commonly perceived that the rapid progress in Guangdong, Jiangsu, and Zhejiang is due to the private sector and the initiative of small firms. For example, some 70% of Zhejiang's economic output is now produced by the private sector.

But Hunan's state sector is still huge. One Hunan scholar said, "In Hunan, some 80% of economic output comes from the state sector. But this state sector is really performing badly. So many of them are in distress."

What is behind the state sector mess? He continued, "This state sector is a government product, designed to serve the government. It has been slow to become market oriented. This has created vast problems for the general economic health of Hunan."

Another local businessman confirmed this diagnosis, noting, "In Shaoyang [another Hunanese city], the top five state sector companies are either already bankrupt or in serious financial trouble. Tens of thousands of employees there have already been laid off. But the state sector situation in this province is not getting any better."

Business insiders in Hunan also point to the serious problems arising from slow state sector reform. For example, countless laid-off state employees in the province live on $20 to $25 monthly welfare payments. Improving the situation will require the state companies to actually produce wealth, but their record so far has not been inspiring.

"Things have completely gone wrong in the entire state sector," said one local business executive in a state company.

What are the problems, then?

He cited his personal experiences: "Some years ago, I was appointed to run a distressed state company. With huge efforts, I quickly turned it around. What is more, our company soon produced sizable profits. But bad things soon happened: For one, my income was less than the previous manager's who had not made any profit, but I had no way to even mention it to the higher bureaucratic offices in charge to ask for a raise. Two, they soon kicked me out and replaced me with a substandard manager."

It would be unfair, however, to say that every state company in the province is doing badly. Some are doing fairly well—the Hunan TV company, for example, which has become one of the top TV stations in China.

The executive further explained the general situation: "If a state company has a qualified leader, it can perform fairly well. After all, China's general economy is expanding and there are all sorts of opportunities out there. Even so, having a stable management is tough. There are huge nonbusiness issues you must handle well. Otherwise, even a superbly performing CEO can be kicked out for no reason whatsoever. Indeed, all it takes is a note from a higher government office. How about wealth creation? No one really cares!"

Confronting a manipulating government power, average citizens have no way to fight back. One local scholar said, "Fundamentally, China's government can hardly provide any single useful service to the business community, but there is no way for the bureaucracy to stop being abusive. That is a true tragedy for Hunan as well as for the rest of China."

Entrepreneurship: The Way Out?

Perhaps not surprisingly, the poor performance of the state sector and its inherited problems have forced Hunanese to turn increasingly to individual private initiative to get ahead. They believe that for the province to move forward, private initiative and entrepreneurship are the only alternative.

As a local scholar said, "Hunan people must use their brains to catch up. In this regard, nothing is more significant than entrepreneurial work."

As in the rest of China, the rise of the private sector in Hunan has never been smooth, but private initiative has been growing. A new class of entrepreneurs is evident everywhere in the province, and some of their companies have made great strides.

One example is Broad Group, a private company started by two brothers surnamed Zhang, which has already become a leader in manufacturing large air-conditioning systems for commercial use in hotels, office towers, and factories. This fast-growing company now has over 10,000 employees, cutting-edge technology, and responsive after-sales service.

Broad Group has come up with a new approach to after-sale services. Since its founding, the company has established an extensive service and maintenance network through a computer system via telephone lines, the Internet, or both. Product users are basically free from daily maintenance. Instead, such work is taken care of by the manufacturer through its computer system.

According to one local businessman, Broad Group "has grown from nothing to a sizable high-tech company, which can compete directly with global giants like Siemens, GE, and Hitachi. The company even owns a corporate jet and two helicopters. This example is hugely influential on young Chinese—so many of them want to venture out on their own, like the Zhang brothers."

Another high-profile Hunan success story is Sany ("Three One") Heavy Industry. Sany was created in 1989 by six local college graduates. They put some academic research to commercial use in manufacturing construction equipment. This company now has many of the leading Chinese engineers and researchers in the field. Also, it is creating numerous joint programs for product development with leading Chinese universities and research centers. By now it is also a famous national brand in the construction business.

Recently, Sany became the first fully floated listed company (meaning that 100% of its shares were made available for open trading) on the domestic stock exchange. The full floating created new opportunities in the capital market for the company and showed management's commitment to creating shareholder value—an impressive achievement in itself in the context of corporate China, where many business leaders have other priorities. It also gave the company new ways to expand; for example, in the future, Sany could use shares to take over distressed state sector assets (see part IV).

One local banker said about the company, "Their success comes from pure entrepreneurial work. They started from some new scholarly work and pursued this to make cutting-edge products. The construction market has huge demand for their products. Some buyers may have to wait for a couple of years to get their products delivered."

The most famous Hunanese entrepreneur of all, however, is Professor Yuan Longping, known as "China's father of super-rice." Now 76, Professor Yuan has devoted his life to breeding rice strains in order to increase crop yields. Despite all the political upheavals in China's recent history and his personal misfortunes, especially during the Cultural Revolution period (1966-1976), his research continued. In this reform era, he has made dramatic progress in creating higher-yielding varieties suited to Chinese conditions.

These efforts have paid off. The innovative rice seeds have become the standard used in some 50% of China's rice paddies, helping to increase crop yields by 20% to 100%, and his strains are now commonly used in Southeast Asia, Latin America, and elsewhere. Instead of retiring, he has continued to work for better results.

In 1999, the highly decorated agronomist (his awards include China's State Supreme Science and Technology Award, the 2001 Magsaysay Award, the United Nations FAO Medal of Honor for Food Security, the 2004 Wolf Prize in Agriculture, and the 2004 World Food Prize) became the co-founder of Longping High-tech Agricultural Products Company, now listed on the Shanghai stock exchange. In recent years, the company has been developing varieties of other plants, such as corn and peppers.

Interestingly, Professor Yuan's company has not sought to register its intellectual patents worldwide. He says, "These products must benefit the entire world. So, it is better not to have any sort of patents for them."

About the new waves of private initiative, a local scholar said, "My province never lacks talented and dedicated people. All we need is a better environment, so that people's creative energy can be best employed. Professor Yuan is a case in point."

Overall, Hunan is moving ahead fast in spite of all the obstacles, because private initiatives have increased dramatically at this point. Local businesspeople predict that the private sector will likely take 50% market share within 10 years.

In the words of a local scholar, "Hunan people must use their brains as well as courage to overcome all the barriers. Please let the world know about our dreams and struggles."

This new mind-set will surely help not only Hunan, but also the rest of inland China, as it tries to catch up with the soaring coast and the rest of the world.

Chapter 12.
A Revolution of Chinese Professions

"China is on fire! Just look how restless the Chinese people have become," a Chinese scholar in Nanjing said to me recently.

True, Chinese people have escaped the confines of the Mao era.

Among all the changes, the emergence of new professions has made a particular difference. Hundreds of new professions have sprouted like wildflowers. This has opened up life in huge ways, but the real meaning is much deeper.

How is today's world different from 500 years ago? Adam Smith's classical concept of the "division of labor" has been one key. The emergence of new professions is a recent world development, representing a sharp departure from the older agricultural age. It is the product of the modern industrial and commercial life that began in the West.

But the actual process of achieving a new division of labor was rather involved for Europe. Cambridge and Oxford Universities were founded in the 12th and 13th centuries, respectively, to train people for civil service, which the old English aristocracies were not interested in. Today, institutions of higher learning are a basic component of any modern society. Since the Middle Ages, Europe has led the way in expanding the sphere of professions.

Indeed, any expanding economy must give rise to a new division of labor and therefore many new professions. The more specialized these professions become, the farther the society advances. This happened first in Europe and the United States followed by Japan and South Korea, among others. Now it is happening in the late-developing nations, China and India included.

In today's China, the quick rise of new professions has made for a dramatic change in the nation as a whole. Whereas in the Mao era the government effectively eliminated all independent living and all professions served only government needs, today new professions are created in the marketplace, independent of the government establishment.

One can only characterize this gigantic change as revolutionary. It is partly through these new groups of independent professions that China has transformed a frozen, rigid society into an increasingly open and dynamic one. In turn, the professions develop even more rapidly in a more open environment, which shows the general direction for the nation today.

A Product of Commercialization

Throughout world history, economic expansions have always created new professions. And the more advanced a nation becomes, the bigger the sizes of its new professions. In this era, India has achieved a fast-expanding economy, especially in the software sector. So India has seen the rise of numerous IT professions. Further expansion is spreading over other economic sectors; thus more new professions are in the making.

In the case of China, development is happening on a much greater scale, as the Chinese economy has been expanding in all sectors. This has given rise to hundreds of new professions that were nonexistent in the Mao era. They are now an integral part of an expanded life in general.

Models

In this new era, the young people may be the happiest, as many professions demand a youthful age—that of fashion model, for example. Fashion models emerged in the mid-1980s in booming Guangdong. At first, the public was shocked in no small way to see these young women in mini-skirts. Some models even quit after a short time. The change was truly a big one. Today, fashion models are everywhere and nobody is shocked even if their clothing covers up less.

Being a Chinese model is not easy, as the field is very competitive. Unlike what happens in the developed markets, a Chinese model must retire by her mid-20s. This seems cruel, but it goes with the territory. For now, millions of young people are eager to become models.

This popular profession can bring quick commercial rewards. As a result, models have quickly joined the middle class. One model in Shanghai told me she could make at least $100 a day. How?

"I give shows at three night clubs every evening," she said.

Modeling as a new profession is getting hotter and hotter as the business rewards get higher and higher. China already has some modeling schools. Recently the models' hottest market has been the auto market. Every auto show of any significance must use models. This concept was imported by international automakers operating inside the nation and has been adopted by the Chinese automakers.

In general, many Chinese businesspeople go the extra mile; today, they employ models for all sorts of business events. Even selling home appliances often involves fashion models. Thus China is becoming a top destination for models around the globe.

More New Professions

Another hot new profession is that of travel guide, popular in part because China has become a top travel destination. Competition to become a travel guide is stiff as well, as there are numerous benefits and many young Chinese are attracted to this type of job. People must have a college education before they are allowed to apply for a position as a travel guide.

There are numerous other internationally oriented professions. Translation is a hot area. China has more than a half-million professional translators, mostly college educated. They work with all sorts of languages, but the most popular one is English.

Many Chinese universities use international textbooks. All college students must pass a national English exam. Getting a promotion in most professional fields also requires passing an English exam. This has made the teaching of English a hot industry. Tens of thousands of foreign teachers teach English and other foreign languages in China now.

More Sectors, More Players

Many new professions involve young people only, but there are jobs for well-trained people who are older also. Indeed, very diverse professions have emerged in all sectors. Today, stockbroker, insurance agent, public accountant, business consultant, money manager, ad agent, lawyer, and fashion designer are among the most sought-after jobs. China now has more than 50 million professionals holding technical certificates in all sectors. This new division of labor underlies the rapid development in this era.

With so many new professions, no society can stay the same. In the legal field, for example, China now has nearly 200,000 practicing lawyers. Going to court to settle disputes is a new way of life. Besides business and economic issues, lawyers deal with increasingly sensitive political cases as well. For example, since 1991, citizens have been allowed to take government units to court with economic disputes, which is a huge change. Because of the unlimited power of the government, there are many cases that belong in court.

A very troublesome area relates to land projects. For example, government units often take over farmers' land and turn it into resorts or other commercial uses for impressive gains. But the farmers frequently receive under-market compensation, or worse. Often they get IOU notes and need to go to court to receive payment. But most do not have the financial resources to do so, as legal fees keep going up. The court fees for a small case may be several hundred dollars, which is beyond the means of most citizens.

Moreover, even when cases go to court, people's rights may not be properly defended. Even so, the new legal option of taking government units to court is significant progress. Having so many lawyers around is a necessary new development given the domination by government power. Furthermore, these lawyers are learning quickly how to defend their clients' interests in order to stay in business.

But unlike their Western counterparts, Chinese lawyers often run into political problems because the Chinese legal system is part of the bureaucratic establishment, which is so designed by the government. Daily legal work is still heavily influenced by the vested bureaucratic interest.[1]

One Chinese lawyer said, "As you know, it is difficult to go by the book. Everything inside China depends on power and power only. There are just too many things you are not allowed to do."

An expanding economy has given rise to other new professions. Some are hotter than others. China now has over 100,000 stockbrokers and over 3 million insurance agents. These professions are responsible for creating booming businesses in these sectors. Furthermore, these professionals have joined the new middle class. Their rising income easily attracts new blood. Now, college graduates are eager to get into these high-paying professions. As a result, competition is very stiff.

One Chinese businessman noted, "These new professions especially in the white collar sector are highly competitive. These professionals are the best educated and best trained in the world. They certainly lack no brains, but they do need more experiences as well as a better environment in general."

The Old Era

Needless to say, the new professions are all a direct response to market needs. But this development has much broader meaning: It has helped China to gradually depart from the old bureaucratic life.

In the Mao era, there were hardly any professions in the modern sense, though there were all sorts of jobs. These jobs had one thing in common: They were all arranged by the government according to its own needs.

The bureaucratic system for a long time completely eliminated personal independence. Even cultural, educational, and artistic professions had to serve the government exclusively. Hence, all writers, painters, dancers, musicians, and journalists were confined to the government world. Even when a person wanted to become a monk, government officials made the decision. Serving the government was the only way of life.

Over the several decades during which this lasted, each and every citizen swam in the bureaucratic ocean. But even this record-level power was not enough for the government, which increased pressure on the population even further. In particular, universities were shut down for 11 years (1966-1977). During that period, countless educated people went through labor camps or worse, provided that they were still around after the previous purges and bloodshed.

More problems surfaced. In the 1960s and 1970s, the bureaucratic economy was stuck in deep mud. Providing jobs for urban high school graduates became difficult. Instead, the government sent over 17 million urban youths to work in rural regions. They could not refuse to go.

In the new era, life has dramatically improved, and gaining prosperity through individual private initiative has become a mandate. People's increased independence has naturally led to numerous independent professions.

The New Era

As a Chinese street expression goes, "What has happened in the new era is the untying of old ropes."

In the old days, bureaucratic ropes were innumerable. Pursuing private interests was a top crime. A common expression was "We want to try things, but they [the government officials] don't let us."

Today people have increasingly become able to pursue their own interests. Since 1978, the old bureaucratic power has declined sharply, which has paved the way for countless changes. Though most good things in life were buried during the Mao era, including entrepreneurial work, which was eliminated by force, one thing survived: the entrepreneurial spirit.

Private entrepreneurship is the biggest change of all and has given rise to one of the biggest new professions. There are now 40 million Chinese entrepreneurs. There are some 4 million private companies, of which more than 90% are family owned. They employ more than 50 million people, about 25% of the urban workforce.[2] The private sector races ahead at full speed today.

This wind of self-reliance is blowing over all corners of the land. Very startling is the fact that more than 200 million rural people are on the move, seeking better opportunities in cities. They do all sorts of jobs, especially jobs that urban residents do not want to do. Their contributions to the economic growth are immeasurable.

Containment vs. Anti-Containment

To many observers, both foreign and Chinese, China has become chaotic, with a vast number of people on the move—all impelled by unbounded desires to improve their lives quickly. Wealth making is a new national passion. Consequently, China now has countless dealmakers and dreamers.

But the underlying truth has to do with the expansion of personal freedom. People are eager to get ahead, whatever it takes. What is behind this massive movement? It is the desire to escape poverty; this desire is the mother of all individualistic ventures. Falling behind is considered shameful.

Today, even under a restrictive environment for travel, 15- to 18-year-old rural girls take long journeys from remote villages to get to the cities. They do all sorts of jobs most urban people don't want to do. Their motive is to improve their lives and the lives of their families by earning higher pay. They are able to overcome countless manmade barriers to achieve what they want.

This resilience is behind the enduring nature of Chinese life. Through private initiatives, finally, China has seen an ever-increased flow of ideas, humans, and goods. The new players, vast in numbers, have transcended bureaucratic containment.

On the new waves of private initiative, one Chinese scholar told me, "If people want a better life, they know how to get it on their own initiative. In this regard, countless Chinese are truly entrepreneurial."

True, people know best how to advance their own interests. But there are tremendous problems still. Today, one fundamental problem is that despite the emergence of new professions, China does not have a true modern *division of labor*. Bureaucratic power still prohibits the existence of truly independent professions, still aiming to contain independent movement. In this setting, merit-based upward mobility is still difficult, to say the least.

Government officials still answer to no one. The worst aspect of this system is that the unchallenged state power is employed by corrupt officials to squeeze people for personal gain. As a result, countless officials have become rich quickly. Consequently many commoners want to join the bureaucratic rank and file in order to experience an easy life.

In this environment, daily life is full of conflicts. Many businesspeople try hard to establish personal ties with officials. Moreover, many businesspeople seek to hold some sort of public title. This is one of the most common ways in which they try to protect their personal interests. As no true ownership and legal protection is in place, making such moves is common.

Demanding improvement still involves high risks. This is indicative of how difficult it is to promote true reform within the system. Examples of corruption are plentiful. One case involved the court in Wuhan. Thirteen corrupt judges in the city's court have fallen. For many years, they used state power for personal gain. They acted as though they were in business and accepted bribes in return for favorable judgments. Moreover, they often teamed up like partners to get the job done. What led to their fall? A convicted businessman in jail reported the corruption.[3]

Yet, under this difficult environment, the real marvel is the sharp rise of countless new professionals and entrepreneurs. Their emergence reflects a new life in the making, the inevitable transformation of the nation from the inside out. This does not mean a completely new society, for the old bureaucratic framework remains in place. Even so, this vast pool of new professions and entrepreneurs suggests the general trend for the nation.

Chapter 13.
What Is the Chinese Bureaucratic Tradition?

Seeking a fair and just society has been a part of all human history. But everywhere, until relatively recently, people's power was limited. Over the ages worldwide, it was a given that the few ruled over the many.

Only in the 17th century or so did the West begin to lead the search for a better society. In old Europe, intellectually, the universal rights of government were first questioned by men like John Locke and the French encyclopedists of the 18th century.

Politically, both the English and the French revolutions were significant in reducing the universal rights of government. (Holland did not need a bloody revolution to achieve a more liberalized society and government; John Locke even stayed there to write two of his books.) Only through profound struggles did Europe escape from the trap of the supreme church-state and find the path it is traveling now.

Now it is China's turn to take this modern path. This requires completely eliminating the old bureaucratic system, which in the Communist era was pushed to its extreme. In fact, in those times the bureaucracy found even more ways to pursue its own interests. For many decades, the entire population became exclusively and completely its servants.

Only today has the issue of people's rights emerged. Even now, it is no small task to challenge the universal rights of the government bureaucracy. For many decades, the Communist bureaucracy completely penetrated into the lives of all citizens.

This chapter and the next cover some basic features of the Chinese bureaucratic system.

China's Basic Political Realities

Up to now, China's governments have been all self-appointed through organized violence. Two basic problems were built into this system over the ages, especially in the Communist era.

The first problem is that by design, China's government body stands against the society and people. As a self-appointed government, it has always had unlimited power over the society and people.

In particular, there have always been strong political ideologies in support of the universal rights of government. The most persistent idea is this: *Everything under the sun belongs to the government.* On the basis of this idea the government has been able to demand services from all citizens, not the other way around.

The second problem is that supervision within the bureaucratic world is ineffective. The supreme government power is overwhelming in its ability to pressure people, but it is rather weak in containing corruption within its rank and file. Renting official power for personal gain is a problem inherent in the system.

Moreover, there is no outside force to counterbalance the bureaucratic ills. As a result, unlimited government creates its own biggest foe — the one within. In short, the old governments all died out from their own weight, like rotten apples falling off a tree.

These two built-in problems were behind the downfall of all the dynastic governments in the past. In other words, it was supreme power and its resultant corruption that buried all the old governments.

Corruption in this era is no more than a continuation of these long-standing built-in problems. The Communist power is nothing new. It is no more than another self-appointed government in the traditional context.

But there is also a fundamental difference: The Communist power has pushed bureaucratic domination to its extreme.

Nature of the Communist Bureaucracy

A basic fact about Chinese history is this: Up to now, China has lacked opportunities to challenge the universal rights of government in any meaningful way. Instead, bureaucratic power increased all the way, reaching the extremes of the Mao era, as reflected in the following set of facts.

First, the Communist bureaucracy has been the largest in China's entire history: 45- to 70-plus million officials in existence today. With its size, this bureaucratic power has penetrated into the grassroots and individual levels more deeply than at any other time in the nation's history.

Second, the Communist power has reached record levels. In the economic area alone, during the Mao era, the government took over all shops, factories, banks, farms, and mining. Such complete bureaucratic domination had never happened before.

Older governments had limited monopoly over certain products and commercial activities involving tea, salt, iron, and mining, for example. But in the Mao era, the private sector was completely buried —

another historical record. What is more, any independent movement was a crime against the state, punishable by death. Vast bloodshed took place for long.

Third, under this unprecedented bureaucratic power, citizens have lost all independence in their lives, as never before. People were given no choice over things like residency, education, employment, and travel. Whatever moves people made, they had to first obtain official approvals for. Even reading newspapers and books required official approvals. Getting married required official approval for many decades, ending only in 2003. Even travel was banned. As such, personal freedom was completely eliminated.

This limitless bureaucratic power has created a perfect bureaucratic society. People were made to serve government needs completely and exclusively. Overall, the Communist government has destroyed true ownership and any semblance of a legal system. Moreover, it has destroyed citizen, consumer, and taxpayer rights, among other modern things. All this has naturally produced record-making disasters after 1949.

The following sections focuses on some basic features of the Communist power of the Mao era in light of China's bureaucratic tradition.

Political Ideals vs. Historical Paths

What is an ideal political system in the Chinese mind? One definition of an ideal government was given by Lao Zi (meaning *old sage*; his exact dates are unknown, but he was a contemporary of Confucius [551-479 BC]).

Lao Zi commented: "The best government is the one that its existence is hardly noticeable as citizens mind their own business in their own ways. On the other extreme stands the worst government that constantly and recklessly preys on citizens by force. Such an abusive government constantly destroys wealth and lives. Hence, its ill-behavior is despised by all citizens."[1]

A modern version of Lao Zi's statement might be the following: Whenever the government is busy expanding its power, disasters must soon follow.

China has seen numerous "golden periods" in the past. These eras had certain common characteristics. The rulers restrained their earthly desires. In particular, they worked hard to keep a troublesome bureaucracy at bay. All this made a difference in the society.

Under a self-disciplined government system especially at the top, people were left to mind their own business. Private, individual work directly produced all wealth. China's government has never contributed a penny to the nation's wealth. Yet, as long as the government could maintain peace, it would be enough for people to focus on wealth making, all on their own initiative and efforts.

Such good times often characterized the early part of a dynasty. For example, one golden era took place roughly in the first 70 years of the Han Dynasty (206 BC-220 AD), and another one took place roughly in the first half of the Tang Dynasty (618-907).[2]

But China has had more periods of disasters, nearly all caused by zealous bureaucratic power. The underlying reason? In general, the rulers had no control over their earthly desires. They squeezed the society and people hard and consequently opened up vast opportunities for abusive bureaucratic power to intrude on people.

Examples are plentiful. In the second half of the Ming Dynasty (1368-1644) and the late Qing Dynasty (1644-1911), China suffered under massive corruption. But this corruption, as always, started at the very top.

For example, He Shen (1750-1799), the most powerful de facto prime minister in the late 18th century, according to the *Wall Street Journal* was one of the 50 richest men who ever lived. He started as a poor man but gained incalculable wealth during his official life. He was one of the key officials who met Lord George McCartney when the latter led the 600-man British delegation to Beijing in 1793.

How did He Shen make his vast personal fortune? He employed his official power to squeeze subordinates and commoners. He even threatened those subordinates who did not bribe him enough. In the end, he amassed vast land and business assets as well as gold and treasures.

After he was punished by death in 1799, his confiscated wealth was equivalent to over five years of total government income.[3] But the deeper problem was this: his death did not mean the end of official corruption at all. Instead, it went more widespread as time went by.

It was corruption that buried these and all other old dynasties, with hardly any exception.

Interestingly, after the fall of the Qing Dynasty in 1911, personal freedom and people's rights became the new buzzwords, but this has not translated into real life yet. In reality, the bureaucrats use these concepts as a cover to advance their own interests. Especially after 1949, bureaucratic power went wild.

In essence, the Communist power is nothing but a continuation of the traditional bureaucratic power. The two basic built-in problems persist strongly in this period of China's history.

The Saga of State Power

Before we look further at the Communist system, it will be helpful to examine some basic features of China's political tradition.

Central to human history, the expansion of government power has happened throughout the world. Until recently, all political bodies around the globe were self-appointed governments that claimed universal rights over people.

These self-appointed governments all tried to rearrange the entire society and people according to their own needs. Though the capability of governments in their power crusades varied from nation to nation, their desires and goals were just about the same.

In old Europe, free thought and movement were banned for ages. European society had a frozen social life, all based on the supreme rights of the government. This environment destroyed upward mobility based on merit. Serfs remained serfs for generations and generations.

Even in the 20th century, various governments used cultish ideologies to expand their power. For example, both the Nazi German government and the imperial Japanese government used the idea of a *Divine Race* to mobilize the entire population for purposes of war. Both governments were very successful in expanding their power by waging wars on other nations.

Although universal rights of political authorities in all nations have been common until recently, the West has hardly experienced the scope and depth of bureaucratic power seen in China. This overwhelming Chinese bureaucratic domination has stopped China from entering a modern society completely for long.

Interestingly, the Confucian school, among others, aimed to provide a counterbalance to bureaucratic greed by imposing moral standards, but its positive effects were rather limited. Instead, the old rulers employed Confucianism for their own ends. The universal rights of bureaucratic power have never been truly challenged.

Behind this ever-expanding government power, an enduring concept has been that *all things under the sun belong to the government.* This idea has been around for ages (beginning with the Xia Dynasty, founded in the 21st century BC). In fact, it is as alive today as it was 2,000 years ago. This cult has become a powerful tool for the bureaucratic expansion for ages. As a result, bureaucratic power has greatly limited the rational development of the Chinese civilization.

For ages, this Chinese government could take over all personal property, including that of the gentry, officials, and even royal relatives, as well as commoners. It could freely demand that people provide services for no recompense. All the great royal places, tombs, canals, roads, and dams were built largely by forced labor.

For example, both the Great Wall and the Great Beijing-Hangzhou Canal (over 1,700 kilometers in total distance and passing through 22 cities as well as the Yangzi and Yellow Rivers) were built by largely forced labor. Working conditions were extremely poor, and huge numbers of deaths occurred in the respective periods.

These were not just isolated projects. People's lives were made much worse by the endless construction of royal palaces and resorts, for example. Furthermore, punishment was cruel. Anyone who failed to follow government orders faced punishment up to death. Moreover, punishment for an individual's crimes could be visited on the extended family.

This cruel environment took a big toll on the old governments. Both the Qin (221-206 BC) and Sui (589-618) Dynasties met an abrupt end. Indeed, massive peasant rebellions took place at the end of these dynasties.

But these two examples are just a few of many. Throughout China's long history, largely forced labor, together with chronic corruption, damaged people's lives in myriad ways. Peasant uprisings took place in each and every dynasty. To date, there have been some 150 peasant uprisings.[4]

One peasant uprising, the Taiping Rebellion (1851-1864), involved more than several million armed peasants. They were angry about bureaucratic abuses and killed countless officials. Along the way, they destroyed numerous cities and vast wealth, especially in southern China. Some historians claim that China's decline in recent times started in that period.

But bloody rebellions did not contain the traditional bureaucratic supremacy at all. Instead, all the succeeding governments tried even harder to lay claims on the people on the one hand and contain any independent movement on the other. The Communist power has only pushed this system to the very extreme.

Bureaucratic Ranking

The making of the Communist society has a long historical background. In reality, it has closely followed the old bureaucratic tradition. But the old rulers and the Communist ones have exactly the same goal: *Make the society and people their servants.*

On this issue, one scholar noted, "There is nothing new about the Chinese Communist government. It has copied all the traditional bureaucratic practices directly."

One area of China's bureaucratic practice is to rank all citizens according to its own needs. Huge differences have existed between life in Europe and China throughout history. In particular, in European history, a person's economic class usually determined his or her social and political status to a great extent. Aristocracies had vast land holdings as well as serfs and therefore would have high privileges in the society.

But this was not the case in China. Instead, it was the government that decided on the political-social status of citizens, rich or poor. This makes for a fundamental difference between China and the West.

Above all, the Chinese bureaucratic power had a complete design regarding all aspects of the society and people. To achieve complete control, all citizens were given a *bureaucratic rank*. Different people were given different amounts of freedom. Overall, government officialdom stood superior to people. Once wearing an official hat, a person gained vast advantages in the society.

Businesspeople had the lowest ranking. They and their children were banned from taking government posts. They were not allowed to wear nice clothes or ride in luxurious carts, for example. Even the size and decoration of their tombs were defined by the government. When businesspeople met government officials, they had to kneel down to show their inferiority, which was in existence only 100 years ago.

Behind all this was the government's fears about potential challenges coming from the business community. Indeed, businesspeople have money, manpower, organizations, and leadership. Hence, in the eyes of the rulers, they could be a serious threat. In addition, they compete with the government for wealth.

Under this environment, independent business interests hardly existed. Businesspeople had to share their profits with corrupt government officials in one way or another as a matter of survival. This kind of bureaucratic confinement existed throughout China's history.

If businesspeople had little freedom in the society, commoners had even less. The government created vast hurdles for people. Whatever people wanted to do required government approval. Once officials could enter all private homes, widespread corruption must follow.

This bureaucratic grip over the society and people reached its height in the Communist era. In fact, bureaucratic ranking was carried out to the fullest possible extent.

In the Communist era, as discussed earlier, bureaucratic ranking determined the degrees of freedom of life for each and every citizen. Even travel was banned for ordinary people. Indeed, the masses lost all their freedom completely. In reality, their survival depended on their service to the government. Any disobedience would invite immediate punishment, death included.

Is the Communist Bureaucracy Different?

What are the general characteristics of the Communist system? One popular opinion is that the Chinese Communist power is different from past dynastic governments. On the surface, the Communist power does differ from the earlier governments. It has a new name, a political party rather than a dynastic ruling family, and a new set of slogans. In addition, Communists have created such entities as the people's congress, women's association, and labor unions. All these things seem new to many observers, both Chinese and foreign.

Indeed, the Communist Party claims that they have created a completely new society. Two popular slogans are "Without Communist Party, No New China," and "Serve the People." But is this Communist power actually new?

Not really! If it is different from the old dynastic governments, why should the Communist government be afraid of free expression and movement? Why should it burn books and close down universities? Why should it be afraid of people in general?

In essence, the Communist power is fundamentally the same as all the dynastic governments. It is no more than another self-appointed government, gaining power only through organized violence and designed to serve itself. According to this mind-set, people exist to serve the government's own needs and nothing more.

Thus the government must be fearful about people, afraid of free expression and information. It must prevent any independent movement at all cost. And it must employ violence against the slightest disobedience.

Under this system, furthermore, people may get some sort of personal freedom, but it must be granted by the government like a *gift*. Also, the government can take back its gifts at any time.[5]

But one fundamental difference does exist. In the past, the concept that all things under the sun belong to the government was difficult to carry out completely in real life, but it has been fully implemented in the Communist era.

Record Bureaucratic Body

The bottom line is about the Communist system is this: the government made the entire society and people its servants, arranging and controlling all lives from birth to education, employment, marriage, and travel.

How could all this manipulation be carried out in real life? Easy. The bureaucratic body was the biggest ever created: 45 to 70-plus million government officials in all. That is, today, there is one official for every 18 to 26 Chinese!

The official statistics show that the government now has 6.35 million officials plus some 29.5 million employees in the public sector in areas such as media, education, research, and medical services. But independent sources claim that the numbers are much bigger. One estimate is that there are over 45 million officials today.[6] Another estimate is over 70 million.[7] Moreover, these 70-plus million people all have governmental roles.

This discrepancy in numbers shows at least that the government's power is much more extensive than it admits. In a way, the top leadership is not aware of its exact employee body even today. One reason is that bureaucratic offices add more clerks without reporting to the higher authorities. Another reason is that many people directly or indirectly employ state power for their living.[8]

This vast bureaucratic body is the mother of all troubles. Oddly, in reality, in the current era the government has been trying hard to trim its official body but has made hardly any real progress so far. On the contrary, the more the government talks about the issue, the bigger the official body grows.

This massiveness of government is unprecedented in China's entire history. In the Han Dynasty, there was one official for every 7,000-plus people compared to the 18 to 26 today. Some 100 years ago, in the Qing Dynasty, there was one official for every 900-plus people.[9]

All the old dynastic governments refrained from extending their power without end. This was true especially with respect to the rural areas, where most people lived. The government relied heavily on the rural land-owning gentry, which acted as a go-between for the rulers and farmers. These educated gentry were very active in matters like collecting taxes and food as well as providing local security.

This arrangement greatly limited direct contact of the officials with people, which in turn limited corruption in significant ways. The role of the gentry class created an *insulating layer* between power and the people, which was extremely crucial for the health and peace of the society as a whole. Furthermore, it significantly increased government efficiency. In short, rural life was relatively self-governed, which was the best choice for the rulers as well.

Without this insulating layer, disasters would soon occur, for corrupt officials would endlessly squeeze people. Wild corruption would destroy everything in its path. China's history is full of examples, both positive and negative.

One extreme case involved the founding emperor Zhu Yuanzhang (1328-1398) of the Ming Dynasty, who decisively banned officials from visiting villages. Why?

He was aware that interactions between officials and farmers would not lead to anything positive because farmers were powerless and officials could easily subdue them. This would lead to corruption, which would topple the government in the end.[10]

In short, it was in the ruler's interest to stop officials from having unnecessary contacts with farmers. Otherwise, official corruption would only damage the ruler's interest.

But the Communist leadership went in the opposite direction. Instead, it believed that having total control over farmers was best. Consequently, farmers have been completely tied up by bureaucratic ropes for decades. Under this environment, all farmers were made servants to the government, a great scheme of the government.

This bureaucratic crusade in rural China has created this reality: the government could take food and other farm produce freely from farmers. In addition, countless bureaucrats could freely squeeze on rural people. All this has meant record disasters for rural China.

Complete Control, Total Chaos

What is the limit of greed? There is no limit. But there are troublesome consequences. In a little story, a greedy man wants to get all the fish in the pond, so he empties the pond. He gets all the fish. Soon he will get no more fish.

The Communist power has gone much further. It not only emptied the pond; in the Mao era it destroyed the pond. By doing so, it created all sorts of troubles for itself.

The disasters under Communism have had no equal in China's entire history. Usually, the early periods in most of the old dynasties were periods of peace and prosperity. But the Communist era saw disasters from the very beginning. Why?

The Communist economic monopoly is one key reason. Hardly any bureaucratic office knows how to manage a business, but this has not kept the government from directly controlling all business assets and their operations. Moreover, banning all private businesses was a natural consequence of the desire to protect bureaucratic power.

Under this monopoly, the government tried in every way to squeeze the people. As one example, to sell and buy gold, citizens had to go through the state banks. For 50 grams of gold sold to the state banks, the seller got 40 yuan, but he had to pay 160 yuan to buy back the same gold—a 300% profit for the government.

But there was no choice, as all private shops were eliminated. This kind of manipulation characterized all aspects of Chinese life for decades. Vast incentives were a part of the motive behind the government's economic monopoly.

Furthermore, the government banned all independent organizations of any sort. Instead, it completely controlled all organizations, including media, schools, hospitals, labor unions, associations of women and youth, and even temples. In short, it created the most exhaustive bureaucratic life on earth.

To maintain order, record-breaking violence was employed. The more economic disasters the government created, the more violent it became. In the Mao era, killing was a daily event. All this produced the greatest bureaucratic paradise, but the worst nightmare for people. With such bureaucratic manipulation, how could China have avoided a vast poverty and stagnation? No way.

The great destructions in the Mao era were unprecedented in world history. According to Joseph Needham and Andre Gunder Frank, China was ahead of Europe in total production even in the early 1800s.[11] For example, around 1820, China had about 30% of global production. Yet in the Mao era, China's total share was reduced to about 1%, the lowest level in its entire history. This vast destruction happened when bureaucratic power reached its height in that era.

It was not just wealth that was destroyed; there was vast bloodshed. Millions of people were killed. But killings could hardly promote the bureaucratic economy at all, which brought vast problems to the government itself. It is under such circumstances that the reform started in 1978.

Chapter 14.
Why Does Beijing Want Reform?

In this era, one of the big buzzwords is *reform*. But what prompted Beijing to push for reform in the first place? This question is certainly interesting, but knowing the answer would be even more important. Government consists of officials who are all humans. Humans have incentives to do this thing but not that. Why do the Communists want the reform? Rather, what do they want to gain from it? And what are they afraid of losing?

A basic answer is this: the government wants to gain more power, not give any away. That is why the old bureaucratic structure remains in place despite all the economic changes.

In reality, Beijing has tried hard to keep this bureaucratic system in place. Consequently, all the reform actions have been confined to the old bureaucratic framework.

What does all this mean in real life? It means, above all, that the government can still make any claims it wishes. It is accountable to nobody and remains to provide services to nobody but itself. And it continues to try to arrange the entire society and people for its own needs. All this has produced a twisted society and life.

Walking out this bureaucratic life turns out easier said than done. A basic reason for this is this fact: Under this bureaucratic power, the society and people remain too weak to challenge the universal rights of government bureaucracy.

A Difficult Start

Most outsiders are little aware of the fact that it was very tough for Beijing to embark on the current reform. Decades passed before the reform began in 1978. This was so despite the fact that as soon as the bureaucratic system was established in the 1950s, all its troubles emerged immediately.

As one example, even supplying enough vegetables to cities was a constant difficulty for the government. Several decades saw a serious shortage of all the essential goods in life.

To make ends meet, the government designed a complete ration system. Every person was given a fixed allowance of items like various food items, tea, soap, clothes, meat, and eggs. Coupons were issued for each and every item. But still, very often, even with these coupons and cash in hand, people found the stores empty.

One well-known writer, Wang Meng (who served as a one-term minister at the Cultural Ministry in the Deng era), recalls his life during the Cultural Revolution (1966-1976); at that time, he and his family were exiled to Xingjiang Autonomous Region.

He writes, "People often needed to get a day break from work in order to buy food. At the time, the city Urumqi had an insufficient supply of all basic goods. You held the [government-issued] coupons in hand for food, tea, and meat, but the stores did not have them in stock often . . . once these items arrived, people rushed in to buy them. There were long waiting lines . . . you must wait for hours. So, taking a day off was all needed."[1]

As another example, the rural people's commune was set up in the mid 1958, but it created immediate troubles: Nationwide starvation was under way at the end of the year.[2]

For the following three years or so, deaths occurred everywhere. To escape, many hungry citizens ran to the former Soviet Union and other bordering nations and regions. For example, hundreds of thousands of people in Guangdong tried to escape to Hong Kong.

As one elderly resident in Guangdong recalled, "Countless people were trying to swim over to Hong Kong and many died in the water. There were countless floating bodies on the water for some time."

Actually, the bureaucratic economy went dead on day one. But for its own sake, the government could hardly correct its mistakes. Instead, more man-made tragedies followed, especially the Cultural Revolution.

With all such abuses, the government risked its own power, to say the least. It was as though monks were trying to burn down their own temple. Only after three disastrous decades did reform action occur.

What has really happened in the government world?

Riding on a Tiger

Something one might not expect about this type of system is this: once it is set up, it creates countless foes. Who or what is the government's biggest foe? *The government itself. Its monopoly over all things under the sun has created problems that were certainly not envisioned by the planners.*

Power brings troubles to the power holder. After all, power is a double-edged sword: It carries vast responsibilities. The more power the government has, the more responsibilities it bears. But it is these responsibilities that government wishes to shed, not the power.

Indeed, the old government monopoly had hugely negative effects on the government's own health. All the responsibilities for providing life's essentials for the world's biggest population turned out to spell complete misery for the government. This nightmare went beyond the *PLAN.*

The government has been trying hard to reform the system all along, a thing the outside world is little aware of. Such efforts have taken nearly all its energy and attention, up to this date.

Even today, the old problems are not resolved at all. But it cannot be otherwise; there are simply no solutions within the bureaucratic framework. Any possible solution would have to come from outside the system, something the Communists are deeply aware of by now.

Yet without any realistic solutions within the bureaucratic establishment, more problems have emerged, naturally. Very unexpectedly, economic failures produced vast power struggles at the top, which quickly spread over the entire society.

By the time of the failures of the Great Leap Forward and the people's commune in 1958, hellish troubles had emerged. Instead of changes in policies, vast purges and killings took place. This first happened within the power circle and soon expanded into all corners of the nation.

The most famous victim was former defense minister Peng Dehuai. Along with him, more than 3 million officials had been purged beginning in 1959. Countless people perished, Peng included.[3]

But the most deadly purges occurred only seven years later, during the Cultural Revolution (1966-1976). Over that time, most, if not all, mayors, governors, central government ministers and Party chiefs fell victim, not to mention low-ranking officials and commoners.[4]

Even Deng Xiaoping was twice a victim during the period. He survived the deadly purges, but Liu Shaoqiu, the state head and second most powerful official, along with many others, perished.

But such power struggles as well as the resultant violence and chaos should not come as a surprise. To put it simply, because of government's monopoly over all things in the society, economy, and market, all economic and social problems are turned into political problems. Moreover, only power struggles and bloodshed could cover up these deadly problems.

Furthermore, because citizens had lost all independence, they could easily be drawn into the political chaos. Indeed, all ordinary people were employed as bureaucratic weapons in the crusade of power. The Red Guards, who were young students, were the best known.

This total madness did not happen prior to the Communist era. But that is not surprising, as the old dynastic governments never amassed the amount of power that the Communists did. *Ultimate power brings ultimate troubles.*

New Games

It is shocking to realize that this system protects no one, not even the most powerful. This has created immense nightmares for the decision makers of the new era. The previous bloody lessons have naturally created the desire for change within the bureaucratic establishment.

To avoid further troubles, the Beijing leadership has cleverly chosen the current path: allowing some degree of freedom to people as long as its grip on power is not jeopardized.

Even in this era, the rights of people remain a foreign concept. The government does not feel that people are naturally entitled to rights. Instead, the amount of freedom one is allowed must be granted like a *gift* by the government.

In the case of the rural people's commune, the government did not hesitate to abolish it in 1983. Buy why? The reason is simple: Allowing more freedom to the farmers would not damage Bejing's power. Rather, abolishing the disastrous people's commune, its own creation, got rid of a number of unwanted troubles.

For ages, Chinese farmers have been highly independent. They are without organizations of any kind, which makes them relatively powerless to defend their rights. This was true 2,000 years ago and remains so today.

Returning to traditional farming has had little effect on bureaucratic interests so far. Millions of old grassroots officials could get new positions in the township-level government units. Today, the rural official body stands at over 14.75 million.[5]

In this era, though Beijing talks much about trimming the official body, little has happened and its size has continued to increase.

Foreign Capitalists vs. the Domestic Private Sector

With the same mind-set, Beijing has given huge space to foreign businesspeople taking part in the Chinese economy and market. Why? Because these foreigners are only profit oriented — they don't really care whom the Chinese emperor is as long as there are profits to be made.

Furthermore, having foreign businesses inside helps the government in many ways. Indeed, this foreign involvement has helped to expand the pie significantly. Under an improving life, it is much easier for the government to maintain its power, which is what it hopes.

But attracting foreign capitalists is no small job. To this end, the government has offered countless incentives to foreign parties. In fact, the government has chosen to become a dedicated service provider to this selected group. Moreover, its service quality has been improving fast. But at the same time, it has continued to deny positive services to the domestic business community in general.

In the 1980s, most foreign capitalists could not take this help for granted. They waited and waited. But by 1992, the situation had changed for the better. Then came the huge rush that immediately made China a new global theater.

On this issue, one Chinese scholar told me, "It is so obvious that the Chinese government has willingly become a great partner with foreign businessmen. With all the privileges, how could foreign businessmen not make fat money in China?"

Evidence for this observation is strong. Within a short time—by 2005—about one-third of China's total industrial output came from overseas companies. The incentives are so high that more overseas businesses rush over. *Very likely, this overseas contribution could reach 50% within a decade.*

But offering more space to the domestic private sector is a different story. After all, the independent private sector could become a political force in the long run. Hence, containing its development is nothing less than necessary for the government.

Market Movement

A truth universally acknowledged is that power can expand only until it runs into opposition. Otherwise, the sky is the limit as far as greed is concerned.

In this era, the traditional bureaucratic power has not encountered any measurable organized opposition. But it has continued to curtail any possible independent movement at all costs.

The fact that China has become more and more open is a great achievement for Beijing in particular. But the old bureaucratic interests persist strongly. The bureaucratic power continues to pursue its interests at the expense of the society and people, just as in the Mao era.

Above all, political power cannot be turned into service unless there is an external force strong enough to make it happen. But today's China continues to lack such an external force. Hence, it is left for the government to try new tactics. That is why all the key institutional and political reforms have been going so slowly.

On the surface, in this era, the government has talked endlessly about creating a law-based, modern market economy, but its biggest effort has been to promote all changes within the old bureaucratic framework.

So far, China's new movement toward a modern market economy has been full of surprises due to the continued existence of an overextended government, all because the role of the government as a squeezer has remained unchanged. Gaining benefits for its own ends is all it cares about.[6]

On this issue, a citizen wrote, "After all these years of reform, evidently there has been hardly any progress on the part of the government. In many ways, it does not do what a government is supposed to do, while it intrudes on countless other things [for benefits]. Clearly, this government does not function in the right way at all."[7]

Today, in spite of the business boom, the state sector is dying rapidly. An underlying reason is that the government has given hardly any independent space to the state companies. Instead, bureaucratic offices have a tight grip over them still, and business dealings turn into bureaucratic dealings. Thus it is next to impossible for the state companies to evolve into truly modern business organizations.

Why is the government afraid of letting the dying state sector revive? Its fear is that it would lose power once the state sector became truly independent. Independent businesses and vested bureaucratic interests do not go hand in hand.

Hence, to have a grip on power, the government would prefer the state sector to die more than anything else. How about wealth or job creation? That is the last concern. Consequently, the state sector has quickened the pace leading to death as now.

Concerning this issue, one scholar noted, "Naturally, the state sector has nothing to do with wealth creation. In truth, it is no more than a political tool for the government to expand its interest. Furthermore, the government would prefer its death instead of independent, market-oriented movement for it."

The Chinese bureaucratic power is somewhat like the European church-state power in the past. Government in old Europe, through its unity with religion, held steady power over the society and people for ages. Furthermore, European society could not produce any effective countermeasure against this church-state. In this environment, the privileged few had unlimited power over the masses. Aristocrats remained aristocrats, while serfs remained surfs, generation after generation.

Even now, the Chinese bureaucratic power has no incentive to turn itself into a modern service provider. Its mentality continues to be to hold on to its power indefinitely.

On this point, a Chinese scholar noted, "This bureaucracy has no interest other than power itself. As a result, the entire society is still held hostage today."

Still, China is fast changing nonetheless, especially at the grassroots level. In some ways, the bureaucracy seems to feel very uncertain about its future. Many bureaucrats fear that a fast-changing society with increasing openness may create barriers to their freedom of behavior. As a result, many want to cash out by stealing.

A popular saying in the bureaucratic world is "Power must be used for personal gain, all before it expires."

Hence, it is easy to see why many bureaucrats are hurrying to steal money. As a Chinese businessman noted, "These corrupt bureaucrats really doubt if they can hold power forever. It is all natural for them to steal as much as possible as if no there were tomorrow."

The WTO Brings Greater Openness

A basic fact is that the closed society of the Mao era aided bureaucratic power in all sorts of ways. Today, Chinese people have great hopes for an open society. In particular, Chinese citizens welcome the WTO as a way to achieve more openness.[8]

Underlying this hope is the fact that up to 80% of the WTO agreement concerns the conduct of government in business and trade. To the Chinese, entry into the WTO marks the first time in which law exists to regulate the government's conduct. This is a huge change indeed.

Specifically, under the WTO accord, lifting bans to market entry for the private sector is mandatory. This finally happened beginning in 2005. By now, Beijing has started to offer the domestic private sector access to the monopolized sectors such as oil, petrochemicals, airlines, banking, financial services, rail, telecom, tobacco, and utilities. Though the private sector is still too weak to participate extensively in these fields, the door is starting to open, representing a basic change.

But such acts have ensued from the WTO accord, which demands that foreign and domestic businesses be treated equally. In its announcement about lifting the ban in 2005, Beijing stated that the domestic private sector should enjoy the benefits given to foreign sectors. This may be indicative of its reluctance to do anything good for the domestic private sector on its own. Rather, what has been done is a result of the WTO accord.

Furthermore, greater openness increases opportunities for reforming the faltering state sector. Countless state companies are dying. Distressed state companies have announced vast layoffs, which has become a very serious problem today. This worsening situation has demanded more action.

Even so, the state sector is still under the tightest control of the government units at all levels. With more foreign players rushing in and competition increasing, the need to reform this dying sector is becoming more urgent. This will lead to greater reform in one way or another. Lately, there have been more dramatic actions. For example, allowing foreign banks and investors to take serious stakes as well as performing hands-on management in key state banks is a huge change (see Part IV).

Acts Impeding Market Movement

Without doubt, the WTO will help to bring about freer movement of goods, people, capital, and ideas. Up to now, China has yet to build a unified national market. The main reason is the various protective measures that are in place, are all tied to bureaucratic interests at all levels. This problem cannot be resolved within the old framework at all, but greater openness is altering the situation significantly. For now, things are moving in this new direction at a faster pace.[9]

To be sure, old bureaucratic practices still commonly militate against a rational market development. For example, the city government in Shanghai banned cars made outside the city from getting a plate in the city. The city government wanted to protect its state company, Shanghai Auto Industry Group, which has several joint ventures with Volkswagen, Toyota, and GM, among other foreign automakers.

Such bureaucratic obstructions are widespread. In one case, in the 1990s, the two mobile telecom operators, China Mobile and China Unicom, feuded in terrible ways, though both belonged to the central government. China Unicom is a relatively new mobile operator, created by three central government ministries in 1994, that was designed to introduce competition in the market.

But for many years, China Unicom consumers had problems making emergency calls, as access was denied by the old telecom establishment. Furthermore, when China Unicom tried to enter the fixed-line business in certain cities, such as Tianjin, there were difficulties in gaining access to the existing network. The problem was resolved in 1999 when the Ministry of Telecom and Information was created, so that one entity no longer wears the two hats of regulator and an operator.[10]

In the small cities and rural regions, bureaucratic obstructions are even more widespread. The small rural city of Han Chuan of Hubei province was the scene of an odd occurrence in early 2006. To protect the local liquor business, the city's government formally ordered that its entire official body drink the locally produced hot liquor, *Little Confused Sage*. The order specified that the government employees must collectively meet a consumption target of $247,000 worth of the liquor per year. Those government units that met the quota would get a 10% kickback. But when the order was exposed by the media, the city government was forced to cancel it.[11]

One may wonder why official groups are so afraid to have less power—after all, less power would mean fewer responsibilities on their shoulders. But the realities suggest that more power benefits the officials in all sorts of ways, as seen recently in a housing project in the city of Zhengzhou in Henan province.

Zhengzhou's city government constructed some apartment buildings that were designated for low-income families—at least in theory. By the time the apartments were completed, they looked more like luxurious buildings with their nice gardens and underground parking. They were sold to government officials and people with ties to the government, all at less than half of the market price. Moreover, the project was never announced to the public. At least 126 apartments went to local officials. Before paying for them, the officials sold the buying rights to ordinary people for profits of $10,000 to $16,250 per unit.[12]

One businessman commented, "This is really nothing. Corruption can be one trillion times worse than this case. After all, no bloodshed occurred and nobody was buried alive."

A Turning Point in History?

For now, an increasingly open environment is injecting huge energy into Chinese life. As if reborn, people have gained new vigor, which is pushing back the old bureaucratic domination in no small ways. But the bureaucratic power remains strong.

As noted earlier, on a global basis, turning self-appointed governments from self-servers into public service providers has been a recent development. Though the West led the way, this task was formidable even for Europe. Even in Voltaire's age, Europeans still lived under the shadow of the church-state. A new way of life emerged only gradually.

For example, it has taken the West a long time to produce upward mobility in general. Europeans living in the time of Charles Dickens had a very different living environment. Today's division of labor, especially the existence of countless independent professions, is a result of this long process.

More significantly for the West, a new political-economic framework enables accommodation to changing realities. The United States and Canada have been more fortunate than the European countries in taking this modern path directly. Intellectually, they have simply taken for granted that the rights of government exist solely to serve society. Consequently, government power has been largely pushed aside. This reduced government power has produced a society based on law.

To me, the most impressive thing about the systems in the United States and Canada is the positive environment for wealth creation. All properties and business assets have well-defined owners or shareholders, who have universal rights regarding their interests. Hence, the United States and Canada have been able to lead the world in modernity and development. In this respect, China can only follow.

Today, opportunities have finally arrived for China to address this issue from the root causes. In particular, vast changing realities have produced new thinking within the government world. For example, Beijing increasingly recognizes that allowing people more room is the best way to avoid unwanted troubles.

One impressive change since the 1980s has to do with the rural election experiment. Beijing has gradually allowed direct elections of leaders at the rural village level. Behind this move are countless cases of official corruption that penetrated into the rural households. Daily abuses threaten general peace and order. With this experiment, a good one so far, Beijing hopes to minimize corruption at the village level.

Today, Beijing claims that some 680,000 villages elect their heads independently. But critics readily point out that this rural village election is rather ineffective in fending off intrusions from the vast bureaucratic body, which can still act freely and happen in the old fashioned way.

But the government has yet to extend the idea of elections to higher levels. Moreover, to truly contain corruption, it has yet to abolish the entire bureaucratic body, which is an absolute necessity for real progress. Moreover, a free media has yet to emerge, which is essential as far as public interest is concerned.

In short, without dumping the entire bureaucratic system as well as the record bureaucratic body, there is no way to establish the modern things: true modern law, true ownership, and true modern government institutions as public service providers. The very existence of this Communist bureaucracy makes a modern, law-based society next to impossible.

But a fast-changing environment presents huge opportunities to destroy the bureaucratic cage completely. Ever-increasing openness, the emergence of independent professions, and the popular desire for prosperity will all help China to move ahead.

But because of the slowness of changes in the basic institutional framework, vast difficulties are present still. For example, in the last five years alone, some 200,000 corrupt government officials were arrested. Given all this, no one should expect fundamental changes to take place within a short time.

Part IV.
China's Banking, Insurance, and Stock Market Reforms

SUMMARY

China's economic expansion has given birth to many new things, especially a stock market as well as a booming insurance industry. But there are tremendous problems still. The basic problem is continuing bureaucratic domination, which has produced vast messes. For example, commercial banks have hardly performed though the nation's economy has been expanding fast.

Resolving these problems now takes central stage. What is really needed is for the government to completely withdraw from the business sphere. But until lately, no decisive actions had taken place. Happily, this urgently needed reform is being pursued more actively now.

Several reform measures are taking place simultaneously in banking, insurance, and the stock markets. These actions are aimed at cleaning up the mess created by overextended government power. In particular, foreign banks, insurers, and investors are being invited to take part in the reform process. Consequently, more opportunities are emerging for international parties. These measures may in the end avoid huge disasters for China.

Chapter 15.

The Explosive Insurance Market

One day recently, while I was sitting in a Beijing hotel lobby waiting for a business lunch, a nicely dressed, pleasant young Chinese man started a conversation. We exchanged business cards, and he turned out to be an insurance man. Scenes such as this, long common in other parts of the world, have now come to China, in a big way.

A rising standard of living invariably brings with it an insurance industry as people try to protect what they have. With more than 3 million workers in the sector, China now has an exciting, fast-growing insurance industry. It is a remarkable change from the recent past.

Only 20 years ago, Chinese citizens had rather a simple life, and perhaps 98% of them did not even know what insurance was. Today, hundreds of millions of citizens hold policies of every sort, from health to life to property. The commercial insurance business has come a long way, from nonexistent during the Mao era to explosive today.

(China's insurance history is this: By 1958, the government shut down all existing insurance companies. In 1980, the very first state-owned insurance company reemerged.)

And the Chinese public has made equally rapid strides in accepting insurance products as a routine part of life. In today's urban China, talking to an insurance agent is nearly as common as talking to your neighbor. Industry observers expect that, in time, holding an insurance policy will become as popular as having a mobile phone. In the rural regions, insurance commerce is also spreading, though not as fast as in the urban regions today.

The business has grown most dramatically in the last 11 years or so, with an annual compounded growth rate of 20% to 30%. By 2005, China's total insurance assets had reached over $190 billion. In terms of percentage of GDP, the insurance sector is still only less than 3%, small compared to some 11% in Japan and 8% in the United States. But as incomes increase further, the insurance market will become more and more significant to the economy as a whole.

These assets are held by some 80 insurance players, both Chinese and foreign. In addition, there are hundreds of insurance brokerage agencies. Most of these insurance issuers and agencies have emerged only within the last 10 years. Their employees are mostly young professionals.

Industry experts now feel that China is well on its way to becoming a top insurance market. One of its biggest strengths is that Chinese life is still family centered. This is true, in general, in the rest of Asia. This is one reason Japan's insurance industry is relatively larger than that of the United States. Indeed, in the 1980s, Japan had the biggest insurance companies in the world, partly due to the strong family ties in Japanese society.

International Involvement

As with most industries in today's China, foreign giants have rushed into the insurance sector. There are already over 37 foreign insurers operating in China, and more are coming. These players include AIG, Liberty Mutual Group, and MetLife of the United States; Samsung Life of South Korea; Mitsui-Sumitomo Insurance and Nippon Life of Japan; Manulife of Canada; and Allianz, Generali, AXA, Royal & Sun Alliance, ING, and Munich Re of Europe.

Due to policy restrictions, foreign operations have been limited to a few major cities such as Beijing, Shanghai, Guangzhou, and Tianjin. Also, most of the insurers operate through joint ventures. In reality, most of these foreign players are only testing the water; as a result, they jointly held only about a 7% market share as of 2005. But this will soon change. As is true for the banking, stock brokerage, and fund management sectors, these foreign insurance players will gain more opportunities soon due to China's entry into the WTO.

The insurance business as we know it today originated in Europe in the 17th century. So the international insurers are nothing if not experienced. But they have few additional tricks to apply to China; rather, their best weapon is manpower. They have to send agents everywhere in the country to get clients. They even set up desks in front of hospitals and shopping centers to find customers, large and small. (The young man at the Beijing hotel, as it turned out, worked for AIG.)

Not every foreign insurance company is committed to China, but the interest is strong even in companies that are not licensed to operate in the country. Very often, foreign insurers send in agents from Hong Kong and other overseas cities to get mainland Chinese clients. Though this practice is illegal, it often gets results. A Hong Kong insurance agent working for a major Western insurance company once told me excitedly, "I just sold an $8 million policy to a Shanghai CEO!"

Building Chinese Insurance Companies

Despite the booming market, most Chinese insurance managers agree that there is still much work ahead in building the Chinese players into strong insurance companies. The biggest problem is that Chinese insurance companies, as with China's state banks and state-owned companies in general, have yet to become truly independent business organizations.

In a scenario that is all too familiar to observers of the Chinese economy, almost all the Chinese insurance companies are tied to an assortment of government units. For example, the biggest Chinese insurance company, China Life, which is already a top-500 global company and listed on the New York Stock Exchange, is run by the central government.

Ping An (Safe Life) Insurance is run by the Shenzhen city government, and Dazhong (Everyone) Insurance is owned by 23 state companies belonging to Shanghai, Zhejiang, and Iiangsu provincial and municipal governments. Another insurer, Yong An (Everlasting Peace) of Xian, has shareholders from numerous large companies in the oil, telecommunications, rail, postal, and other sectors, all of which are controlled by the central government.

This organizational structure is standard for the entire state sector. The biggest state companies are run by the central government, while small and midsize state companies are run by provincial and local governments.

This structure means that there are enormous frictions among the various state companies. The companies belonging to the central government get more privileges. For example, in the past, they were allowed to play in national markets, while companies belonging to various provincial and local government units were allowed to operate only in their own areas.

But the insurance sector has some noteworthy exceptions to the general rule. Some insurance companies run by city- and province-level government units have outperformed. In particular, within the last two decades of its existence, Ping An Insurance has taken the second spot in China's insurance sector. This is mainly due to Ping An Insurance's strong leadership. The company has appointed more than a dozen senior executives who have previously worked for global financial and consulting firms. Under their strong management, the company has been able to attain a dominant position among domestic insurers.

One regional executive working for a big-four global accounting firm has been very impressed by the Ping An management. He said, "They are very pro-international and eager to follow global professional standards. This has become a top strength for the company."

Many international investors agree with him, and some foreign giants like Morgan Stanley, Goldman Sachs, and HSBC have become significant shareholders in the company, which is now listed on the Hong Kong stock exchange. In particular, HSBC has continued to increase its stake in Ping An and now holds 19.9% of the Chinese insurer, a limit set by Beijing for a single foreign shareholder.

Behind this increased foreign interest is a satisfying performance sheet from the Ping An management. In 2005, its sales reached over $8 billion and profits were $530 million, which makes the insurer a top performer in China.

But many other Chinese insurance companies have had lackluster performances so far. The basic problem is built into the system. That is, these companies are organized in parallel to government structures, and their top managers are government officials, not insurance professionals. This bureaucratic establishment has already created disasters for China's banking and brokerage sectors. It is casting a shadow over the insurance industry as well.

Under this bureaucratic environment, numerous Chinese insurers have already suffered tremendous losses despite the rapid growth. Some highly inexperienced and substandard decision makers have involved their firms in high-risk deals such as highly illiquid real estate projects, which predictably resulted in financial distress.

But the chronic problem of separating business and government will not be resolved soon for the insurance sector any more than for China as a whole. The bottom line is again the weakness of the society and the unlimited number of ways in which bureaucratic power can continue to expand.

Limited Investment Choices

Another important challenge confronting China's insurance sector, as well as the financial sector as a whole, is the very limited choices for company investments. Insurance company investment portfolios are restricted to mainland China only, which has posed a huge problem.

For example, Kong Tai (Prosperous Life) Insurance of Beijing puts about 80% of its assets into bonds, and most other domestic insurers do about the same. This portfolio structure limits asset appreciation and therefore the long-term health of the industry.

One investment officer at a Chinese insurance company told me, "We badly need to widen our investment choices and go global. For now, we are so limited."

The ability to choose the most promising from a vast menu of global investments allowed today's global insurance companies to become powerhouses in the first place. The Chinese insurance and financial companies must follow their example. Many Chinese investment professionals are aware of this.

The former chairman of a leading Chinese investment company strongly affirmed that globalizing Chinese financial businesses is a must. "The sooner, the better. Otherwise investment limitations will damage the health of China Inc. in general."

Unfortunately, at this point, the government is behind the curve. It has imposed innumerable restrictions on the ability of Chinese companies, especially financial concerns, to move capital out of China. Even moving capital to Hong Kong is next to impossible. Business decisions are still turned into bureaucratic issues. This has always been the top problem for Chinese insurers as for Chinese companies in general.

Making policy changes in Beijing is always two steps forward, one step back, as both the old government mentality with its traditional protective measures and the officials' desire to retain their influence over businesses remain strong.

Gaining Independence

An even bigger concern than optimizing investments is achieving independence from government influence. This would mean nothing less than survival for the insurance companies in the long run.

In China's state sector, all key managers are appointed by government offices. Compared to Western professionals, these managers are hobbled because their activities and careers are dependent on maintaining the approval of those who appointed them. Privately, most business managers in the state sector deplore this situation and would like nothing better than to operate their firms in the same way as their colleagues in developed nations.

In this bureaucratic world, business managers stand lowest on the bureaucratic ladder. But without direct power to change the situation, they have tried to promote their interests in other ways. The most realistic options are to become a publicly listed company, have international partners, or both. Taking these actions has helped Chinese managers to protect their professional interests.

As with the rest of the state sector, Chinese insurance companies are eager to get listed, especially on overseas markets. Both listing and foreign tie-ins promote better-quality corporate governance, which benefits the most competent managers.

In the state sector in general and the insurance business in particular, there are enormous internal tensions within the organizations. Since hiring and promotions are not done on merit, it is extremely difficult to improve the quality of management. Furthermore, leadership transitions are troublesome. Often a management change in these state companies may lead to collapse.

In general, there is little trust between government offices and managerial people. In practice, a constant war goes on. The government officials want to expand their interests by tightly grasping business assets and managers, but managerial people wish for room to employ their professional talents as well as rewards based on merits. This eternal conflict has severe consequences for wealth creation.

Among all the issues, one is most basic: Who is to protect wealth creation? Under the current system, there is no one to do this. The solution lies outside the existing political-economic system.

Becoming More Service Oriented

A huge gap in quality of service still exists between most developed-country industries and their Chinese counterparts. Putting market needs first is a new concept to China Inc., and insurance companies are no exception. Behind it, moving away from bureaucratic domination is easier said than done.

In general, Chinese insurers have performed well in sales — getting new clients. Their great weakness thus far has had to do with truly satisfying client needs, especially with respect to after-sales service. Professional service standards remain weak. This means that consumers can easily fall victim to abuses.

Quite often, consumers encounter problems when they need help from their insurance companies. Effectively responding to claims has been an issue, and there have been numerous cases of companies failing to deliver on their promises to clients.

In today's China, it is easy to find disgruntled insurance customers; the litany of complaints includes misleading descriptions of coverage and the delay of refunds for months or even years. One dissatisfied auto insurance policyholder said, "It has taken more than a year to get my claims refunded after I had a car accident."

In most countries, a government consumer protection agency would be responsible for assisting the public in such cases. But in China, government watchdogs are more often than not ineffective in protecting consumers' interests. The deep entanglement of businesses and government bodies has certainly not helped the situation. Indeed, the governance problem is built into the system. Helping aggrieved insurance customers would in effect require one government unit to fight another.

Naturally, this bureaucratic structure can hardly protect the average consumers. In reality, consumers can easily become victims. Until this problem is addressed, the industry cannot reach its full potential. In fact, all Chinese businesses in general and insurance players in particular are well aware of the holes in the existing system. That is why some businesspeople are not afraid to commit abuses against consumers. Punishment is so light that abusive practices are highly rewarding. Turning the tide is simply beyond the power of consumers.

Headhunting Reveals Intense Competition

One sign of hotter competition in the sector is headhunting for the most competent managers; recently, for example, Kong Tai Insurance hired a top marketing executive away from Ping An Insurance. The Ping An management now calls the company an insurance training school, a characterization its competitors agree with.[1]

But Ping An has continued its expansion programs nonetheless. To do better, it has intensified its employee training programs. By mid-2006, the company had set up a sizable training school in Shenzhen, costing $56 million that can provide extensive classes for 900 students at a time. These programs are joint ventures with several leading international insurance and financial organizations and schools. For example, the Wharton School, LIMA, LOWA, and AICPCU, as Ping An's partners, provide teachers and textbooks for some of these programs.[2]

Also, there are the ambitious international players. A key concern for Chinese insurers going forward is the possibility of losing their top management talent to deep-pocketed foreign insurers. In addition, more and more foreign insurers will hit the ground running as they enter China after 2006, when WTO commitments will require further liberalization in the industry. Some executives might even take their best clients with them.

Actually, this is already happening in a big way; many international players are trying hard to woo Chinese insurance executives. The insurance market has become a hot battleground in general. All players are doing their best to move ahead. At the same time, many insurance executives are trying to jump over to greener grass. All the familiar scenes in the established markets have come to China's insurance market.

As it turns out, the insurance market demonstrates that the biggest value in a business organization is human talent. With respect to gaining talented employees, the Chinese insurance industry is an example: The employers are increasingly showing respect for their employees. This is a new wave for China in general.

Increasingly, good employees wish to be treated as partners rather than mere employees. This new mentality is eroding values in the state sector, where employees are treated poorly and their creative energy is little appreciated. Growth along these lines will push organizational development forward, which remains a key need in China today.

In spite of such issues, overall, the looming competitive pressure from foreign-invested companies is impelling the Chinese firms to work harder and is therefore a positive factor in the insurance industry's development. Greater openness will promote greater competitiveness, which will help to create a healthy industry in the long run. In the end, Chinese citizens will be the biggest winners: Millions of them are gaining access, for the first time, to the "peace of mind" that is ultimately the insurance industry's only product.

Chapter 16.

Chinese Banks on the Move, Finally!

June 17, 2005, was no ordinary day for the Chinese banking community, as news spread rapidly that the Bank of America had injected $3 billion for a 9% stake in China Construction Bank, China's third biggest state bank. By the end of the year, the bank floated in Hong Kong, raising $9.2 billion in cash.

Behind the cheering, most Chinese bankers were aware of a great paradox regarding China's economy. For the past 26 years, even as China's GDP raced ahead like a bullet train with annualized growth around 9.6%, the only aspects of the banking sector that were growing seemed to be the bad ones: mountainous nonperforming loans, capital misallocation on a mammoth scale, and malfeasance by bank officials.

Indeed, China's banking sector has been stuck in such deep mud for so long that it has cast a huge shadow over prospects for the sustained development of the country. As time has passed, the banking holes have only widened, a threatening trend for banking insiders.

But, at last, real change seems to be in the air: The urgent need to clean up the banking mess has become clear to Chinese society. All of China's "big-four" state banks (Bank of China, China Construction Bank, Industrial and Commercial Bank of China, and Agricultural Bank of China) are suddenly in a hurry to restructure, reform, and generally clean up their houses—to be reborn, in fact.

The opening up and listing of this once tightly controlled sector may be called, without exaggeration, a banking revolution; and one of the most important steps in the revolution is the introduction of foreign banking partners.

Banks Dragging the Chain of Economic Reform

A key cause of the banking mess was the same underlying issue that has faced the entire state sector of China's economy—employment by the government of the state sector for its own use. Practically, this meant that the state companies and banks served the needs of the government, not markets.

This twisted economic structure produced vast problems for China's economy and society. As a result, even as other "Asian tigers" boomed after World War II, poverty ruled mainland China for several decades, made worse by waves of political chaos.

Since the economic reforms began in 1978, private initiatives have reshaped China in huge ways. Even the state sector has gone through vast changes. Two of the most significant changes were the involvement of foreign investors and the booming domestic private sector, which has become a major player in the Chinese economy alongside the state companies and banks.

Against the background of the resultant booming economy and the record-setting speed and scope of economic development, China's banks conspicuously lagged. Their fortunes did not improve with the brightening economic picture; on the contrary, they have depended partly on periodic capital injections for survival.

The underlying reasons lie in the history of China's banks since 1949. For some six decades, the state banks have not acted like "real" banks — that is, independent businesses that are, at least in theory, accountable to shareholders for their successes and failures. Rather, they have operated as government units. Above all, they have served as cashiers for the government.

All measures were taken to protect the government's interests. In particular, all the key banking managers were government officials appointed by the central government. Their actions were controlled by countless government units at all levels. The local and provincial governments were given the task of co-supervising the banks. As a result, the appointments of local and regional bankers were often influenced by provincial and local government units in the area.

The bureaucratic organizational structure implies that these banks must constantly follow orders given from higher government offices. Furthermore, because of the high level of official control, in order to secure their positions the bank managers had to pay constant attention to the government officials who had the power to influence their positions. Their conduct was closely monitored by the higher government units.

Unsurprisingly, this affected their professional conduct. They could only follow orders from above. With the banking sector an integral part of the government system, bureaucratic interest groups have gained unlimited power over bank funds.

But this banking system is only part of the general bureaucratic economic system that has dominated China since mid-1950s. Under this system, all aspects of economic and business activities were completely and exclusively controlled and managed by government officials alone. Of all this, the central government in Beijing has acted as the supreme planner, organizer, rule-maker, executer, and decision-maker.

Inner Workings

In reality, the whole banking system has been completely built into the bureaucratic framework since day one. Prior to 1984, commercial loans, in the Western sense, were nonexistent. Instead, all bank funds were allocated by the government exclusively and completely.

Indeed, the entire business life was carried out by the government bureaucracy. The banks did not need to study the creditworthiness of aspiring borrowers. Instead, they simply needed to follow government directives as to how much money to hand over, when, and to whom. Moreover, all the state companies were treated as government units, so there was no need for a commercial credit system. *In short, all commercial and economic activities have completely turned into bureaucratic activities.*

Payment collections were also a governmental affair. The government simply took away all the profits all companies made each year no matter what.

Actually, prior to 1980, the words *commerce, market, consumers,* and *goods* did not exist at all. The government completely controlled all goods and services as well as their allocation, among countless other things in the entire economic universe. Only since then has liberalization gradually taken place.

For decades, all companies were part of the bureaucratic establishment. If a company needed funds, it had to go through the relevant government offices at different levels. Actually, it was not the companies that decided whether they needed funding or not; the decision was made by the government offices. If a company needed money but the bureaucratic offices did not see it that way, the company could not get a penny. Conversely, if a company did not need a penny but the bureaucratic offices thought otherwise, it could get billions.

Dozens of government agencies at all levels were responsible for carrying out money allocations. The most important government agencies were the *Economic Planning Commission* (at central, provincial, and local levels), which decided on the needs of individual companies and projects, and the *Economic and Trade Commission*, which supervised and monitored the funding and business process.

In particular, these two organizations within the central government have been most significant in the entire money allocation process. They decided how much money and what projects different regions, units, and ministries should get each year. Subsequently, the lower government units decided how to allocate the money to their subunits.

Below these agencies are countless government agencies in charge of different business sectors. Each and every business sector, such as retail, consumer electronics, machinery, food and drinks, trade, and construction, has answered to a particular government agency. These specialized agencies are still responsible for the funding needs of companies under their control. All companies stand at the bottom of the bureaucratic ladder and are treated as mere workshops for the government.

In reality, the companies are responsible only for taking care of orders and production quotas issued from above. Also, they must ship their products to buyers designated by the government. In addition, numerous government agencies decide on the employee body as well as employee salaries and benefits, among countless other matters.

On the surface, this whole game is called *Central Planning,* but in reality, little planning has taken place.[1] Instead, all the government units are nothing but special interest groups. Since day one, they have been fighting with each other to gain more power and hence more business assets, as well as all the associated benefits.

Of all, the central government is the ultimate boss who makes all decisions, as well as obtains all associated benefits.

Indeed, it is government offices that have managed all banks and business transactions completely. This is how the banking and corporate system worked prior to 1984. *Thus all banks served solely as cashiers to the government, a term widely used by Chinese bankers today.*

Under this environment, vast destructions of wealth have taken place for long. The government controlled all aspects of market and economy as well as labor and financing. All people must serve the government's own needs. In particular, whatever people wanted to consume, including bikes, clothes, and even toothpastes and soaps, were in short supply. Even having enough food took a huge struggle.

But the government did hardly pay any attention to it. Instead, it allocated vast bank funds and business assets on other things especially the military industrial complex. In addition, vast bureaucratic chaos especially the Cultural Revolution caused more destructions of wealth.

In short, this so-called central plan has been a tool for the government bureaucracy to take over all banking and business assets for its own use. This is the very nature of this bureaucratic domination in the economic field.

Naturally, this system was bankrupt as soon as it was established. In reality, vast government projects were bankrupt before they were completed. Also, countless other government companies have gone bankrupt. Behind it, it is that these companies served the government's own interests, not markets at all.

A New Way

Since 1984, the state banks and companies have gradually been allowed to become more market oriented, at least in principle. But still, governmental influences are overwhelming. Above all, all the old government agencies have continued to exist (many of them have new names), and they perform business in nearly the same way as before. This implies that the banks and companies are without true owners and true legal protectors above all.

Furthermore, the banking situation is made worse by the fundamental absence of professional management and accountability. In reality, banks and state companies, still being on the lowest ladders of the government establishment, have gained hardly any autonomy. The dominating government power has made reform highly difficult if not impossible.

True banking and state sector reform would separate the government from the banks and state companies. Naturally, no government officials involved with banking and the state sector (which involves many millions of bureaucrats) would be pleased by such an outcome.

Again, throughout this era, there has been no accountability whatsoever within the government or banking and state sector systems. These banks and companies have had no meaningful owners in principle or practice. Bank losses have been more than common, as nobody is held responsible. Under such circumstances, it is no wonder that there have been seemingly unstoppable pileups of nonperforming loans.

For many decades, the big-four banks have faced this dire situation: For every $10 loaned, only $8, or less, was collectible.

Today, all honest Chinese bankers are aware of the banking mess. One loan manager working for a big-four bank told me, "It would not surprise me a bit if my bank goes bankrupt 10 times in a single day." But good bank employees are rather powerless to deal with the banking mess in general.

The need for reform of the sector companies and banks has become so clear it cannot be ignored any longer. Unfortunately, in Chinese society, the same entity that has the most to lose from reform—the government—is also the only entity that can initiate reform. The sometimes-halting progress of reform efforts has reflected this dilemma.

All things considered, reforming the banking and state sector mess requires reforming the entire political-economic system. After all, it is this system that has created an ownerless banking and state sector. But very unfortunately, the weak Chinese society does not have means of imposing its will on the government. As a result, resolving the banking problems waited for decades, until these problems threatened the very power of the government.

In this regard, the Asian financial crisis of 1997-1998 was a great lesson for Beijing. The ugly chaos and vast depression following the crisis in many Asian nations alarmed Beijing in no small way. Indeed, in Indonesia and several other crisis-filled nations, the old governments were toppled by angry citizens, which shocked Beijing even more. Since then, fast actions relating to the banking sector have occurred without stop.

The History of Bank Reform

Serious banking reform began only in 1999, the year the average nonperforming loan rate for the big-four banks reached a crisis level of 39%. This rate was even worse than that for the distressed South Korean and Thai banks, which had nonperforming loan (NPL) rates around 35% during the Asian financial crisis of 1997-1998. But the Chinese public was little aware of the risks involved.

There has been some media coverage, though not very extensive. Serious investigations have yet to take place. But one can hardly blame the Chinese media for naming the big-four banks "troublemakers" — they created huge troubles indeed, given that they controlled up to 70% of China's financial assets.

Since 1999, major loan write-offs as well as capital injections have taken place. The first write-off amounted to $170 billion for the big-four banks and occurred around the same time as an injection of about $33 billion of fresh capital into these capital-depleted banks. Beijing did not have the money, so it sold bonds to get the needed funds.

Second, beginning in 1999, four asset management companies (AMCs) have been created. These four AMCs are designed along the lines of the United States' Resolution Trust Corporation (RTC), which was formed in 1989 to clean up the savings and loan mess. Through these companies, Beijing hopes to break the deadlock for the banking sector. Also, very significantly, by 1999, Beijing had stopped the old practice to cover up the banking mess.

By design, the four AMCs are responsible for handling the written-off assets from each of the four big banks. Each was given a capital injection of $1.2 billion by Beijing.

The AMCs have tried in all sorts of ways to dispose of debts. The percentage of original capital they have recovered has typically been only 20%, or less, of the original book value. Their activities nonetheless represent a highly positive change, despite the fact that these organizations are reportedly tainted with corruption.

This new venture has international dimensions. Not only Chinese buyers, but also many leading international banks such as Citibank, Morgan Stanley, UBS, Deutsche Bank, and HSBC have actively acquired assets from the AMCs, to the mutual benefit of both sides. Indeed, resolving the Chinese banking mess has become an international business.

On the institutional side, huge efforts have focused on reducing the unwanted interference coming from government offices at all levels. In particular, the People's Bank, China's central bank, has replaced several dozen old provincial and municipal branch offices with nine new regional offices. By design, these new offices are independent of local and provincial government establishments; it is hoped that this will allow for more effective, independent banking supervision.

Lastly, in 2003, one additional dramatic change occurred with the establishment of the China Banking Regulatory Commission (CBRC), which has taken over the oversight role formerly performed by the central bank. In general, the banking reforms to date have been heavily influenced by the previous experience of other countries, particularly, though not exclusively, the United States (for example, China's AMCs were also influenced by South Korea's KAMCO agency, which very successfully performed an RTC-like role after the 1997-8 crisis).

The CBRC's Reform Strategies

The CBRC is pursuing three new strategies for banking reform. It has been learning how to create a new banking industry. So far, several significant measures have been adopted.

One is to list all Chinese banks, especially on overseas stock markets. To gain market confidence, the government has been injecting more capital into the big-four banks. Also, it has warned small retail banks about potential closure if they fail to perform satisfactorily. Because these small banks are tightly controlled by local and provincial-level government units, the issuance of this warning indicates the government's level of determination regarding banking reform.

But Beijing faces enormous difficulties in carrying out its supervision. The fundamental reason is that the big banks under Beijing's management have performed much worse than the small banks, thus damaging the credibility of the central government in huge ways.

One banker working for a small bank said, "My bank's performance is indeed ugly, but it is still far better than the big-four banks'."

Indeed, the big-four banks under Beijing's management have performed particularly poorly. So far, much more than $300 billion in cash has been wasted. Under the present system, there will likely be more tensions between Beijing and regional government units in the future. This aspect of the issue has no easy solutions under a centralized structure.

The second strategy, equally significant, is a new accountability measure. If internal abuses occur, then the two managerial layers above will be held responsible. If this measure works as intended, it will be a tremendously positive shock to the banking system.

This new measure is hugely significant due to the notoriously high level of malfeasance within the ranks of bank management. Thousands of corrupt employees, including hundreds of senior bankers such as Liu Jinbo, the ex-chief executive officer of the Bank of China (Hong Kong), have been arrested for stealing funds.

But there are even more corrupt government officials who steal bank funds. So far, there has been an absence of countermeasures against corrupt government officials in general. Such measures are simply beyond the power of any single government unit within the system.

Today, internal misconducts and crimes remain widespread. For example, in the period of February 2005 to mid-2006, 1,769 cases of banking frauds and misconducts were uncovered, which involved more than $1 billion in bank funds. A total of 1,887 abusers were prosecuted and additional 6,624 people were disciplined.[2]

The third strategy is to allow Chinese banks, including the big four, to form strategic partnerships with foreign banks, along with permitting foreign entities to buy shares in the banks. This has naturally opened the door for a much greater foreign presence in the Chinese banking sector.

In this case, WTO requirements have forced the government's hand: Foreign banks will gain complete access into China by the end of 2006 under WTO rules. So time is running out to clean up the banks, which adds enormous pressure on Beijing. As in other sectors of China's economy, the sight of incoming foreign "wolves" is causing the domestic "sheep" to run faster.

It must be noted that in the absence of outside involvement, China's banking and state sector reform would have been little more than bureaucratic reshuffling, simply because the Chinese bureaucratic establishment has been so weak in terms of accountability. Furthermore, the government continues to ban private Chinese parties from entering the banking field.

Foreign Involvement

As a result of the CBRC's moves, numerous foreign investors and banks have become significant shareholders in Chinese banks. In particular, HSBC holds 19.9% of Communication Bank, China's fifth largest bank, whose shares are newly listed on the Hong Kong stock exchange. HSBC also was allowed to have a seat on the board as well as two vice presidential positions at the bank.

At some smaller banks, the government has willingly allowed foreign investors to become controlling shareholders. This is what happened with Shenzhen Development Bank, a Shenzhen-based small retail bank whose shares trade on the Shenzhen stock exchange. The new controlling shareholder is Newbridge Capital, a U.S. venture capital firm. Since late 2004, it has reorganized the bank's management; the new chairman and CEO are two highly experienced U.S. bankers. Under their leadership, a massive restructuring program is under way inside the bank.

In another transaction in the making, Citibank, together with some international partners, proposed to buy a majority stake in Guangdong Development Bank, a highly distressed bank run by the provincial government. Once this deal is approved by Beijing, Citibank will run the bank on its own. This will push banking reform a step further as far as foreign management is concerned. But by mid-2006, all parties were waiting for the green light from Beijing (which is still very reluctant to give the green light).

Such hands-on foreign management has pointed toward a new way to shore up China's dire banking situation and may turn out to be a more realistic avenue for future progress. The foreign involvement also suggests how difficult it would be for China to create modern banks without the employment of modern management and accountability and well-defined ownership.

It should come as no surprise that borrowing international knowledge and experience could effectively hasten China's movement toward a modern financial sector; this has been true in many other areas of the Chinese economy. But the new government mentality of learning from outsiders is nonetheless very meaningful. After all, the gradual creation of modern banking systems has been a universal phenomenon in developed countries; in no case did countries start their development with a fully modernized system.

In this respect, the United States had many hard lessons, among which the 1929 stock market crash, which resulted in a comprehensive set of financial reforms, is only the best known. Indeed, for several years following the crash, American depositors refused to put money into banks, and banks were afraid to open their doors and incur withdrawal runs. Only after all that was the modern U.S. banking system painstakingly created, despite all the imperfections we are aware of today.

Banking reform through openness has been a strategy successfully employed by many nations, including those in Asia. The South Korean case, in which greater foreign ownership and an AMC-like NPL clearance agency were employed, is now widely seen as a major success story that helped the country bounce back quickly from the 1997-1998 Asian financial crisis.

At the same time, of course, achieving this new openness is not easy. The Japanese banking system has struggled since the 1991 collapse of the bubble economy to extricate itself from the financial meltdown created by traditional cross-holdings between banks and their corporate clients, among other causes.[3]

Japan Inc. has been trying hard to introduce foreign talent, permitting foreign participation in the financial sector and adopting international standards to deal with the problems. These are certainly positive changes. But it remains unclear whether the Japanese reforms have been as successful as South Korea's, or whether Japan's economy can ever recover the upward momentum that now characterizes China's.

Behind the Foreign Buying

Though the Chinese government sees the banking morass as a huge burden, many foreign banks and investors see the potential for great rewards. The invitation from the Chinese government to the world has already led to a rush on the part of global banking and investment communities.

In the case of Bank of America's buying into China Construction Bank, the potential upside is large indeed. From Bank of America's point of view, China has fundamental advantages over the United States: a much faster-developing economy (although the U.S. economy remains larger, and will for some time) and access to the vast personal savings of the Chinese, who have among the highest savings rates in the world.

Today, the personal savings rate in China is around 40% in general and was 46% in 2005. The pool of Chinese savings is rising steeply year after year, while U.S. personal savings are flat. By the summer of 2006, total Chinese personal savings reached over $2 trillion. Though China remains a poor nation today, but as its economy continues to expand, more opportunities will emerge. This expanding pie looks like a gold mine to all competent banks.

In short, buying into a huge Chinese bank like China Construction Bank was perceived as the quickest way to tap into this immense and growing pool of capital. Indeed, if these Chinese banks were in the right hands, they could become huge profit-generating machines. So, this long-term picture attracts foreign interests in no small way.

China Construction Bank is the third biggest bank in China, with 14,500 branches that serve 136 million retail clients and all the top Chinese corporations. Its principal business focuses on infrastructure and large business projects. In 2004, it had around 13% of China's total deposits and $472 billion in assets.

By making itself both a shareholder and a hands-on partner, Bank of America has immediately established itself as a major player in China. But Bank of America's involvement is not limited to capital investment. It wants to send 500 bankers to help manage the Chinese bank, especially the risk-control aspects of the business.

This hands-on involvement by foreign bankers is welcomed by the Chinese reformers as well as the public. In fact, the more these international professionals are involved in the daily operations of the Chinese banks, the more effective will be the transformation of the banks into modern organizations. To most educated Chinese, this aspect of involvement is more meaningful than the capital injection itself as far as modernizing Chinese banking is concerned.

The Bank of America-China Construction Bank deal has certainly been a harbinger of further foreign activity in the sector. It seems very likely that the three other key banks — Industrial and Commercial Bank, Bank of China, and China Agricultural Bank — will also gain significant foreign partners. As a matter of fact, this has been happening since mid-2005.

By now, a crowd of international banks and investors has rushed into the Chinese banking sector. They include names like Goldman Sachs, Allianz, American Express, Royal Bank of Scotland, and Temasek. These companies took significant shares in the top four Chinese banks before their listing in overseas markets. In June 2006, Bank of China, the second biggest state bank, raised $9.73 billion in Hong Kong. (The various international strategic partners of the bank got an immediate, huge profit on the books as they paid much less than the initial offering price. Based on the closing price on September 1, 2006, their profits reached over 110%.)

A major motive behind the four banks' desire for foreign partners is their aspiration to be listed overseas as soon as possible. Selling shares to international strategic partners at huge discounts reflects this urgency. But a great deal of work with regard to internal restructuring and improvement remains.

Surely, huge problems have accumulated for many decades, and reaching the present level of a slightly improving financial picture has already required massive efforts. All things considered, fundamental change remains at the absolute beginning.

Today, reform actions are welcomed by the global investment community. The warm reception of China Construction Bank and Bank of China's new listing in Hong Kong shows that overseas investors have great hopes for Chinese banking reform and the long-term positive prospects.

One can hardly deny that bringing outside partners and investors in to foster a progressive atmosphere is a very positive step toward resolving the banking mess. Furthermore, the selling price tag for prelisting buyers is very low, according to some. This possibly shows some desperation on the part of Beijing.

Lessons for the Future

Openness to the outside world, in terms of both equity investment and the deliberate adoption of "best practices" from overseas, is indispensable in resolving the banking mess. Greater foreign involvement will bring modern, professional management much faster than could be developed from China's resources alone. Overseas managers can help China's banks to achieve greater transparency, accountability, and superior risk management, ultimately leading to globally competitive financial institutions.

Above all, foreign involvement can lead to well-defined ownership for these banks. Without foreign participation, there is little way to introduce modern ownership. The most important lesson of the bank saga is that banking problems will inevitably become government problems if the banks are built into the government structure.

Without true ownership, the mess in the banking sector in particular and the state sector in general has created vast problems for the government as well. The government has been trapped by its own design.

A basic lesson is this: there is no rational resolution at all within the bureaucratic framework. Furthermore, falling into this trap caused the country a great deal of pain and loss of economic opportunity, from which it is only beginning to escape.

For a "real" bank, every $10 in loans should bring back $10 in principal, plus a variable amount of interest. The simplicity of this benchmark will make it obvious whether or not China's banks have become "real."

But achieving this will demand a complete package—well-defined ownership; clear, consistent government regulation; and accountable management. For the past six decades, because these basic elements have been absent, disasters have been wholly natural.

Moving the banks' problems from the political sphere back into the business sphere will bring many long-term rewards: Independent banks will be able to direct capital to the enterprises that need it most rather than toward bureaucratic interests. This basic change will provide China's economy with the sustained boost that it needs to complete its historic task of catching up with the rest of the world.

Chapter 17.
Lessons From China's Stock Market

On the morning of May 9, 2005, the employees of a leading Chinese investment brokerage in Guangdong, returning from the nine-day Labor Holiday, were surprised by an unusual memo from company management that contained some alarming news.

They were told that tough days were ahead following the government's announcement that formerly nontradable shares in Chinese companies would soon be allowed to float freely. The managers predicted that the Shanghai stock index could fall another 10% to 20%, perhaps to the 900-1,000 levels, as a result of the reform measure.

Sure enough, even though the measure to float nontradable shares had long been expected, the immediate reaction of the market was a sharp dip. By that afternoon, retail investors were calling the day another "Black Monday." Both Shanghai and Shenzhen saw a wave of selling, with the Shenzhen stock index dropping 4% and Shanghai 2.44%. This selling pressure lasted for several weeks before stabilizing.

In the many months that then passed, the market went up and down. The key question on the mind of 73 million Chinese investors was, where is the bottom? China's stock market, beset by confusion and worry, reached an eight-year low in June 2005, having seen a greater fall than even the overinvested NASDAQ in the United States as measured by bear time.

The depressed markets made a dramatic—and to naive outside observers, inexplicable—contrast to the sizzling economic numbers China presents year after year, which have not stopped the continuous panic selling of domestic shares.[1] The truth is that most Chinese stocks were overvalued for many years. But the reasons are complex and are more political than economic.

What Went Wrong?

The "Great Bear Market of China" had many causes. China's two infant stock markets were established only in 1992. Disturbingly, a legal charter for the markets emerged only in 1997—a clue to the uncertainty of officials as they experimented with market-oriented reform measures.

Numerous bull and bear markets have come and gone. During the bull periods, stock prices rose wildly, often reaching price/earning ratios over 60. Many unprofitable companies had their glory days, as if unprofitability was a minor detail.

Under such an environment, the end of the party was all too predictable. The bear market that began in late 2000 erased some 60% of the market's value. Chinese investors experienced shock after shock during this period. Many listed companies went virtually bankrupt; hundreds of senior executives were sent to prison; and widespread financial abuses became a daily feast for the Chinese business press.

In this environment, the nontradable share reform measures struck many investors as unwelcome, bitter medicine. Nontradable shares are shares that have been held by various government units as well as legally defined entities. Their sale would put enormous downward pressure on the markets. The reason is that nontradable shares constituted 64% of market value, 74% of which belonged to the state. To investors, it seemed unacceptably risky to hold mainland Chinese stocks. The resulting exodus of capital pushed down the markets even further.

Historical Background

Why did the government decide to sell the nontradable shares on the open market? The answer requires a brief history lesson.

Prior to the mid-1990s, official China had a different mentality: It was believed that holding a controlling stake in large companies would ensure the government's continued control over these enterprises. This is the reason 90% of the listed companies are still state owned.

In fact, between the mid-1950s, when virtually all industrial companies were nationalized, and 1978, when the economic reforms began, essentially all economic activities were government run.

Government bureaucrats ran all factories, mines, banks, farms, and shops, with the minor exception of shoe and bike repair shops. Government power expanded along with state economic control, reaching heights unparalleled in China's long history. This gave rise to chaos and poverty and brought the nation to a halt for three decades.

Furthermore, the government monopoly also created vast problems for the government itself. Chinese officialdom inevitably faced the quandary that the greater their power became, the more unmanageable their responsibilities.

The government monopoly over all aspects of life was disastrous for the government in all possible ways. Providing life's essentials, jobs, and happiness for 1.3 billion people would be a tall order for even the most efficient organization imaginable. Most significantly, the burdens on the government were so big that they threatened its supreme power in all sorts of ways.

By the late 1970s, China's creaking bureaucracy showed clear signs of beginning to buckle under the weight of this self-imposed burden. This opened some space for the independent development of non-state sectors. The market reform policies that began in 1978 were most significantly motivated by the need to address this problem, and the dramatic changes that resulted are well known. One of the most noticeable changes was that foreign capitalists and Chinese businesspeople were encouraged to play a significant part in the economy, along with the state companies, which continued to exist.

Along the way, other effects became evident. The introduction of a stock market in 1992 was widely regarded as a sign that the reforms had become irreversible.

Huge economic progress has been achieved in the reform era; the vast wealth destroyed by the bureaucratic power is quickly being restored. But unresolved issues remain. The most basic issue is how to transform a government-run economy into a market-oriented economy. The fundamental reason for the difficulty of this transition is the continued presence of vast bureaucratic power.

That issue has brought one fundamental conflict to the fore: the double role being played by the government as it attempts to be both a "player" and a "referee" in the economy and marketplace. This basic conflict of interests tempts government officials to utilize excessive government power, left over from the Mao era, for personal gain. It is little wonder that official corruption has reached a historical high in this era. Nowhere are the effects of the player-referee conflict more visible than in the stock markets.

China's Stock Market Woes—and Their Cause

Building a stock market with 1,400 listings in a short time is an impressive achievement. Furthermore, the Chinese stock market is already ranked in the top six worldwide. But the market has had built-in flaws since day one.

In theory, stock markets follow a competitive principle: Investors put money into good companies, and not into bad ones, which allows the good companies to grow with the help of investors while the bad ones die out. In the end, wealth is created. But the Chinese stock markets have hardly followed this rational path so far. They have run into all sorts of nightmares because of continued bureaucratic domination.

To begin with, the number of companies that want to be listed is hundreds of times greater than the number of listing slots available. Listing rights are controlled by multiple government units, at central, provincial, and local levels. This arrangement has naturally led to record-breaking corruption.

Under this environment, it is hardly surprising that listing rights frequently go to companies whose business qualifications may be less than sound. Furthermore, companies frequently fudge their financial numbers in order to meet listing requirements. While regulatory bodies exist that are theoretically empowered to stop such abuses, in practice they have been too weak to do so. Actually, internal corruption within the regulatory organizations is common. Seeking to rent official power is a quick way for corrupt officials to make personal gains.

Once a company is listed, the reward mechanism that should operate is greatly weakened by the prevalence of manipulative practices. There are many sources of "hot money" in the Chinese markets: state-owned banks and state sector companies, for one, and government offices for another. These hot funds are without true owners, and therefore insiders employ these funds for private gain.

Under this system, in reality, these public funds are without true owners or protectors. That is why manipulators want to put their hands on such funds in the first place.

On this issue, one investment banker said, "Obviously, countless government officials wish to make quick personal gain by using public funds under their control. If the money is lost, no one is held responsible. If there is profit, they pocket it immediately. This sort of game has been going on since day one."

Along the way, "pumping and dumping" has become very popular. Hot-money investors push weak stocks to sky-high prices by buying in massive quantities, then sell quickly for a fat profit, leaving small investors holding the bag.

Regrettably, various investment brokerages have become involved in these practices by making short-term loans to such speculators. Worse still, they sometimes play the game with their clients' money by promising clients fat profits. This sort of practice has been widespread, and has led directly to the collapse of more than a dozen brokerage houses, mostly government owned.[2]

The lack of effective regulation and legal supervision has created an "anything-goes" atmosphere around the Chinese financial markets. The manipulators have done well for a long time without getting punished, attracting even more who would commit abuses.

A high-profile case involves a "Chinese Enron," De Long. It was founded by four brothers surnamed Tang in the 1980s. For many years the company borrowed heavily and tried to manipulate the stock market. The founders were convinced that their company was "too big to fail"; but they were wrong, and De Long collapsed recently, leaving huge uncollectible debts—believed to amount to billions of dollars—to various Chinese banks, companies, and individuals.

The company's manipulation was very extensive. It borrowed some $8.4 billion, which was partly used to take exclusive and complete control over three stocks. At the peak, it controlled over 91.5% of these shares. Pumping and dumping went on between 1997 and 2004. But De Long collapsed abruptly in 2004 when the bear market lasted a bit too long.[3]

Without doubt, this company has had countless corrupt officials involved as well. As one scholar says, "For a long time, this group of corrupt businessmen were very busy in putting state assets into their pockets. They had countless corrupt officials and bankers as their partners. How come no officials have been arrested in this case so far?"

The greatest damage done by stock market excesses is that they are impeding China's critical goal of transforming and modernizing Chinese companies, both state and private. With capital flowing so freely, the listed companies have little incentive to introduce modern, professional management, to say nothing of transparency and accountability.

This problem is exacerbated by the fact that 90% of the listed companies are still controlled by various government entities, making them directly responsible to government officials—not to the market or to investors. Indeed, government officials, as controlling shareholders, can effectively control these businesses through such means as the appointment of key managers. The net effect is to turn market transactions into bureaucratic transactions. This bureaucratic tie means that building modern professional, merit-based business organizations is next to impossible.

Furthermore, such bureaucratic interference blocks China's transition into a law-based market economy. In reality, bureaucratic interests have continued to lead to a twisted market. As pointed out by a Chinese scholar, "This government domination in all aspects of economy and society is a deadly virus for China."

Naturally, financial wrongdoing, in all its multiple forms, is hardly exclusive to China; every country with a stock market has witnessed a certain amount of manipulation and sleaze. Behind the bursting of the Japanese stock bubble, for example, was the widespread practice of cross-holding among banks and their corporate clients, which helped to prevent Japan Inc. from instituting professional, merit-based management. China Inc.'s key problem — bureaucratic meddling — may be different, but escaping the traps created by past practices will be easy for neither country.

Split-Share Reform as an Aspect of Privatization

On the plus side, the atmosphere in China has become more conducive to systemic reform. There is a broad consensus in society that the government should withdraw from the business world and concentrate on the referee role. Sales of state assets in general have picked up recently. The split-share structure reform policy fits these general developments.

At the same time, the government entities involved have a huge financial interest in the outcome. Privatizing creates enormous wind-falls for them and thus provides enormous incentives. In general, government units must have direct incentives in order to act on anything.

Consequently, Beijing, which sees asset sales as a convenient way to dump troublesome enterprises and generate hard cash at the same time, is actively trying to list more state assets, both within China and overseas.

Now, even the big-four state banks — Industrial and Commercial Bank, Bank of China, China Construction Bank, and Agricultural Bank — either are already listed or are trying to get listed. Two listings, China Construction Bank and Bank of China in Hong Kong, created new IPO records for recent years worldwide. Actions in this direction are accelerating, as Beijing sees more and more incentives.

But average investors remain worried. On the basis of past experience, they fear that even needed reforms are just another government ploy to get their money. So, selling government-owned shares, as desirable as it might be in theory, has had the practical effect of pushing the market down even further, and no lower limit is in sight.

Crossing the River by Feeling for the Stones at the Bottom

An old Chinese saying is "Messes are best cleaned up by their makers." Indeed, Beijing is trying to get out of a stock market mess of its own creation. The only problem is that the market is nervous. Beijing's solution to these jitters is to carry out the plan gradually over a long period. The government hopes that proceeding in this manner will avoid large-scale disruptions.

For a long time, the government had promised not to float these state shares. Going back on this promise was another cause for confusion and fear among investors. To allay popular discontent, the government had to offer incentives to encourage potential investors. But Beijing has chosen to let individual companies decide on the benefits to investors rather than present a grand scheme.

So, in the immediate term, Beijing has chosen to sell the remaining shares of four companies as an "experiment," with the aim of finding practical ways to meet the ultimate goal of fully floating the entire market. Beijing's approach to the problem is clever. The procedure for selling the four stocks is something like a bargaining game between regular investors and the entities holding nontradable shares. The latter must offer some incentives to the regular shareholders in order to gain the ability to trade the shares.

Superficially, this new game is reminiscent of the old Chinese game of pitting people against people. But this time, Beijing wants to act as a neutral arbiter of others' disputes, which represents tremendous progress.

For one of the "experimentally" listed companies, Sany ("Three One") Heavy Industry, the proposal is that the holders of formerly nontradable shares give both cash incentives and shares to regular shareholders before being permitted to freely trade their holdings. The proposal calls for regular shareholders to get three free shares plus $0.97 in cash compensation for every 10 tradable shares held.

Announcement of the proposal caused the regular shareholders of the company to immediately calculate their gains and losses, and indirectly is causing all investors to do the same. Market reaction to the new plan was positive: Sany and two other "experimental" companies traded up smartly for a few days.

The government introduced 42 listings in the second round of the experiment in the summer of 2005. The gradualist approach may work out in the end for the remaining companies. This process began to accelerate late in the year. By mid-2006, the initial phase was over, as about two-thirds of all listed companies had reached floating settlement. The government predicts that the remaining listings will achieve full floating by the end of 2006.

So far, so good. Many investors now agree that having a fully tradable stock market is unavoidable, even if some investors will have to pay more than others. Fortunately, the market fundamentals are improving. By mid-2005, the average listing had a 2005 price/earnings ratio of about 16, which most global investors would consider reasonable. Many already feel that these listings are a good investment. Consequently many investors, both Chinese and foreign, are interested in buying quality shares.

Since the summer of 2005, the market has rebounded as much as some 65% to 75% from the lows set in June 2005. This turn of fortune signals that the worst time for China's stock market may be over. Many investors feel that some of the listed companies have noticeably improved their management quality. This has attracted new buyers and thus led to a strong rebound.

In general, unwinding the government's business stakes is necessary for China to truly move forward. Despite the short-term pain, this will be positive in the end as the stock market becomes more like a "real" one. The reforms also represent a larger trend: China is increasingly embracing international norms with respect to matters such as ownership structure, corporate governance, and professional management.

But caution is still warranted. In the entire process, the government still makes all the decisions. Moreover, there is neither transparency nor accountability in the government structure. This reality could bring additional disasters to China's stock market in the future. The persistent bureaucratic shadow still hangs over the market.

The Road Ahead

The trends are in the right direction, but two basic issues remain. First, there must be a decisive separation of government interests from the business sphere. The government must irreversibly commit itself to being only a dutiful watchdog, not a market competitor. China cannot establish a sustainable, modern economy without this change.

Second, all existing state and private companies must be transformed into modern business organizations using up-to-date management methods. Above all, business organizations must be held accountable to law and to their customers.

China has never lacked creative, diligent people, but they must have the right environment in which to perform, and the entire society must be responsible for producing the necessary support for their work. Accordingly, curtailing excessive government power is a necessary goal for the Chinese civilization. In this reform era, China has taken a giant step forward in this direction, and continued progress is the only way China can achieve its national goals.

Part V.
Chinese Multinationals vs. Global Giants

SUMMARY

Chinese multinationals must enter global markets sooner or later. For now, events show that they are in a hurry to do so. What is behind these new ventures? The answer: These companies must expand overseas in order to survive, due, at least in part, to increased needs for oil and industrial materials on the one hand and chronic overcapacity in manufacturing on the other.

In some ways, they are following the trail of the United States and United Kingdom in the distant past and Japan and South Korea in the recent past.

However, so far, China Inc. has only tested the water. Today, there are tremendous limitations with respect to these ventures. One major difficulty comes from the home market. Most Chinese companies are financially weak due to cutthroat competition at home. Another key difficulty comes from various barriers in the outside world. *But the most fundamental problem is the linkage between business and the bureaucracy.*

Because of these difficulties, Chinese international expansion can occur only slowly. Even so, some small progress has been made. In particular, forming international partnerships is a highly realistic strategy for China Inc.'s international program. There are numerous interesting examples already.

Chapter 18.

The Coming of Age of Chinese Multinationals

Chinese multinationals caught the world's attention in December 2004 when Lenovo suddenly took the global stage. The bluest of blue-chip multinationals, IBM, got out of its personal computer business by selling out to Lenovo, making this faceless company the third biggest global PC player. This naturally raises questions for the world.

Are there other Chinese brands that could take the world by storm? A basic reality is that Chinese companies are still terribly weak in general. It will take huge effort and a fundamental overhaul before they can mount meaningful international ventures.

Major Chinese Players

Most sizable Chinese companies cover oil, telecom services, energy, minerals, banking, and insurance. Currently, 19 Chinese companies are already in the 500 club, including several telecom operators, four banks, State Grid, China Southern Power Grid, three construction companies, China Food Group, China Life, and Baosteel. Also, new members of the club are China First Auto Group and SAIC, two Chinese automakers that have joint ventures with GM, Toyota, and Volkswagen, among others.[1] They are all state run.

State monopoly in these business sectors is one key reason for the existence of these sizable companies. In addition, the economic and consumption surge has played an important role.

China now builds a new power plant every week. The prize goes, mostly, to State Grid, China Southern Power Grid, and five other major state power companies. These seven state power companies formerly constituted the old State Power Company, the state monopoly over the power sector for many decades. In the late 1990s, it split up into seven independent companies.

Today, private investors and overseas parties are allowed to enter the field as a result of the reform, but nobody can yet compete with State Grid and the six other giant state power brands. They have proved as powerful as the government, and complaining about their poor service invites trouble.

In the past few years, however, State Grid has been behaving more like a company, improving its management and services substantially.

This energy company is already ranked 32nd in the club. It could become a top-10 player as China's energy needs grow. However, China has seen frequent power cuts over the past few years, even though it is the second biggest energy producer after the United States. Naturally, there is room for more investment.

Among state companies, China National Petroleum Company (CNPC) and Sinopec are already global players. These two, together with China National Offshore Oil Corp (CNOOC), constitute the state monopoly in China's oil and petrochemical market. Their annual profits could reach over U.S.$100 billion. In 2005, Sinopec was ranked 23st and CNPC ranked 39th in the club.

A booming Chinese economy has offered these three giants all the perks. Since 1993, China has been a net importer of oil. In 2005, it consumed over 7% of global oil supplies. By 2020, its oil demand will likely more than triple. Thus, CNPC, Sinopec, and CNOOC must go out and acquire both supplies and assets.

So far, CNPC is competing with Sinopec head-on at home and overseas. Both have already cut more than a few dozen deals around the world. Both are aggressive and go anywhere there is a whiff of oil. Their trails are in regions from Latin America to Africa to Central Asia. Interestingly, these Chinese executives are warmly received by governments and businesspeople around the world.

The third oil player, CNOOC, which is much smaller than the other two, is also moving rapidly around the globe. It gained huge publicity in its failed attempt to take over the troubled U.S. oil concern Unocal in 2005. But it has enormous opportunities in other regions.

For example, in April 2006, CNOOC spent $2.3 billion buying an offshore oil asset from the Nigerian National Petroleum Corporation in Africa. The company is becoming more active in its efforts to acquire additional assets around the globe.

These three oil giants are clearly ahead of the curve of China Inc. in terms of international expansion. There are also several other sizable players for the future. China Mobile and China Unicom are examples. They hold sway over China's mobile communication market because private companies are barred. China is already the biggest mobile phone market. Each month, 4 to 5 million new users are added. By early 2006, there were over 400 million connections. With billions in cash and over 400 million consumers on hand, China Mobile and China Unicom should be able to go far. But the truth is that they have yet to gain international experience.

International expansion is the buzzword for China Inc. today. For example, Shanghai-based steel mill Baosteel is expanding fast beyond

China. It has joint ventures with CVRD in Brazil and Hamersley Iron in Australia.

China's steel market is already bigger than those of the United States and Japan combined. Fast economic expansion is creating ever-increasing demand for metals, steels, and cement, among other basic industrial raw materials. As a result, more Chinese companies are reaching out to places where supplies are plentiful: Canada, Australia, Africa, and Latin America. More deals should be expected in these areas. Actually, in recent times, more than half of Chinese international investments have gone to oil and natural resources.

New Players

There are dozens of relatively new entrepreneurial Chinese companies more than eager to trot all over the planet. These include TCL, Huawei, ZTE, Haier, Galanz, Chonghong, Ningbo Bird, Hisense, and Konka. They are all manufacturers, still growing and wanting to expand beyond China.

Among these companies, TCL, Chonghong, and Haier focus on white goods and consumer electronics. They have now added telephone handsets to their product list. ZTE, Huawei, and Ningbo Bird focus on handsets or telecom networks. One of three handsets in the world is produced by Ningbo Bird, TCL, or other Chinese companies.

Galanz is the premier manufacturer of microwave ovens worldwide, with a global market share around 40%. In Europe it costs $90 to produce a simple microwave oven; it costs Galanz only $30. Hisense is a company to watch too. It could become a leading global cooling product maker by acquiring Kelon, recently a major cooling product manufacturer. Hisense has also started international expansion.

How will these companies enter the big boys' club? Well, for a start, they are players in the world's fastest-growing consumer market—China. In 2005, China produced 83 million television sets, 60 million air conditioners, and 300 million handsets. TCL alone produced some 23 million TVs and over 10 million handsets.

Some of these companies have set up international units as well. But this group of manufacturers is still weak in general, and their profits are often far below international norms (see Ch. 19).

Unsettled Issues

There are many issues to be settled before these Chinese firms can morph into competent multinationals. In general, again, Chinese businesses are still weak. One most basic reason is that they are still confined to the bureaucratic establishment above all.

To move forward, China will first need to transform all state and private companies into modern business organizations. Achieving this goal will involve huge work, as was seen with China's stock market. For example, in January 2005, about a dozen listed companies were found to be abusing the market and several dozen senior executives were arrested.

The fundamental issue is separating government from the business sphere so that well-defined ownership can be established together with a modern legal system. These are the basic elements on which modern enterprises must be founded.

At the next level, the overcrowding in every business sector needs to be solved. China has about 70 TV makers and more than 100 car manufacturers. Having all these firms can only mean needless price wars, which could pull down the stronger ones. Therefore rational consolidation must take place. If China's consumer electronics and home-appliances makers—now numbering 1,300—could be reduced to half a dozen companies, those remaining would become some of the biggest multinationals globally.

Chapter 19.

Behind Chinese Multinationals' Global Efforts

The world community now pays much attention to Chinese multinationals. Especially of late, this attention is on the rise as several Chinese companies have tried to buy established business assets in the developed markets. But the truth is that this Chinese international expansion is nothing new, as China Inc. is only following the paths set by its counterparts in the developed nations.

For now, China's international investments reached less than $50 billion by 2005, which is very small compared to the overseas investments inside China. Western nations were the first to reach out globally, followed by Asian companies in more recent times, with Japan and South Korea leading the way. China and India are new entrants into this venture. Chinese and Indian multinationals have the limelight at present even though their work remains at the early stages.

But each nation's international expansion may be very different from that of others. Today, there are numerous unique aspects to the Chinese multinationals. The Chinese are able to do very few deals, as they are not ready to go international in a big way. Even so, they get more media coverage than many of their international counterparts. This in itself is a great surprise to the Chinese public back home.

Buying Oil and Other Natural Assets

For now, the biggest Chinese buying spree involves oil assets and supplies as well as other natural resources. For example, in 2005, the majority of China's overseas investments went into oil and other natural resources assets. This trend will only increase in the future.

Behind such buying is the ever-increasing domestic demand. Indeed, most new supplies are shipped back to meet the Chinese appetite at home. China has fast-rising demands for energy and raw materials because of several factors.

First, China's biggest progress in this era has been in the manufacturing sector. This sector naturally has the greatest demand for energy and raw materials, but China does not have sufficient supplies at home.

Second, over 70% of foreign investments inside China have gone into the manufacturing sector as well. As a result, factory demands for energy and raw materials have been continuously climbing.

Furthermore, most of China's exporting is carried out by foreign parties. This suggests that China's energy and raw material demands are tied directly to global consumption. That is, the increasing needs of China come also from the overseas demands for products made in China. This interdependence will only increase as time goes by.

Third, a fast-improving living standard at home further increases needs for energy and raw materials. For example, whereas only 10 years an air conditioner was considered a luxury, it is now a household item, especially in urban regions. Also, several million new autos are added to the streets every year. The supply of oil and raw materials must keep up with the rising demands.

Fourth, China's energy and natural resources supplies are limited. There are insufficient reserves to meet the increasing needs. This is somewhat like the situation in Japan, where most energy needs are supplied by international markets. Hence, China is quickly following Japan's trail and is actively searching the entire globe for more supplies and assets.

In 2005 alone, China's consumption of industrial materials reached a staggering level on a global basis: about 40% of the cements, 7% of the oil, 30% of the plastics, 30% of the steel, and 25% of the aluminium. Such consumption will only go up as the economy expands further.

China's energy consumption is rapidly moving away from traditional coal to oil and gas. At this time, about 80% of the energy resources still come from coal. But consumption of oil and gas has skyrocketed to meet new industrial needs as well as a changing lifestyle. Naturally, the need for more oil and gas means that the Chinese must increasingly look to the global markets for additional supplies.

A basic fact is this: China's international buying is purely business oriented and has little to do with ideology. Indeed, any nation with an expanding economy needs to consume more energy and raw materials. China is no exception. After all, foreign investors had more than $620 billion in China as of 2005, so it is natural for the Chinese to invest in the outside world.

Many international China watchers agree that this Chinese expansion is almost all business oriented. William Ratliff, who closely follows China's business in Latin America, observes that the Chinese are there for business reasons, with no interest in ideology.[1]

China's increased international effort has also a particular background: A decade ago, no Chinese decision makers predicted that the domestic demand for oil and minerals would increase shapely. If the rise had been foreseen, China could have acted sooner and more effectively, especially when oil and minerals were priced very low a few years ago.

In short, China has lacked a realistic national energy strategy for a long time. But many other nations do not have an energy strategy.[2] Confronting explosive energy demands, partly from the emerging economies, is a new global issue. Even for the developed world, this is a huge challenge to deal with.

New Reality

Only recently, Beijing has started to increase efforts to obtain sufficient supplies. One specific aim is to build an oil reserve for 60 days or more. Slowness in procuring an adequate oil supply has already caused serious damage to the Chinese economy. For example, since mid-2005, many coastal regions have not had enough gas for car owners.

To deal with such supply problems at home, the three Chinese oil players have sharply increased their efforts. Several impressive transactions have taken place between these companies and outside parties since early 2004. Over $10 billion of Chinese capital has gone into buying overseas oil assets and supplies. Much bigger deals are in the works.

More accidental than planned, such activities have brought China into closer contacts with many regions, from Latin America and Africa to North America to Australia and Central Asia. These regions, especially Latin America, Australia, and Africa, are the biggest suppliers of minerals to China. Through such activities, close business ties are established.

So far, the biggest oil deal was China National Petroleum Corporation's $4.18 billion takeover of PetroKazakhstan Inc in central Asia. Another sizable deal is being done with Iran. China has signed a $100 billion agreement with Iran to import 10 million tons of liquefied natural gas over a 25-year period in exchange for a 50% Chinese stake in the development of Iran's Yahavaran oilfield. China also wishes to build a pipeline to Iran via Kazakhstan.

But industry insiders feel that these new assets will make a very small difference to the hungry market at home. Naturally, more international buying will take place.

One Chinese oil industry expert told me, "China must buy more oil supplies and assets. Otherwise, how can it sustain growth?"

At present there are other areas of acquisition as well. More and more Chinese companies are going elsewhere to find supplies in minerals and steel, among other resources. For example, a major Chinese aluminium company, Chalco, is proposing to buy a midsize aluminium mine in Australia. And it wants to pay top dollar.

In all these activities, there are additional accidental effects. China has gained broad contacts with various nations in all corners of the globe. Furthermore, all this has helped to move many natural resource-rich nations, such as those in the Middle East and Latin America, to a higher level in the global economy. For example, Sino-Latin America trade reached $50 billion in 2005, with China now the region's third largest trading partner. This is a very positive development for all parties.

Besides buying oil, gas, and other natural resources, many Chinese companies are setting up factories of all sorts in many regions, especially in the developing nations. All this should bring added benefits to the various trading partners.

Equally significant, such new developments lead to new forms of international economic interchange. In the past, many poor but resource-rich nations made transactions almost exclusively with the developed nations. The situation is beginning to change as so many late-developing nations step into the picture. The developing nations have enormous benefits to share with each other as well. This is a sharp departure from the situation even in the recent past. Through such cooperation, more and more developing nations are taking their place on the global stage in bigger ways.

Searching for New Markets

Today, China's international expansion is visible in all other business sectors. This follows the overall economic development at home. Going international has become a mandate for the Chinese players. Chinese manufacturers are increasingly interested in tapping into international markets through acquisitions. Their motives are very much like those of all other global multinationals: They are looking for new markets, better technology, established brands, distribution networks, or some combination of these.

The underlying factors are the vast manufacturing force China has built up and the chronic overcapacity at home. Cutthroat competition is part of daily life. Hence, going international is about nothing less than survival.

One Chinese executive told me, "The only way for Chinese companies to survive in the long run is to become fully globalized. That is what global multinationals have done. The Chinese companies must follow their lead."

International expansion is risky for any multinational. But the risks are much higher for China Inc. as the least experienced group in the international market. Many outsiders feel that the Chinese companies are very strong already. But the truth is that they are still weak in general and have enormous difficulties growing, due mainly to the huge unsettled issues at home.

Under an overcrowded market at home, most Chinese companies find it extremely difficult to make reasonable profits. This tough reality forces them to target only financially troubled assets when they search for merger and acquisition opportunities in the overseas markets, but this may lead to additional problems.

Acquisitions

In a way, China Inc. has become a trash collector. The Chinese have been forced to acquire assets others wish to dump. Does this make business sense?

For now, one key difficulty for China Inc. is how to quickly gain sufficient knowledge and know-how to turn around newly acquired assets in the outside world—clearly a very tough proposition.

TCL, a leading Chinese consumer products company, has been a leader in reaching out. The company had plentiful lessons to learn following its recent acquisitions of Thomson's TV unit and Alcatel's mobile phone company. Both units were unprofitable when acquired. In 2003, Thomson's TV unit incurred a loss of $217 million, and Alcatel's handset unit lost over $83 million. TCL is going through a tough time in the hope of turning these new assets around.

On the plus side, TCL was able to double its TV production after gaining Thomson's TV assets. In particular, it has acquired the company's RCA brand as well as its research centers and distribution network. Now TCL manages five R&D centers in Europe, China, and United States.

But making these units profitable is extremely hard, further requiring that the company have very effective control over the combined assets. Achieving this goal is easier said than done. One key reason is that TCL's management has yet to become fully internationalized. But finding suitable international managers has turned out to be difficult.

On these deals, one Chinese commentator noted, "TCL's buying gains only a short benefit. The purchased technology will last only shortly. Even Thomson's distribution network is limited for TCL's global expansion . . . but the costs are very high and TCL must fight to turn these distressed assets around."[3]

Examination of TCL's difficulties suggests that several key tasks are essential for the company's success. The first is very effective integration of the different assets under the TCL brand. Second is very efficient financial and management control over these new assets. Third, the company needs to get help from highly experienced international managers who can turn the poor performance of the newly acquired companies around. Getting the new assets to perform satisfactorily is the most significant.

These tasks are very daunting. Very significantly, TCL has been rather slow to find qualified managers for the new assets. As a result, operation of these units has been troublesome, which has added a huge financial burden. Now the company has to borrow more money, though it has not been profitable lately.

Commenting on the company's overseas work, one Chinese researcher said, "It is natural for TCL to pay a hefty tuition. After all, it has no other way to learn. But the only problem is that most Chinese companies are too weak to pay a high price."

Lenovo's recent purchase of IBM's troubled PC unit has naturally led to some difficulties. So far, Lenovo has been doing much better than TCL, as it has been able to produce profits for the combined assets. The new Lenovo has achieved a very positive first step in restructuring. Interestingly, in terms of quality and services, the new Lenovo seems little changed from the old IBM days, as noted in one international report.[4]

So far, its international business has been performing well except in Japan. In Japan, Lenovo's business has declined seriously due to Japan's sensitivity with regard to the ownership change. There are some other sensitive issues also. For example, in the spring of 2006, the U.S. State Department raised the issue of security with the IBM computers it has bought.[5]

After the merger, Lenovo has aimed to become a true international company. Of its 21,400 employees, about half are outside China. Its CEO and many other senior executives are international professionals. Also, Lenovo's headquarters are in New York rather than Beijing. Following international standards is the only way for the company to go forward from here.

Currently the new Lenovo is going through a restructuring program, which is being carried out according to global business norms. For example, in March 2006, the company announced its plan to cut the employee body by 1,000 and reorganize the various units in order to make more business sense. This merger is a test case for China Inc.'s ability to become more internationalized.

Performance in the first year, 2005, was mixed: Sales reached $13.3 billion with $22.2 million in net profits, but the restructuring program had cost $70 million already.[6] The company's profitability was indicative of a very strong performance especially given that IBM's PC unit had seen losses for many years before the sale. Lenovo's products are sold to 66 markets worldwide and the company now competes directly with Dell, HP, and everyone else.

All things considered, international expansion for the Chinese companies is only beginning. Getting ahead of the game is by no means easy. Learning by doing seems to be an art of living for the Chinese. Naturally, along the way, they will have to pay high tuition.

In addition to business issues, political obstacles are increasingly coming especially from the developed world, which tends to view these types of Chinese business activities as political moves.

In most cases, Chinese multinationals have chosen to directly set up international shops. Most of these shops are very small, aimed at testing the water in different markets, although some are sizable.

For example, Haier, the biggest Chinese consumer products maker, has entered the U.S. market by setting up a factory there. Its employees are mostly U.S. citizens. Its country CEO is a highly experienced U.S. manager. Haier has also set up numerous plants in India and many other countries. In so doing, it does not need to go through the hurdles of buying existing assets. Haier is already a key global consumer products maker. In 2004, its sales reached $12.2 billion, almost high enough for entrance into the global 500 club.

Partnerships

Another popular approach is to expand through partnerships. Both Huawei and ZTE, two top Chinese telecom equipment manufacturers, have followed this model. They have formed numerous strategic partnerships in various markets around the globe. Huawei's many key strategic partners include Motorola, 3Com, Siemens, NEC, and Ericsson. The aim of these partnerships is to achieve new product development, distribution, or technology transfers. Such work has helped enormously in the efforts of these two Chinese brands to go global.

Their specific strengths come from both intellectual work and the low price tags for their products. Though they are the new kids on the block, they have achieved far more progress in the global markets than most Chinese companies.

Overall, again, international expansion for Chinese companies remains at the very early stage. China Inc. will face an uphill situation with regard to its international trials. But development should become more rapid once China Inc. has gained solid experience in the first stage.

Hiring experienced international managers and advisors will make the going smoother for companies trying to expand internationally, which is one of the new lessons the Chinese are learning. But internationalization is a long process that the Chinese companies must become completely familiar with in its entirely in order to make much business sense out of it. There won't be any shortcuts. For this, the Chinese will have more tuition to pay.

Building a Strong Home Base

The more serious issue facing China Inc. is how to build a strong home base. But there is no easy solution given China's general overcrowded market. Overinvestment has created cutthroat competition, which has destroyed possibilities for healthy profits in most sectors.

Rational consolidations have yet to take place in a large way. Without such consolidation, building a strong home base with reasonable profits will be extremely difficult. This is one of the most serious problems for China Inc. in general.[7]

However, other business models have turned out to be more positive. One highly successful case is Galanz, the Chinese leader in microwave ovens. Galanz's key strengths are low costs and an original equipment manufacturer (OEM) business model (OEMs manufacture products for other firms to sell under their own brands). The same microwave that costs $90 for a European company to produce, Galanz can make for $30.

As a result, Galanz has attracted many dozens of OEM clients from all over the world, including GE and Philips. Most interestingly, many of its clients have shipped their entire assembly lines to Galanz's home base in Guangdong. Galanz has used this model to become a worldwide leader with a global share of some 40%.

The company has recently expanded its product lines to include air conditioners. In 2004 alone, it shipped 1.56 million air conditioners to the international market, making it the Chinese export leader in this category. At the same time, Galanz remains a minor player in the domestic air-conditioner market.

For now, it is expanding its production and hopes to reach 6.5 million air conditioners per year, mostly for export. Although the yuan revaluation will reduce Galanz's price advantage, the magnitude of the change is too small to alter its competitive advantage, and most export-oriented firms in China remain in this category.

But most Chinese companies are not as lucky as Galanz in the home market. There is a chronic oversupply in most sectors. Profit margins keep being squeezed. The ultimate solution is rational consolidations, which have yet to happen on a large scale.

Chapter 20.

China's Technology Development

Made-in-China products have flooded the globe. But most Chinese products stand on the low end of the value chains. Will China Inc. move up in the value chains? The answer: It must, but the transition will not be easy at all. This chapter examines China's technological development, both progress and challenge.

Product Development

Question: What is the most active area in China's current tech development?

Answer: All areas are active, especially high-growth and high-volume sectors.

Question: Can you be more specific?

Answer: The first highly active sector has to be telecom. China is already the biggest telecom market, especially for handsets. This is certainly an exciting sector for all telecom equipment companies worldwide.

Question: Who are the leading Chinese telecom manufacturing companies?

Answer: The top three players are Huawei, ZTE, and Datang. Both Huawei and ZTE are located in Shenzhen, Guangdong, while Datang is in Xian and Beijing. Huawei reached $8.4 billion in sales in 2005, while ZTE reached over $5 billion. Datang is smaller, but it holds the third-generation TD-SCDMA patent, which could help its future growth.

Both Huawei and ZTE are better known internationally, as they have some 50% of international business. Huawei conducts business around the globe, while ZTE is catching up quickly. They have established numerous partnerships in many markets, which has become a major strength for their international programs. Both companies rival leading global brands like Cisco, Siemens, and Nortel in technology and R&D. Both now produce networks as well as handsets. They each have more than 25,000 employees and are still adding more.

Question: Do they dominate China's telecom sector?

Answer: Not really. Each global brand has been in China for a long time, but nobody dominates. Interestingly, they compete with each other on the one hand and have joint programs on the other. This is a trend for the Chinese market. For example, Huawei has joint product development programs with Motorola, NEC, and Siemens, among others. So joint ventures have become a new avenue for product development.

Consumer Products

Question: What is the next most exciting sector?

Answer: Perhaps consumer electronics. In this sector, China Inc. has been a later developer, as key technologies for TV, DVD, and other products have been dominated by leading global brands. But Chinese companies have huge manufacturing capability. In 2005 alone, China produced some 80 million TV sets and over 100 million DVDs. Also, lately, Chinese companies have increased their efforts in R&D. It is a matter of survival. More efforts are badly needed.

The hottest competition is with next-generation, high-definition TVs and DVDs. In this area, Chinese players are doing better than before.[1] But there is still a drawback, in that international players still hold patents for all old technologies. Chinese companies can hardly bypass them.

For example, several Chinese companies hold their patents on the next-generation high-definition DVDs. But these new products must be made compatible with the old DVDs. However, the existing patents are all owned by key international players. Hence, Chinese manufacturers must continue to pay royalties for these old patents. This situation will not change for a long time.

All this also shows the absolute need for continuous intellectual development. This situation of backwardness is a major bottleneck for China Inc. today. At this time, most leading Chinese high-tech companies are still small and homebound. They have very limited resources in R&D, among other things. How do you change this for the better? Tremendous effort will be needed. But the good thing is that the Chinese have a much better understanding today about the need for intellectual development.

Question: What about computers?

Answer: For computers, China Inc. is as advanced as international players on the manufacturing side. But intellectual development is a dramatically different story. Chinese chip technology is still at the early development stage, which is many years behind Intel and AMD. Catching up won't be easy.

Question: Which Chinese company is leading in chip designs?

Answer: One interesting Chinese chip player is a start-up, Vimicro, already listed on NASDAQ.[2] This company was created by a group of returning Chinese students who studied and worked in the United States. Their research capability is high, but they have yet to prove their worth in a crowded market dominated by a few giants like Intel and AMD.

Software

Question: What about the software industry?

Answer: China now has more than 8,000 software companies, mostly tiny. In 2004, the total market was about $27.8 billion, but it is already bigger than India's, which had $22.9 billion in sales in 2004. But most Chinese software companies are tiny compared to the leading Indian software players. Very few Chinese software companies have reached the $100 million mark in sales. Their strengths are much less than those of their Indian counterparts in general.

Question: What kind of software do they use the most?

Answer: Linux has become a very popular tool, but all software forms are used. For now, many Chinese software companies wish to develop more with Linux, where nobody dominates.

Question: How about business management software?

Answer: Both international and Chinese software companies are active. In some cases, international software products for accounting, CRM, and ERP, among others, cannot directly fit the Chinese markets. This is simply because China may have different business organizations and market behavior.

In the case of ERP, many joint ventures in China bought international software, but soon found out that using it required significant modifications. This means that Chinese software providers can have an edge in making localized products. That is the reason for the strong performance of two leading Chinese accounting and ERP players, User Friendly software in Beijing and Kingdee in Shenzhen.

But foreign software companies can easily improve their products to meet the local needs. As such, competition between the two parties is hot, which will become hotter as time passes.

Question: Any other interesting software companies?

Answer: Most interesting Chinese software players are in the Internet arena.

Question: Why is that?

Answer: For one thing, nobody dominates Internet development the way Microsoft does in computers or Intel does in chips. For another, China's Internet is already the second biggest market, with more than 123 million users as of early 2006. Very shortly, China will become the number-one Internet market. This will certainly attract all sorts of investments and therefore plenty of efforts in research.

Question: Any interesting Chinese Internet players?

Answer: Several. One internationally known Internet software company is QQ.com (the company name is Tencent), which provides Internet instant messaging software for global consumers. It already has over 500 million global users.[3] This company is now listed in Hong Kong and is adding new features and services all the time. For example, it has recently added gaming and telecom services.

Question: Please name more players.

Answer: Another interesting Chinese Internet company is Shanda, which focuses on Internet gaming. It has hundreds of games in Chinese. It is already listed on NASDAQ. It is the most popular Internet gaming brand in the Chinese language. Its young client base is fast expanding. But Shanda and most other Chinese Internet companies face the task of developing their own intellectual products, which is the biggest challenge for them.

Question: Any other names?

Answer: Sure. To me, one of the most promising Chinese Internet players is Alibaba.com. It is basically a Yellow Book, but it has some 6 million global corporate clients, who trade with China directly. In addition, it has an Internet auction business, which is like eBay. But its auction business is domestically oriented.

Question: Is this the company Yahoo has bought a major stake in recently?

Answer: Yes, it is. Yahoo spent $1 billion to take 40% of this company and is the biggest shareholder. But Japanese Softbank is a major shareholder as well. So, they both want to ride with this Chinese company.

Question: So, China's Internet development is tied to global development in many ways?

Answer: True. In this area, China moves at about the same pace as the United States, for example. But China has yet to produce global brands in the way the United States does. In particular, going beyond China is a difficult issue. Hence, most Chinese Internet companies are homebound still.

Question: Any other interesting areas?

Answer: All sorts. For example, Chinese companies are active with IC products. These products cover computers, consumer electronics, machinery, and home appliances. In these fields, China has a huge manufacturing capability in particular. Furthermore, biotech has become popular, but most Chinese biotech companies are small still.

Future Trends

Question: What is the general stage of China's high-tech?

Answer: It's still at a beginning stage, and there is a huge gap with the outside world. But it is developing very fast, due particularly to the ever-increasing international involvement. At this time, more than 900 labs have been created by leading global multinationals. They cover all sectors and have a global aim.

At the same time, more and more Chinese companies are putting more resources into R&D, which is very healthy. One should expect quicker tech development from now on for China. But closing the gap will take a long time.

Question: How does China Inc. grow so fast?

Answer: That is a great question. On one hand, it may surprise people elsewhere that China is moving forward fast in its high-tech development. On the other hand, one should note that despite quick growth, the quality of the Chinese economy in general and of high-tech companies in particular is very low. Up to now, nearly all Chinese high-tech companies have been small and homebound. Furthermore, their profits are smaller even compared with those of the leading Indian high-tech companies, not to mention the global giants.

Question: Are you worried about this slow progress in China's high-tech industry?

Answer: In most ways, China's development is just beginning, especially in the high-tech area. It will take a long time for China's economy to reach the level of the developed world.

Question: What is the best way for international high-tech companies to tap into China?

Answer: Each company should develop a unique strategy in China. This is simply because China's market is in the transition stage. Gaining maturity takes time. Hence, international players should learn about and need to know this market inside out.

Part VI.

The Taiwan Issue:
Current Affairs and Trends

SUMMARY

A peaceful resolution between Taiwan and mainland China is one of the most pressing issues China faces. There are no easy solutions. The problem is made worse by the fact that it involves huge international interests; this tends to cloud the situation.

However, the picture is fast improving today as economic ties are being created and vast human interactions between the two parties are occurring. In this fast-changing environment, one very realistic resolution would be a federal system, which could produce win-win results. This federal alternative has a solid foundation in the ever-increasing economic and human ties across the strait. Furthermore, it would lead to a peaceful and productive outcome in a global context.

Currently there is also increased political feasibility for this outcome. Under the federal approach, the island of Taiwan could gain enormous advantages. For China as a whole, this approach would also provide a solid foundation for fundamental progress. Furthermore, it would promote stability and long-term peace for the region and beyond.

Chapter 21.

Federation:

The Best Choice for Taiwan and Mainland China

The realities between Taiwan and mainland China are "economically hot, politically cold." Their ever-increasing economic ties demand far better political relations, not to mention other things. *A federation would seem to be a highly feasible solution. Economically, the time is right; politically, it is only a few steps away.*

A federal system would mean more autonomy for Taiwan than Hong Kong and Macau enjoy. For Beijing in particular and China as a whole, it would mean the revolutionary concept of a unified China with multiple power centers.

Under a federal system, the island would keep its own government, military, judicial, and other systems. Its political leadership would not bow to Beijing. In short, the relationship would be a political partnership between equals. Both political entities would be subject only to a "federation" law. And anything is open for discussion under the "one China" principle.

Taiwan's Love Affair With the Mainland

Economically, Taiwan and mainland China are well connected. The mainland is Taiwan's biggest trading partner as well as its number-one export market. In 2004, total cross-strait trade reached U.S.$61.6 billion, a jump of 33.1% over 2003; of this, Taiwan's exports accounted for $45 billion, by Taiwan's own accounting.

Besides ever-increasing trade, investment is another major activity. In 2004 alone, Taiwan Inc. invested $6.94 billion in the mainland. Officially, Taiwan's total investment stood at about $60 billion by 2005. By some estimates it is $100 billion or more. This discrepancy in numbers is the result of numerous government restrictions on Taiwanese investment in the mainland; many members of Taiwan Inc. may go to the mainland from a third location. One popular way is via tax-shelter islands.

Behind the ever-increasing trade is an ever-increasing tide of investment from Taiwan Inc. The mainland, Taiwan's biggest destination already, now has over 60,000 Taiwanese enterprises. It also has more than 1 million Taiwanese residents. Shanghai alone has more than 300,000 Taiwanese residents. Fujian, Guangdong, and Beijing, among other places, also have huge crowds of Taiwanese residents.

In general, living and working opportunities in the mainland will only increase for the Taiwanese residents, as there are more opportunities for them there. Some surveys show that the majority of educated Taiwanese youth are interested in living and working in the mainland.

Cross-strait trade has made a huge difference in the island's economic health. Lately, nearly all the island's growth has been attributable to mainland trade. In particular, cross-strait trade has created 1 million jobs in Taiwan. There are vast additional benefits as well. In fact, without the mainland market, Taiwan's economy would have stagnated in the past few years. This strait trade could reach over $100 billion within five years.

In reality, room for improvement is huge, as there are numerous restrictions in Taiwan against bilateral trade and investment. For example, Taiwan's largest energy company, China Power, is allowed to buy only up to one-third of the coal it needs from the mainland. Consequently, China Power must spend more money buying additional coal from places far away.

If such bans were lifted, cross-strait trade could easily double. Better political ties are required in order for both sides to enjoy all the benefits from their huge economic cooperation.

A Big Step Toward a Solution

Like Hong Kong and Macau, Taiwan is moving fast in integrating its economy with that of the mainland. This process has been accelerating year after year. Taiwan has gained enormously, and its economic benefits will directly promote better political relations.

The current cross-strait difficulties are caused by the unfinished business of the long-term civil war between the Communist Party and the Kuomintang (KMT), the nationalist party that lost the Chinese civil war and fled to Taiwan. For now, the KMT has become more involved, with official visits to the mainland often today.

Despite all the political uneasiness, the general direction can hardly be reversed. Indeed, in the past six decades, there have been dramatic improvements, from past exchanges of bombshells (ending in 1979) to vast human and economic exchanges in this new era.

Above all, there are enormous opportunities for Taiwan to explore. Simply put, the more rational measures Taiwan's leadership adopts, the more advantages it gains. This is something the island's government has yet to learn.

Despite all the frictions between Beijing and Taipei, the road for peaceful resolution is wide open. The recent trips to the mainland by KMT Chairman Lien Chan were a very healthy start, also opening the door wider for more direct exchanges between Beijing and Taipei. Immediately following Lien's first trip, James Soong led his People First Party on an extensive trip in the mainland as well, followed by numerous other political groups from the island.

For both parties, being Chinese is their greatest strength and nothing is more significant. For now, there are also positive signs from Taipei. In particular, Taipei is considering increasing access for mainland Chinese tourists. Widening peaceful contacts and dialog are occurring. All this points to bright prospects for both sides. By now, visiting the mainland has become very popular among the island's various political groups (except the current government administration).

In the long run, the most crucial factor determining the ultimate outcome of the unity issue is sustained progress in the mainland, both economically and politically. A progressive and prosperous mainland China will change the dynamics of cross-strait relations. This is indeed the top concern for most Taiwanese people today.

Happily, by now, mainland China is entering a new era of deepening institutional and political reforms, besides possibly new rounds of economic advancement. This will fundamentally enhance a peaceful resolution of the unity issue.

At the same time, as the mainland liberalizes further, the choices for bringing about unity are also great. *A new federation for a unified China is the best choice on the table.*

Why Federation?

The central concern is that the island's government fears becoming a "local government" under a traditional central government in Beijing. Instead, it wishes to maintain itself as an independent political center, having all the autonomy possible. It wishes to keep its independent government body, military, currency, and judicial system, among other things. In short, it does not intend to be subject to a higher central power.

For Beijing, the concern relates more to political unity. Beijing has become very pragmatic in its thinking and dealings. In its mind, anything can be and should be discussed provided that there is one China. This position means that Beijing has left behind the traditional mentality that a unified China must be governed under one centralized government. This change in mentality and policy lays the political foundation for a federation.

Already, Hong Kong's and Macau's returns to China are exemplary. The situation is different from the U.S. federal system, for example. In the United States, the governor of New York State is elected by the state's residents and his actions are independent of the central government in Washington, DC. However, federal law overrides state and local statutes. Financially, the central government levies a federal tax on New York residents.

But Beijing does not have tax claims over the residents of Hong Kong and Macau, which are highly self-governed cities, though politically Beijing remains the central authority. This reality shows a new way in the governance of China.

However, the good will of Beijing goes far beyond the degree of autonomy for Hong Kong and Macau with regard to special case of Taiwan. Indeed, Beijing's position is that Taiwan can gain much more autonomy in the future.

For a long time, Beijing has been proposing that the island maintain its government and key institutions. Its political leadership would not be subject to Beijing. Anything could be discussed under the "one China" principle. So, China has already taken a significant step toward a federation, though Beijing has not used the word "federation."

In April 2006, Beijing announced again its intention to talk with Taipei on an equal basis over the unity issue as long as the "one China" principle could be maintained.[1] Indeed, Beijing's stand on this unity issue has become more clear.

The federal approach is revolutionary for China, as it has no historical precedent. Throughout Chinese history, a unified nation implied only one government that administrated the nation through an official body directly appointed by the top leadership. A federal system means that a unified nation can have more than one political center. Indeed, under a federation Taipei would become another political center.

Having multiple political centers would certainly be new to all Chinese. Enabling the Chinese public to understand this type of structure will require huge efforts. But this resolution is demanded by the current realities and is the best possible option for accommodating the needs of the various political entities. Furthermore, even under a federal system, there will be new challenges, though in a different context.

A New Trend in the Mainland

The federal concept fits well with changing realities within the mainland. In the past three decades, the mainland has embraced a gradual decentralization process that offers more and more economic autonomy for the various regions.

This increased regional autonomy is a major way to deal with the ills of the old centralized system of the Mao era. This policy change has already increased self-reliance and creative energy in all regions, which have directly promoted regional and national development.

Indeed, regional competition and self-initiative are a significant boost to China's progress in general and economic dynamics in particular. For example, the new growth in Guangdong province has become possible only through a sharply increased autonomy. As a result, Guangdong has been able to move ahead of the old powerhouse Shanghai, which gained more autonomy only beginning in the early 1990s.[2]

Though such regional autonomy has been limited so far to the economic field, its positive influences have gone well beyond that. Even without the Taiwan issue, a continued increase in regional initiative and autonomy will happen one way or another in the mainland as time passes. There is no way to reverse the trend, as the central, provincial, and local governments have all benefited from the new arrangement, despite its limited scope to this point.

Overall, mainland China must completely reform its entire traditional centralized system toward more modern, liberal governance. That is, regional autonomy and self-reliance must assume more prominence in a modern society. This is strongly warranted by the changing realities, whose future development is already outside the traditional centralized framework.

Taiwan's Advantages

Would this federal alterative do Taiwan any good? It certainly would. Above all, it would eliminate all unwanted political tensions and lead to innumerable opportunities for Taiwan. In short, the island's political establishment would gain all the advantages, and the existing positive institutions and ways of operating would remain.

A federation would give the island more opportunities to expand its interests in the mainland. This extra advantage would also be welcomed by the mainland Chinese because increased and open competition would promote more progress on both sides of the strait. This in itself would mean a great leap forward for all China.

Naturally, the opposite extremist stand would be full of risks for Taiwan. Indeed, continued cross-strait tensions will cause unnecessary, even catastrophic, damage if they escalate. Fundamentally, any separation measures taken by the island could backfire against its interest. Its economy would suffer severely. Furthermore, hostility toward the mainland with its 1.3 billion Chinese would be most irrational as well as unacceptable to all Chinese around the globe. A change in mentality and approach would open the door to a better world for all involved.

Most importantly, those involved are all Chinese, separated only by unfinished business stemming from a painful civil war. The Chinese people now have opportunities to move forward creatively and productively. A federation would mean peaceful unification for the Chinese people living on both sides of the Taiwan Strait. It would root out all the elements underlying political tensions and the unwanted consequences. Both sides will benefit directly from peaceful unity.

Rational resolution of the cross-strait tension will enhance peace and progress everywhere, not just for China. For many decades, and even centuries, the Taiwan issue has been a key destabilizing factor for East Asia and beyond. Especially today, unwanted tensions across the Taiwan Strait could trigger disasters beyond the region.

All in all, a peaceful and progressive outcome would bring benefits to the entire world. So the outside world has every reason to be supportive and constructive in promoting a peaceful resolution. The federation concept is the best choice.

Chapter 22.
Taiwanese Business in the Mainland

The ongoing business and human flows from Taiwan to the mainland are both natural and inevitable. They follow from the basic economic principle: Humans go where opportunities lie, and so does capital.

To date, Taiwanese businesspeople have made strides in the mainland, with impacts of many dimensions. For one, they have helped to integrate the island's economy with the mainland's in all sorts of ways. For another, they have gained huge room for growth. In addition, they are helping to foster a new environment for a possible peaceful resolution of the unity issue.

A Vibrant Taiwanese Force

In the current era, the Hong Kong and Macau business communities went to the mainland far sooner than their Taiwanese counterpart, but the reasons were exclusively political. For Taiwanese residents, traveling to the mainland has been allowed only since 1987. Quickly, cross-strait life changed dramatically. By now, Taiwanese businesspeople have made as much of a mark in the mainland as those from Hong Kong and Macau.

Why has Taiwan Inc. put such huge capital into the mainland despite all the political tensions? Their motive is simple: The mainland offers immense opportunities, much greater than those on the island. Indeed, the early birds have already benefited greatly, which has hastened the rush.

As with their Hong Kong and Macau counterparts, the greatest strengths of the Taiwanese businesspeople come from their vast numbers. Today, most Taiwanese players are small and medium-sized companies. They cover all economic sectors, ranging from consumer products, real estate, and retail to IT and equipment manufacturing.[1]

These Taiwanese companies are mostly niche players, but they have numerous advantages. They are aggressive and flexible and are quick learners. Being Chinese, they can adapt to the mainland environment very quickly and effectively despite the different political surroundings. The explosive growth in the mainland market has become a new profit and growth haven for them.

One mainland Chinese businessman is very impressed by the capability of Taiwanese businesspeople in the mainland. "These Taiwanese businessmen know what they are doing and they are doing better than we mainland businessmen in getting top opportunities over here," he told me.

High-Tech

Taiwan Inc. plays an increasingly important role in the mainland economy and market. One highly significant sector is information technology. Thousands of Taiwanese high-tech companies are operating in this sector. Most are OEM players that provide services to global markets. Their clients include numerous international multinationals such as Dell, HP, Sony, Philips, Apple, Toshiba, and IBM. By now, many Taiwanese high-tech companies have also become significant suppliers to mainland Chinese high-tech companies such as Lenovo, Founder, and Great Wall.

Furthermore, many Taiwanese high-tech companies have greatly expanded their business lines. In particular, many Taiwanese OEM companies like BenQ now make their own brand of personal computers and notebooks, which are directly sold in the mainland and beyond. At the same time, the Taiwanese IT sector is helping the mainland to reach a higher level of technology and know-how. This has become a natural development for both parties.

In this context, one high-profile chipmaker, Semiconductor Manufacturing Corp (SMIC), stands out.[2] It is a start-up about six years old that now trades in Hong Kong and New York. Its cofounder and CEO, Richard Chang, is a native of Taiwan and formerly a Texas Instruments engineer. The company's seed money has come from various sources, including mainland Chinese and overseas investors.

Under Chang's leadership, this company has made good progress. By now, several sizable chip plants are established in Shanghai, Tianjin, and Beijing. Chang's ambition is to become the world's biggest contract chipmaker. The rising chip demands in China offer bright opportunities. By early 2005, SMIC overtook Singapore's Chartered Semiconductor Manufacturing to become the world's third largest contract chipmaker. It now plans to take over some badly managed state chip companies.

This company's sudden emergence as a sizable chip player poses a new challenge to the established semiconductor world, Taiwan Semiconductor Inc. included. As one result, more and more overseas chip companies are coming to the mainland. The aim of all this is partly to meet rising chip demand in the mainland.

By some estimates, China will have become the biggest IT market in the world by 2012. Currently, mainland China consumes about 20%, or more, of the global chip supplies. As the biggest consumer products market, China has become a place no overseas high-tech companies can avoid, Taiwan's included.

There are other advantages in the mainland for Taiwan's companies. First, the labor and land cost in Taiwan has gone up sharply. As a largely low-end player in the value chain, the Taiwanese business community must find alternatives in order to cut costs, as a matter of survival.

Second, many leading clients of Taiwan Inc. are international multinationals with mainland operations. Getting closer to these end buyers is another advantage, without which the Taiwanese companies may lose their competitive edge.

Third, entire business chains within Taiwan's manufacturing sector have been transferring to the mainland. Naturally, more and more components makers follow. As a result, by 2005, the island's high-tech sector had invested more than $10 billion in the mainland.

Business movement has its own merits. Once a major manufacturer sets up its factory in the mainland, its suppliers must also follow. This is why Taiwanese component makers are rushing to China.

I once asked a senior manager of a leading Taiwanese computer component maker, "What has prompted your company to set up factories in the mainland?"

He replied, "The reason is obvious: All our buyers have moved to the mainland. So my company has no choice but to come."

One of the biggest success stories is that of Hon Hai Precision Industry, one of the two global Fortune 500 players from Taiwan. It is a leading high-tech components maker with clients that include most global high-tech players like IBM, HP, Toshiba, and Dell.

By now, the company has moved most of its manufacturing facilities to the mainland, which has significantly helped in its rapid growth. In 2005, its mainland business reached $15.6 billion. This company's success in the mainland, with all the resultant benefits, in turn attracts more players away from Taiwan.

Other Sectors

The food and soft drink market is another strong playground for Taiwan Inc. Besides countless small firms, there are several sizable companies in this sector. One popular brand is Tingyi (whose company name is Ting Hsin International Group), which is the biggest fast noodle maker in the mainland and is expanding into soft drinks and other food products. Recently, Asahi, the biggest Japanese brewer, and Itochu, the third biggest Japanese trading company, injected $424 million for a 50% stake in Tingyi's soft drink division.

After being established in the mainland, Tingyi went back to acquire a leading Taiwan-based food company. Playing in both markets helps the company to get the best of both worlds. Tingyi very cleverly made the mainland its home base; from there it wishes to expand globally.

Another food company, the President Group, the most famous Taiwanese food concern, is also a top player in the mainland today. Unlike Tingyi, it was a major food brand in Taiwan for a long time. By entering the mainland, it has gained much more room for growth. Having become established in the mainland, President hopes to become the world's biggest food group by 2020. Being in the mainland makes this goal more realistic than ever before.

In the general retail industry, Taiwan Inc. is also very active. The mainland has built a vibrant retail chain business, though only about 12 years old, that took about 30% of market share in 2005. Chinese consumers prefer these chain stores for their better products and quality, so the profit potential is huge for all participants.

At this time, all retailers, both domestic and international, are competing to set up more stores. Several fast-growing Taiwanese-managed supermarkets, such Guandong-based Trust-Mart, have shown quick growth. Trust-Mart was established by Yu Rijiang, who arrived in the mainland in 1987. In 1997, he created the franchise outlet, which had expanded to 107 megastores by mid-2006, located in several dozen cities. Trust-Mart has already become a major franchise retailer in the mainland. Even some major international retailers are interested in these franchises, which provide a quick way to expand into mainland China.[3]

In general, Taiwanese companies cover all business sectors. They are also a very significant player in specialty chemicals. In numerous ways, Taiwan Inc. is helping to create more channels to link mainland China's economy to the global markets. One way is for Taiwanese employees to work for companies in the mainland. Increasingly, mainland Chinese companies want to hire experienced Taiwanese engineers and marketing and managerial professionals.

Ping An Insurance, for example, the second biggest insurance company in the mainland, has hired several Taiwanese professionals for senior positions. These professionals previously worked for leading international insurance and financial companies. Such international experience is highly appreciated in China.

Taiwan Inc. has become a powerful player in the mainland already, and its presence there provides great opportunities for future development. But the prerequisite for sustained development of Taiwan

Inc. is complete participation in the mainland. Otherwise, this island of 23 million people could have a small future. Indeed, a retreat from the ongoing economic exchange would push the island's economy south at once. This is already a common understanding, though the current government administration under Chen Sui-bian is reluctant to admit it.

What's Next?

So far, cross-strait trade and investments have brought Taiwan enormous direct benefits. On the whole, Taiwan benefits more than China. This is so partly because mainland Chinese companies face political barriers to entering the Taiwanese market directly. In addition, more than 2,000 products made in the mainland are banned from entering Taiwan.

Even so, mainland businesspeople have found numerous ways to do business in Taiwan. One most common is via joint ventures with Taiwanese companies, mostly to sell products. But their scope and reach are very limited. As of now, mainland businesspeople are not allowed to set up shops in the island.

It has not been easy for the Taiwanese business community to move to the mainland, mainly because of barriers imposed by Taipei. But creative Taiwanese businesspeople have found ways around this containment. They may go through a third location before putting money into the mainland.

Still, man-made barriers are plentiful. For example, Taipei has opposed direct flights. As a result, people crossing the strait have to stop in Hong Kong or Macau. So, cross-strait business life has a complex backdrop.

Due to political considerations, Beijing is keen to offer more benefits to the island. For example, Beijing recently lifted tariffs on the sale of numerous Taiwanese farm products to the mainland. Since the mainland is a huge market, Beijing can afford to be generous.

The more Beijing tries to offer incentives, however, the more the current Taipei government wants to avoid. Taipei has recently increased efforts to block its business community from investing in the mainland. One way is to impose fines. A more extreme measure has been to threaten those who refuse to withdraw from the mainland with legal action and punishment.

Richard Chang was fined $500,000 and threatened with prosecution. Confronting such threats, Chang has simply given up his Taiwanese citizenship and has applied for a mainland passport instead. Other Taiwanese businesspeople face similar hard choices.[4]

Such irrational acts on the part of Taipei could backfire further. Specifically, they could potentially cause difficulties for Taiwan's economy. Popular discontent is on the rise against the separation-minded Chen government.

On the latest measures, one Taiwanese businessman said, "Chen is going nuts. Does he understand that the island will go broke if it cuts off from the mainland?"

Will Spring Follow Winter?

Chen's administration has not yielded, however, but instead has taken more extreme actions. In early 2006, it abolished the National Unification Council together with the National Unification Guides. These had constituted the most important platform for official communication between Beijing and Taipei since the early 1990s. Furthermore, with this action Chen has abolished the status quo of Taiwan as part of China.[5] The move shows how desperate Chen's administration has become in its drive for independence, regardless of the harm to the interests of the island.

Nevertheless, prospects for the future do not look that bleak. On the contrary, very positive developments are occurring with the many direct contacts between people on the two sides, including high-level political leaders. One may predict that when Chen's term is over, the stand will likely become less hostile, regardless of which new group of politicians is elected. Changes will not be limited to business policies. Unity talk will likely pick up steam after Chen's term.

The real marvel is that the integration of the two economies has been accelerating year after year despite all the political barriers. The human interactions are accelerating at an even faster pace. All this can hardly be reversed by any political interest.

At the same time, without fundamental political and institutional reform toward a more liberalized society in the mainland, the path toward peaceful resolution with Taiwan will hardly be smooth. Still, the general trend in the mainland is already in this direction, and more positive progress should greatly enhance cross-strait relations.

This political reform issue in the mainland is actually a major concern for many Taiwanese. One Taiwanese businessman told me:

"Most Taiwanese people want to get a peaceful union with the mainland. But many of them are not comfortable with the Communist system. Once the mainland achieves more progress in political reform, there won't be any serious problems for the unity issue."

Work on the unity issue will move forward as cross-strait exchanges intensify along with deepening political reform in the mainland. Despite all the political uneasiness, the general direction cannot be reversed. More rational measures for improving cross-strait relations will offer the island's political leadership huge advantages. Despite all the frictions, the economic benefits from ever-increasing cross-strait ties will promote peaceful resolution.

Part VII.

India vs. China:
Moving Ahead at the Same Time

SUMMARY

Today China and India are moving fast in tandem. In both cases the new growth, which started from a long-standing poverty, is led by new entrepreneurial armies in an increasing open environment. Involving more than 2.3 billion people eager to improve their lives through their own efforts, the growth, development, and modernity of these nations will impact humankind in no small way.

At the same time, the growth paths of the two countries have been somewhat different. This has created unique strengths and challenges for both nations. However, one reality is this: There are mutual benefits for them to share with each other. Closer ties between them will do the world only good.

Furthermore, with the development of these ancient societies just beginning, sustained growth will demand fundamental changes — institutional and government reforms in particular. All this demands greater openness as well as greater individual private initiative for both nations.

Chapter 23.

China and India: Can They Do Better Together?

In this era of globalization, the elephant (India) and the dragon (China) both have a sense of urgency about catching up with the developed world. There is a high degree of rivalry between the two nations, but this competition will produce a creative and productive partnership in the end. This new trend is already gaining great momentum.

Mutual Benefits

The mutual benefits of an India-China partnership are many. India has built up a world-class IT army while China has created a fast-expanding manufacturing force. Their strengths are complementary in numerous ways; all they have to do is team up in a more productive fashion.

So far, India's IT army has successfully courted the big boys' club in the developed world, but there are limits to how far this can go. Indian software companies are service oriented. They have not had large space for developing their proprietary products. China can provide them that space.

China Inc. will benefit from this partnership as well. Although the Chinese companies have developed an extensive manufacturing capability and can produce nearly anything, China has lagged behind in terms of intellectual development, especially in software and design. This is where the Indian software giants come in. Leveraging on this combination of knowledge and production, India and China together will be able to supply the world better and cheaper products of all sorts, which will promote greater growth for both nations as well.

One could estimate that trade between China and India should reach $200 billion in two decades or so. But in comparison, the present level is very low. In 2005, bilateral trade reached $18.71 billion. That was a record, up nearly 38% from 2004. China is now India's second biggest trading partner and will likely take the top slot soon. All this points toward a mutually beneficial partnership in the making. More and more Chinese and Indians now understand the importance of increased collaboration.

Reaching this stage of cooperation between the two nations has required huge efforts already. In many ways, businesspeople in the two countries are far ahead of the governments, having sensed the potential for partnership much earlier and tapped into each other's resources quickly.

China Inc.'s presence in India is increasing as time goes on; this is especially the case with respect to manufacturing and R&D centers. Konka and TCL, two leading Chinese consumer products companies, have extensive operations there that target the Indian consumer market. Haier, the biggest Chinese consumer products maker, is adding a handset factory in India as well as expanding its durable goods production. Haier aims to become one of the top three players in India by 2010.

With regard to Chinese R&D centers in India, a high-profile example involves Huawei, the biggest Chinese telecom network manufacturer. Huawei has been operating a sizable R&D center in Bangalore for several years now, with some 700 employees, mostly Indians, and an investment of $80 million. Satisfied with the general environment and the talent base, the company is putting in another $100 million to expand its programs there. ZTE, the second biggest Chinese telecom network maker, is also active in India.

The booming Indian economy also has great market potential. As of 2005, all Chinese consumer products companies wished to tap into India's $4.8 billion home appliances market. When the Indian economy grows further, the consumption market will become explosive. For now, India has some 60 million handsets; this number will rise to over 400 million in a few years, as in China.

When it comes to the presence of India Inc. in China, the most interesting development involves the Indian IT sector. Many Indian technology companies have already been active in China. In fact, all the top Indian software firms are in China today.

Among these, NIIT, a leading consulting and educational concern, has been operating in China since 1998. The company has set up more than 125 training schools in the major Chinese cities, each with thousands of students. This is done through partnerships with Chinese businesses and universities. In addition, it offers extensive consulting services to China Inc. as well as conducting international operations inside the nation. Given the initial success, the company aims to expand its programs further now.

The other leading IT names, such as Infosys, Wipro, TCS, and Satyam, all have a significant Chinese presence. They can definitely play a big role in helping China move to the next level. Their international experience is also a huge plus.

Moreover, plenty of Indian manufacturing companies are operating in China. China offers them both a factory and a market. At the present time, consumption in China is way ahead of that in India. Again, China has plenty of component suppliers, offering vast choices for Indian manufacturers.

Another important area of cooperation between the two countries involves cotton, steel, and mineral products. India has increased its efforts to sell more of these products to China. Chinese businesses want to buy more of them in order to meet ever-rising demands at home. Indian steel and mineral producers have become very active in tapping into the Chinese market.

Sharing Managerial Skills

Another very significant area of increased cooperation involves managerial skills. Economic development in these two nations has had much in common. Sharing managerial skills will be even more significant in the long run.

Why should India and China share their managerial knowledge? They face many similar development issues and problems. As late-developed nations, they have had to walk a long way to become participants in the global economy.

From deep isolation in the past to current active engagement with the world, both nations employ openness as a grand strategy for development. At the same time, both confront the challenges of achieving progress with very limited resources. Their weak companies must compete directly with international giants. Getting ahead of the game takes very special skills and efforts. In this regard, the two nations have rich knowledge and experiences to share with each other.[1]

In many ways, the new managerial experiences and knowledge of the two countries are highly relevant to each other. Broadly speaking, as late developers, they should understand each other's strengths and weaknesses better than anyone from the developed world. Therefore, sharing managerial talents is natural and should bring enormous benefits to all participating parties.

At this time, China's Indian operations are aimed at building localized management centered on Indian managers, while Indian companies in China are keen on hiring more Chinese talent. These types of moves seem natural and will become more popular as times passes.

But more can and should be done by the two nations in sharing managerial talents. If Chinese multinationals hire experienced Indian managers and Indian manufacturers get help from Chinese executives, the combined forces will be much stronger in the end. Such managerial sharing should not be limited to narrow fields but should be as widespread as possible. Today, this kind of venture is beginning to come to life.

New Global Players

For a long time, each of these nations lived in isolation. This caused vast problems as far as modern development is concerned. In the past, they opened up only when forced to do so by foreign powers. Now both nations have chosen to embrace the world and have taken giant steps to participate in the global economy and community.

So in many ways, both India and China are being reborn under openness. Their prosperity is great news for the world. The more prosperous they are, the easier it will be for the developed world to tap into these huge markets. The biggest gainers will be the multinationals, with their shops already set up in these countries.

Fundamentally, it is an explosive entrepreneurial spirit that is leading the growth of the Indian and Chinese economies at the present time. Millions of entrepreneurs are changing the very basics of these two traditional societies. And, as pointed by Amartya Sen, development in these nations should help to expand personal and social freedom, with both moving forward by leaps and bounds in this new direction.[2] In this new environment, their large burdensome populations are being turned into a productive force.[3] Interestingly, they have become the new champions of global development.

Still, development in these countries is only just beginning. There are still enormous barriers to be overcome. Both nations face the task of creating a truly entrepreneurial culture, this in turn demanding a reshaping of the government structure from the traditional bureaucratic power into a modern service provider. Such issues are becoming most urgent today, which is the focus of the next chapter.

Chapter 24.

Uneven Development: India vs. China

Both China and India have already overcome enormous man-made barriers to reach their current stage of development. To move forward, they need to institute greater political and institutional reforms, aimed at clearing away bureaucratic problems. A basic fact is this: Their openness to the world should make the transition much less painful.

Commonalities

China and India have several characteristics in common as late developers. One of these is their mammoth populations. In recent history, it has been in the less populated nations that development occurred first. The largest developed nation is the United States with its 270 million people. This is a small population compared to those of India and China, which together have more than 2.3 billion people — over one-third of humankind.

The movement of so many people into the world development orbit is a new chapter in the story of humankind. Indeed, their advancement will be influential to an unprecedented degree. Once these countries move solidly ahead on this new path, life on earth will rise to a new level.

In the past, the massive populations in these nations were a huge burden, which was made worse under a closed society. Today, the people of India and China are becoming a hugely productive force. The creative outburst of over 2.3 billion people is something the world has never seen before. Countless Chinese and Indian entrepreneurs have appeared seemingly from nowhere.

Second, these late developers are advancing rapidly, more or less in tandem. The reason is obvious — development in both cases is closely tied to the outside world under globalization.

The outside world has been surprised to see how quickly Chinese and Indian products and services have flooded the globe. But this new development started at an extremely low level for both nations. Only a few years ago, they faced starvation. Despite the quick growth, the room for further growth is huge. After all, the productivity in both nations is shockingly low and the average income is even lower — only a tiny fraction of that in the developed countries.

Third, fully embracing globalization is a new path willingly and firmly chosen by both nations. This openness is transforming both nations from the inside out. Their contributions to the world economy have already altered global production norms significantly.

Even so, the stories of the two nations in this era are very different. There are tremendous lessons to be learned from their development. Above all, as late developers, both nations have huge opportunities as well as challenges ahead.

From Isolation to Global Engagement

Throughout history, both China and India have been predominately inward-oriented societies and had mostly self-sufficient economies at home. This self-sufficiency and inwardness meant that they went their own independent ways over the ages.

In more recent history, both nations were forced to open up mainly by the expansionist West. As a consequence, defending national independence took priority over development.

These negative foreign experiences left vast impacts on national life in the two countries. But the reactions of the governments did even more harm. As soon as the foreign powers were gone, both nations turned inward again. Indeed, after World War II, they went through a tightly closed period. A closed society was extremely harmful to their development, not to mention other issues. Under isolation, poverty ruled over both nations for decades.

The price paid was massive. In the case of India, even under British rule its international trade was much bigger and its connection to the global economy much wider. For example, in 1913, India's international trade took 4.5% of global share. But in 1983, its trade share was reduced to a mere 0.5%.[1]

Furthermore, gaining openness has been a rather complex proposition for India. The key reason: the government power increased sharply. One Indian businessman recalls:

"When I went to work in the sixties I discovered that we had become economically enslaved and socialism was leading us to statism. By the time I got married . . . Indira Gandhi was creating dynastic rule and leading us into a ditch. . . ."[2]

This Indian author maintains that the economic reform initiated in 1991 put India on the right track of growth and global engagement. In particular, the sharp rise of the Indian IT entrepreneurial army has become a powerful force in leading India to reintegration with the global economy and community.

The closed society in China was even worse. In the Mao era, China's total foreign trade was much less than that of the city of Shanghai in the early 1930s. Under a closed society dominated by government bureaucracy, even mighty Shanghai completely lost its glory after 1949. With the nation's economy in total disarray for decades, human flourishing was constricted beyond belief. Even simple things like installing a phone at home or travel became a bureaucratic privilege.

In this era, both nations have reversed the course of history and now actively participate in the world economy and community. Being open to the world has made a huge difference. Though only at the very beginning stage, their future development will continue to coexist closely with global development. By tapping into global resources, both nations have gained unlimited opportunities for development.

Even in this era, though, these two nations did not start their current growth paths at the same time. China started to open up to the world in 1978, while India did so in 1991. This time gap has had noticeable consequences. China's growth picked up steam ahead of India's. As a result, Chinese income growth has gone ahead.

Prior to 1983, India's economic output per person was slightly ahead of China's. But over the next two decades, the relative income per person reversed sharply. Today, India's GDP per person is less than half of China's. Why?

There are many reasons, but the most crucial one is China's greater openness during this time period. As a result, China had gained over $620 billion in foreign direct investment by 2005, over 10 times more than the figure for India. This foreign direct investment not only transformed China, but also served as a powerful bridge between China and the world economy. Today, the majority of China's export is conducted by overseas-funded businesses inside the nation.

Why has China been able to attract so much more foreign capital than India? One reason is China's fast-rising domestic consumption. Indeed, China's quick rise in personal income and the resulting consumption have played an essential role in attracting foreign involvement.

The difference in consumption growth between the two nations is staggering. For example, China's home-appliances market was about $50 billion as of 2005—around 10 times the size of India's. Moreover, this Chinese consumption reached its current level from next to nothing within only three decades. Naturally, all international technology and consumer products makers came to China first.

International multinationals have no patience for future profits; they want immediate rewards. Most put their money only into markets where transactions can take place right away. China's explosive domestic consumption has made this possible.

Without doubt, India will follow this same path in attracting foreign direct investment as time goes by. Once India's domestic consumption picks up steam, the nation will be able to attract more foreign capital. Indeed, this is already happening today, as India is moving forward fast in growth in both income and consumption. But it will take time for India to catch up in attracting foreign capital.

Another striking difference is that China excels especially in manufacturing whereas India does especially well in software and IT services. The different development roads have also made huge differences in their economies.

Indeed, China's fast-expanding manufacturing sector has created demands for everything else. It requires complete business chains as well as all sorts of participants, technology, management, and capital. Therefore, huge investments have had wider effects in China.

Besides factories, the business chains must cover power supply, roads, ports, and other items of infrastructure. Over the past three decades, China has constructed more than 33,000 kilometers of roads. There are extensive logistical services as well. For example, both Shanghai and Shenzhen's ports are among the top 10 in the world as of now. They could move up to the top two positions within a few years. Naturally, these investments have helped to connect China's economy to the global economy in big ways.

Furthermore, made-in-China products can compete in global markets. Though their brands are little known, they are highly competitive because of their low prices. Also, quality has improved continuously. All this has helped Chinese growth.

In the case of India, the pace of development has been fast in certain sectors, most outstandingly in its info-tech service sector. Some other sectors such as the booming steel industry are also doing fine. At the same time, India's development in infrastructure and other economic sectors is lagging seriously behind at present. Moving to higher pay scales is another huge task. Moreover, the IT sector employs only about a million people. The steel industry is booming, but its employment power is also limited. Wider development will take time.

India's backward infrastructure in particular is in need of more attention. It surprises visitors to see that India's roads are ridden with potholes. Ports and rails remain underdeveloped as well. All these improvements call for huge investments.

But the deeper issue is that such issues cannot be resolved in an isolated environment. Greater openness is needed in order to attract more foreign as well as domestic capital. This is an area in which policy changes by the Indian government are most urgently required.

Overall, India is moving ahead very fast, with over 6% annual growth in the past decade or so. But it has yet to catch up with China. Experts say that with the current growth rate, it will take over 15 years for India to reach China's current general domestic product per head.

All this having been said, however, in many ways the quality of Indian economic development is ahead of that in China. Part of the reason is that India has a stronger private sector based on modern ownership law. As a result, the Indian banking sector, for example, performs far better than its Chinese counterpart. In this context, it will take more time and effort for China to achieve quality in development.

Huge Challenges Ahead

Some Indians claim that China has an advantage in its vast pool of overseas Chinese who bring huge capital back home. True, the overseas Chinese are the biggest investor group in China today, but there are still the deeper issues. Internal bureaucratic interference remains the fundamental weakness for both nations. All things considered, many of the greatest obstacles come from within. Only when these nations modernize their political-economic institutions will sustained development become possible.

In the case of China, its state sector has hardly become a winner despite huge economic expansion. Up to 90% of Chinese state sector companies are in distress today. Thus the state sector continues to cause enormous woes. True reform demands a complete disconnection between the government and business spheres, which is a mighty task due to the vested interests of the government bureaucracy.

In many ways, however, India also confronts an out-of-date government establishment. Without a fundamental overhaul, India will run into problems similar to those in China. Hence, leaving the bureaucratic framework behind is an urgent goal for both nations.

A Great Puzzle

One puzzle about today's India is this: It has had a democratic system, but it has failed to reduce man-made barriers, as well as official corruption, in any serious way. The Indian bureaucracy is responsible for countless hurdles in the way of development.

For example, setting up a new company in India requires very lengthy governmental approvals. A recent World Bank survey, *Doing Business in 2006*, shows the depth of problems in India as far as conducting business is concerned.

In January 2005 it took 11 procedures, 71 days, and 61.7% of per capita income on average to start a business. The annual report ranked India 116th among 155 nations or regions in terms of general business environment.

As a matter of fact, this was already a significant improvement in relation to the past. A few years ago, registering a company involved some 45 government procedures, or more. Starting a new business is by no means easy in India.

But starting a business is still the easiest part, with countless bureaucratic hurdles following. I asked an Indian businessman about this. He said, smiling, "It can become smooth if you know your way around."

I asked him to explain.

"It is no secret that bribery smoothes things a lot," he said.

"Can you reform the system instead?"

He replied, "The Indian society is so weak against the countless interest groups within the government establishment. Changing the system will demand more efforts and time."

Restrictive policies are only part of the total picture in India. There are more extensive problems stemming from backward institutions and the resulting corruption.

Another major problem is the state sector, which has not performed well despite the general development in the nation's economy. For example, the Indian state auto companies make very little business sense, but opening the auto market to global competition has yet to take place.

The Ills of China

Some Chinese refer to India's corruption as "Indian ills."[2] But China's reality is no better. All the Indian ills are also present in China, only worse.

The bottom line is the character of the Chinese bureaucratic body, its inability to provide any useful service to the people and society. In this reform era, bureaucratic interest groups have invented all sorts of strategies to benefit themselves.

In daily life, an art of living for Chinese businesspeople is to coexist with the corrupt bureaucratic power and even take advantage of it. As a popular street slogan has it, "Corruption is the catalyst for development." This shows how widespread government corruption is at the present time. But the society still does not have the strength to challenge it. The built-in holes are numerous, and the chances of corrupt officials getting caught are not high. Rather, the idea of supreme state power gives them strong cover.

In a coastal Chinese city I once walked into a government building that was filled with local businesspeople waiting to get official approvals for their projects. I was very troubled by the scene. I said to a government clerk whom I knew slightly:

"What a great business your office has! But so many government demands on businesses will drive international multinationals to India instead."

The clerk said, "Well, I hear that the Indian government also makes countless demands on businesses, just like us."

Among the variety of ways in which corrupt officials can pressure people, an increasingly popular tactic is to sell government titles. To get promotions, lower officials bribe their superiors. This sort of corruption is widespread.

One case involved several hundred officials in Heilongjiang province over the period of the 1990s through to 2003. Among the senior officials in this case was Han Guizhi, who was the deputy chief of the province's Communist Party and chairman of the province's Political Consultancy Conference, the top government advisory board.[3]

As one researcher noted, such corruption means that bureaucratic misbehavior has reached a new level:

"Selling government posts is the highest corruption in the nation. Corrupt low-ranking officials squeeze on people directly; middle-ranking officials find opportunities to rent their power for personal gain, while the senior-ranking officials sell government posts directly. Hence, selling government posts is the biggest corruption."[4]

Some people hope that democracy is the way out of these problems. But that path is difficult. The fact that the Indian democracy has not been able to contain corruption causes the Chinese great alarm. One cannot hope that an elected government will always behave perfectly or that a democratic system can resolve all problems forever. In reality, progress will not result merely from elections. Instead, the focus must be on creating a better-functioning society and better institutions.

Elections are not the answer to the issues a nation like China or India faces. India aside, the democratic systems in Russia and Latin America have also run into huge problems. They also have been unable to contain widespread corruption. All this shows that building a market economy is a more formidable task than instituting an elected government. This problem is something the developed world has not experienced, but it is common in the developing world.

Power, without counterbalance, can only feed on itself. Even under a democratic system, overextended bureaucratic power can easily find ways to expand its interests, as happens so commonly around the globe. This reality may surprise people who regard democracy as a recipe for doing away with corruption once and for all.

On this issue, a Chinese scholar in Hunan province says, "A better China demands to contain its traditional bureaucratic power. But let us not dream about achieving it by electing a government through votes. India is one good example where a democracy has failed to contain wild bureaucratic power."

But in China now, controlling bureaucratic power is a mighty task simply because China does not have the socioeconomic forces required to mount a direct challenge. Rather, so far, all efforts to reduce the overextended bureaucratic power have been indirect. Raising the power of people remains a formidable task.

Going Forward

At this time, both China and India stand at a crossroads. In order for these nations to move ahead, bureaucratic influence must be contained. Obviously, neither nation lacks entrepreneurs, but they have limited influence over institutional reforms. Hence, ending bureaucratic domination is an absolute requirement if the Chinese and Indians are to fully employ their creative energy toward prosperity.

Abusive political power has been common throughout human history. It is difficult for a European today to remember the difficulties of even the recent past. It took Europe centuries to pull down man-made barriers. Only some 150 years ago, traveling from Paris to Berlin was rather troublesome. With all sorts of fee collection checkpoints, it was normal for people to have to pay fees hundreds of times. Getting rid of such bureaucratic intrusions was no small matter for Europe.

Similarly, sailing for China and India will not be smooth. Both nations have taken the first step, the most significant one, in moving forward on this growth path. This will make it much easier for them to resolve the deep-seated bureaucratic problems at home. Once these problems are resolved, both nations will become more open and dynamic than many others, including those in Europe.

Part VIII.
The Japan-China Issue:
Evolving Relations in Light of History

SUMMARY

Japan has been a major source of problems for East Asia and beyond for more than eight centuries. In the distant past, Japanese pirates and Japan's government caused vast bloodshed in the region. But the greatest Japanese aggression took place between 1894 and 1945, causing unspeakable miseries to many people and nations and killing tens of millions.

Yet, unlike what has happened in Germany, this dark Japanese past has not been addressed or condemned. Though the German government has willingly and openly discussed and condemned the crimes committed in the Nazi era, Japan's government has not addressed it past aggressions.

Now, entering the 21st century, the Japanese government has continued to behave irrationally and irresponsibly in all sorts of ways in dealing with the crimes of the imperial Japanese government. This type of behavior causes continuing widespread anger among the victimized nations. At the same time, it reflects Japan's difficulties in becoming more open and leaving its traditionally tightly closed society behind.

Economically, in this era, Japan and the nations it victimized have engaged in ever-increasing trade and investment activities. Interdependence has become a foundation for a new era.

Despite this improved economic picture for the region, today the Japanese government continues to irritate its neighbors by glorifying its past aggressions, honoring war criminals, and altering history textbooks, among other acts. This has naturally produced new tensions in the region, and creates a shadow over relations in general and economic relations in particular. So, what is at stake for Japan and its neighbors, especially China?

A sound analysis shows that, for a variety of reasons, the economic relationship between Japan and China may be more significant to Japan than it is to China, limiting the Japanese government's freedom of action. Ultimately, Japan must play its role rationally in order protect its long-term interests.

But there are more significant issues for Japan. Today, the basic problem of Japan is its closed society and market, which have already harmed its economy and general health in no small way. For Japan to move ahead and become a true solution provider in a new era, the key is to become an open society and market. Such openness will above all benefit the Japanese people.

Chapter 25.

Japanese Business in China

In the past three decades, Japan and China have enjoyed ever-increasing economic ties, but their political relationship has lagged seriously behind. The ongoing political rows cast a shadow over the economic ties. So what's really at stake?

Japan Inc. in China

Japan Inc. has been the third most important investor in China, after "Overseas Chinese Inc." and U.S. Inc. By 2005, Japan had invested over U.S.$72.59 billion in equity in China, while Japanese banks are leading international lenders to China. At the same time, the booming Chinese economy has become an engine for Japan's economic recovery. Recently 50% or more of the total increase in Japanese exports has been attributable to China.

In this era, Japanese investments in mainland China have come in three waves. The first wave, which really only tested the water, was in the 1980s. Japanese investors at that time felt that the Chinese lacked sufficient buying power to make investments worthwhile. As a result, only small investments were made.

The second wave occurred in 1993-1995, as Chinese growth began to accelerate. Still, however, Japanese investments remained limited in scope and reach. China was treated as a factory, not a market. Goods made in China by Japanese manufacturers were largely sent to overseas markets.

But by the late 1990s, seemingly all of Japan Inc. rushed in — creating the third wave. By 2005, not only giant Japanese multinationals, but also many small and medium-size firms had arrived. Greater Shanghai alone has more than 40,000 Japanese residents. Japanese schools operate in major cities such as Xian, Dalian, Beijing, Shenzhen, and Shanghai. In 2004, the number of people traveling between the two nations reached 4.35 million — a new record.

Basically, Japan Inc. is now completely hooked on China. This should not come as a surprise — China has become the largest consumer market in the world, besides being a top manufacturer and top trading nation. In 2005, China had nearly 400 million handset users and sold more than 16 million personal computers, giving it, respectively, the first and second biggest global market for these goods.

Using China as a growth engine has become a fundamental strategy for Japan Inc. It has taken more than two decades for the Japanese to reach this conclusion. Naturally, huge Japanese investments have rushed into China accordingly.

By now, countless Japanese firms are established in China, including Mitsui, with more than 110 joint ventures; Matsushita, which runs more than 49 factories and is adding more; and Canon, Hitachi, and Sharp, which intend to make China their biggest market and site of their biggest factories. Japanese auto giants Honda and Toyota are already top players. Clearly, the fortunes of Japan Inc. are already seriously tied to China.

Furthermore, many Japanese companies are setting up R&D labs in China and lining up Chinese research institutes and universities to support future R&D efforts. Outsourcing is another major activity. Sony alone has more than 3,000 China-based suppliers, and Japanese firms are increasingly turning to China, rather than India, for their software outsourcing.

Japan Inc. is active in all economic sectors, not just manufacturing. Retail giants like Jusco, MyCall, Ito-Yokado, and 7-Eleven (which has been Japanese owned since its Japanese subsidiary purchased it from the Southland Corporation in 1991) are all established in China. Increasing Chinese consumption has become a gold mine for these retailers, who are competing with Wal-Mart, Tesco, Carrefour, and everyone else to set up more stores.

The rising real estate price in China has brought over countless Japanese land developers, who have been busy building innumerable hotels, office towers, and shopping centers in places like Xian, Nanjing, Tianjin, and Suzhou. Japanese banking and financial service giants are increasingly active in China as well. In particular, venture capital companies are arriving in crowds. Top venture capitalist firm Softbank is already a major investor in numerous Chinese Internet and IT companies.

China Inc. and Japan

Chinese exports to Japan have been increasing rapidly. By 2004, China had replaced the United States as the top exporter to Japan. Chinese products in Japan are mostly consumer products. Their penetration has been greatly aided by Japan Inc.'s operations inside China.

Relying on low costs in China, Japan Inc. has adopted a strategy of manufacturing its vast range of products in China, then selling them in

Japan and elsewhere, including China itself. The cost advantages are tremendous, since the average Chinese manufacturing job pays only around $115 a month and the labor pool is vast. What is more, there is no labor law to protect the interests of the Chinese workers. As a result, employers have unlimited power over employees.

In addition to its trade activities, China Inc. has become increasingly active in Japan. Among other things, some Chinese companies are interested in acquiring Japanese assets as a way to obtain better technology, distribution networks, or both.

Several high-profile cases come to mind. First, Shanghai Electric Group acquired a bankrupt Japanese manufacturer of high-tech printers, Akiyama. Another purchase came from Guangdong-based Midea, a major home-appliances manufacturer, which acquired the entire microwave oven division from Sanyo Electric Co. Also, the Chinese company 999, a Shenzhen-based pharmaceutical and consumer-chemicals business, has an active joint venture with a Japanese pharmaceutical concern, the aim being to cross-sell each other's products.

Chinese purchases like this have shocked Japan Inc. But they have benefited all parties. Actually, unable to find buyers inside Japan, many distressed Japanese companies try to find buyers from the outside world, including China.

In the case of Shanghai Electric Group's purchase of Akiyama, made basically for its printer factory, the Chinese factory had been in distress itself. Before the acquisition, the Chinese firm's technology was three decades behind. Buying the Japanese asset benefited the company tremendously, and it now offers popular printers for the Chinese market and beyond. As such, it has saved numerous Japanese jobs on the one hand and produced better Chinese performance on the other.

Such acquisitions have become a popular way for Chinese firms to upgrade their technology and gain a new market at the same time. This has naturally concerned Japan Inc., which has always been more interested in building business empires headed by Japanese than in actually making money.

But China Inc. may not need to buy Japanese assets to advance its interests. Chinese firms can simply hire Japanese talent to work for them, for example. As a matter of fact, this is already happening.

This is what Skyworth, a leading Chinese consumer electronics company, did when it recently hired a veteran Matsushita engineer together with many of his research colleagues. The Japanese engineer has become a senior executive at Skyworth. Due to such activities, and for other reasons as well, the technological gap between Japan and

China is narrowing fast—faster than expected. The eroding of technological advantage has increasingly become a concern for Japan Inc.

In addition, many leading Chinese companies are actively expanding into Japan. So far, these efforts have met with limited success. The main reason is that Japan's domestic market has always been notoriously closed to foreign companies. Surprisingly, in many ways, Japan is not as open as China. This closed situation is not going to change anytime soon.

Typically, a more effective way to penetrate the Japanese market is via joint ventures with Japan Inc. So far, most of these joint ventures have been aimed at the Chinese market. But this is gradually changing, as more Chinese companies attempt to invest in Japan as well.

In more recent years, leading Chinese multinationals such as ZTE, TCL, and Haier have all increased their efforts to tap into the Japanese market. In particular, Huawei, a top Chinese telecom equipment manufacturer, has established joint ventures with NEC and Matsushita dealing with third-generation (3G) mobile phone technology.

One key reason behind Japan Inc.'s interest in forming joint ventures in this context is the quick development of many Chinese companies. Finally, China Inc. has achieved enough development that the Japanese multinationals must pay attention. All this was unheard of only 15 years ago.

Interdependence and Beyond

As the world's second largest economy, Japan has both advantages and challenges. The biggest advantage is that Japan has hundreds of truly global companies that are well equipped to operate anywhere it is beneficial for them to do so.

The biggest challenge is at home—Japan has had a two-decade economic slump. Deep-seated problems include high costs, low efficiency in many industries, and rampant overstaffing. The banking sector is still recovering from massive numbers of bad loans made during the "bubble economy" period and is also running into more bad debts.

These problems run very deep and are not likely to go away in the near future. The tightly closed Japanese market has backfired. Domestic stagnation virtually compels Japanese businesses to expand overseas— and China has been their overwhelming first choice.

At a deeper level, Japan Inc. is confronted with this reality: It needs to generate fat profits from overseas in order to sustain its declining operations — which are very often losing money — at home. This compels Japan Inc. to do even more overseas and in a hurry.

Unfortunately for an increasingly globalized Japan Inc., the Japanese political establishment has been behaving in a way that is contrary to its interests. The political leadership is keen to re-establish Japanese assertiveness, politically and militarily. This unresolved conflict has been causing wide debate within Japan.

Business interests never stand alone. Recent street protests in China and Korea concerned Japanese textbooks that minimize war crimes committed by the former imperial Japanese government; Japanese political leaders' glorification of war criminals; Japan's alleged interference in the Taiwan issue; and conflict over certain islands claimed by both China and Japan, among other issues. These events have heightened the conflict of interest between Japan Inc. and the Japanese government.

At the same time, Japan Inc.'s competitive edge is no longer as sharp as it was back in the 1980s. For example, both the EU and the United States surpassed Japan in total trade with China in 2004. China's trade with Australia, Eastern Europe, Latin America, and the rest of world has been growing fast.

Also, South Korea Inc. is investing more in China. Lately, the Korean investment has gone ahead of the Japanese. Leading South Korean names like LG, Samsung, and Hyundai have made huge progress in China, although they were late entrants into the Chinese market. LG did $10 billion in business in China in 2004, a level even the biggest Japanese brands have hardly reached.

So, Japan Inc. feels great pressure to do more in China, and do it bigger and better, for fear of losing out to Japan's global competitors. This reality is behind the current all-out commitment by Japan Inc. in China.

For now, China is less dependent on Japanese investment than it has been in the past, partly because international investment in China has been so massive. By 2005, more than $620 billion worth of foreign investment had entered China, with Japan accounting for only a fraction, about $72.59 billion.

Although Japanese investment is still significant, its relative importance is decreasing. The reason is that in all sectors where the Japanese invest, there are crowds of other players, both international and Chinese. Actually, at present there is overcrowding in all business sectors.

Especially in the past 10 years, domestic Chinese companies have developed significantly, and tens of thousands of them have become able to produce all sorts of products. China has become the top manufacturer for over 100 manufactured goods.

Furthermore, Japan has a high cost structure, while Chinese buyers generally prefer low-cost, but highly competitive, products and services. For example, both Indian and Russian software companies are far better equipped to sell in China than Japanese companies are.

Overall, even without the ongoing political disputes, Japan Inc. faces an increasingly uphill battle in China. Its entire business line faces tough competition from both China and international firms. Japanese products no longer have unique advantages as they did in the 1980s.

In the auto industry, for example, Honda and Toyota face competitors like GM, Volkswagen, and Hyundai. In home appliances and consumer electronics, which have been traditional strengths for Japanese firms, the domestic brands are improving fast, along with intense competition from other international brands. At this time, Japan Inc. has a small share in China's consumer products market.[1]

Japanese business competitiveness is being challenged from all directions. Therefore, finding new markets like China has become a top strategy for the Japanese to employ in order to increase their competitiveness. According to one international reporter, Japan is experiencing "a rude wakening."[2]

In general, Japan Inc. must continue to focus on China as its top growth strategy. This is why Japan Inc. put $6.53 billion—a new record—into China in 2005 despite the disagreements between the two nations. The Japanese multinationals are now in hot pursuit to expand in all business sectors, especially auto, telecom, financial services, consumer products, chemical, retail, and steel.

The increased Japanese efforts to tap into China do surprise many Chinese today. Such efforts are especially surprising given that the right-wing Japanese government is pursuing an opposite course, which continues to cause tensions in Asia and beyond.

One can predict that the opposing interests of Japan Inc. and the Japanese government will impact Japanese foreign policy more in the future. Traditionally, the close ties between business and the Japanese government have made it difficult for the government to act in a way that is contrary to the interests of the business community. Japanese foreign policy is more influenced by domestic politics than is widely believed. The government has every reason to try to make Japan part of the solution to regional conflicts rather than part of the problem. Japan's neighbors are watching eagerly for signs of this.

Chapter 26.

Japan's Past Aggressions vs. Current Affairs

Most people are aware of Japanese aggressions only in the period of 1894-1945. However, the reality is that Japan has been a key source of problems for Asia for more than eight centuries. Although these problems reached their height in the first half of the 20th century, Japan's past aggressions produced vast miseries for itself as well as for many other nations.

Has Japan changed? Japan has a democratic system, but this can hardly stop the government from whitewashing Japan's war atrocities, nor can it stop political leaders from honoring war criminals memorialized in the Yasukuni Shrine, which was founded by Japan's state religion in 1868.

The most basic issue is that Japan has yet to become more open. In this era, Japan has had a huge outward economic expansion, one that has reached the entire globe. But the society and market have been kept closed as much as possible. A closed Japan has produced vast adverse consequences not only for the outside world, but also for Japan itself.

This reality means that becoming part of the solution for a new century is still a difficult task for Japan. In the end, the Japanese people, and the world, could be misled again. Hence, there is every reason for the Japanese society to become more open.

Earlier Invasions

Starting in the 13th century or earlier, Japanese piracy was a major menace for East Asia, ending only at the close of the 16th century.[1] But this was no ordinary piracy, as tens of thousands of invaders were involved. They raided East Asia's coast, looting and killing, with the ultimate aim of establishing a permanent settlement on the continent of Asia.

In that period it was coastal China that suffered the most. Indeed, the Japanese pirates were a powerful military force, highly organized and well equipped. Also highly mobile, they often used a hit-and-run strategy. Each invasion involved several dozen battleships carrying thousands of armed men. They could raid any large coastal city, then move on to raid other places. Major Chinese cities such as Nanjing, Hongzhou, Ningbo, and Weihai fell repeatedly.[2]

These pirates may be comparable in some ways to the terrorists of our era, but the destruction they caused was much greater. Imagine the scale of disaster if 30,000 terrorists like Bin Laden raided New York one day, then moved on to Boston, Houston, and San Francisco. Only after a four-century fight was Japanese piracy eliminated.

By the mid-1500s, the Japanese threat became so great that quick action was needed. By then, several very creative Chinese generals had emerged. One of the most impressive was General Qi Jiguang (1528-1587), who is now remembered in somewhat the same way General Grant is in the United States. His army won many battles in Fujian and Zhejiang provinces.[3]

Soon the Japanese invaders became fearful about General Qi and his army. Indeed, he was a highly creative leader and man of mission. He built a new army from scratch, devised his own way of fighting, and won. He took a unique and careful approach to enlistment, personally selecting only honest, bold men. They were trained extensively under his personal guidance. This army became known as the *Qi army*.

The decisive battles took place on land in the early 1560s. By that time, the Japanese pirates had won many victories over the Chinese. More significantly, the victorious pirates built numerous land bases. Once on the land, the Japanese pirates lost much of their mobility and speed. They were more easily attacked by the Chinese army. Interestingly, Qi's army did not have the numerical advantage, but it was more determined and highly organized and thus become a fearsome fighting force.

But piracy was only a small part of the Japanese problem during that period. By the end of the 16th century, events took a nasty turn. This time it was the Japanese government army that invaded its neighbors. Though Japan eyed China for eventual occupation, it first wanted to establish a base in Korea. So the Japanese military invaded Korea in between 1592 and 1598.[4]

Again, the powerful Japanese army had a major weakness: Once they landed onshore, they were attacked from all sides. At the time, Korea had a weak government and army, and it was relatively easy for the Japanese army to land there. But the Japanese invaders were defeated quickly. The Korean citizens took defense into their own hands, and after some bitter fighting, the Japanese were expelled.

Modern War

By the late 19th century, beginning in 1868, a newly industrialized and united Japan emerged, but this meant more bloodshed in Asia and elsewhere. By then, Japan had a much better war machine, especially a modernized navy, millions of armed men, and bigger ambitions. Imperial Japan's aim was to become the master of the world if at all possible.

Apart from having better weapons and more armed men, imperial Japan pushed its state religion to a new height. The claim was that the Japanese were a "divine race," and the aim was to subdue all other people. Also, imperial Japan created a new slogan: "Commonwealth for Asia."

At the time, both China and Korea were very weak, and each confronted vast problems. Hence, no force was strong enough to contain the Japanese invaders. The superior Japanese force attacked anywhere and everywhere its battleships and army could reach. Again, both China and Korea fell victim in the new waves of Japanese aggression.

But that was not all, as victories produced more aggression. In 1941, imperial Japan went to Pearl Harbor. One might suspect that if the nation had had more resources, it would have invaded more regions.

Historical Parallels

There are close parallels between the Japanese piracy of the past and Japan's imperial aggression from 1894 to 1945 as far as war strategies are concerned. In the recent period, Japan's war machine again aimed at taking over Korea first. After its conquest of Korea, it took over Taiwan as booty for the war victory over China in 1894-1895. These two regions became footholds for Japan's all-out aggression in China and elsewhere beginning in 1931.

In its first move in 1931, from occupied Korea, Japan invaded northeastern China. From a strong base there, war efforts soon became full scale. In the second wave, as before, an invading fleet was sent to occupy the Shanghai-Hangzhou region in 1937. From these two bases, the invaders moved on into the hinterland.

In another parallel, both the early and the more recent invaders used a lightning strategy in both Korea and China, which was repeated at Pearl Harbor in 1941, as well as in other regions in Asia, including Malaysia, Indonesia, Thailand, the Philippines, and Singapore. The lightning strategy was especially successful in the first half of the 20th century.

Atrocities

The world is well aware of the war atrocities committed by Nazi Germany, less aware of the crimes committed by the imperial Japanese army. Hardly anyone could understand the reason the Nazis wanted to kill countless civilians. Hardly anyone could explain why the Japanese army killed tens of millions of innocent people, which served no military purpose at all.[5]

Today, Japanese citizens, nicely dressed, have the very best manners, which makes it difficult to imagine the barbaric acts that occurred only six decades ago. Indeed, massacres took place everywhere the invaders put down their boots, from the Philippines to Singapore and Malaysia to Korea and China.

In particular, rape by Japanese soldiers occurred on a huge scale, much greater than among the Nazi Germans. Countless prisoners, Westerners and Asians alike, suffered inhumane treatment. But the most extensive and prolonged killings took place inside China. The Nanking Massacre in 1937-1938 is best known to the world, but this was by no means an isolated case. There were many massacres. Killings that took place in rural regions are less well known even today. Innumerable villages were wiped out, especially in northern China.

In one case, many thousands of Chinese villagers were killed when they were suspected of helping some U.S. pilots. This happened during a U.S. bombing mission on Japan in 1942. Short of fuel, some of the pilots made emergency landings in southern China; naturally they were helped by Chinese. Soon afterward, the Japanese soldiers took revenge by killing thousands of villagers in the rescue region.

The most dreadful reality is that for thousands of years, Japan has been a good student of China, learning eagerly about Chinese culture, technology, and arts, among other things. Japan's written language, fashion, architecture, arts, and literature, among many other components of civilized life, have all been heavily copied from China. Several leading Japanese cities, for example, were built through imitation of the Chinese capital, Xian, in the Tang Dynasty.

Among the war atrocities, it is little known that imperial Japan employed chemical germs against civilians, even in their occupied territories. Imperial Japan had a massive, secret, and well-executed plan to develop biological weapons from experiments using human guinea pigs. These and other acts of imperial Japan were outside any civilized boundary. Perhaps the aim of these barbaric acts of killing was to enforce the idea of the Japanese as a "divine race." After all, a "divine race" must prove itself in front of "inferior" races. Indeed, this was how the Japanese were taught in the war period.

A new book, *A Plague Upon Humanity: The Hidden History of Japan's Biological Warfare Program*, presents much evidence on Japan's biowar atrocities.[6] The biowar took a huge toll. The author calls it "genocide" to underscore the fact that a stunning 580,000 people were killed in this way. The victims lived in many parts of China, ranging from northeastern provinces to central and south coastal provinces. Furthermore, many wartime germs still remain in numerous sites, continuing to cause harm.

War Criminals at Yasukuni Shrine

Huge changes have taken place inside Japan since 1945, but vast problems have remained. True, Japan established a democracy under U.S. supervision. Yet this Japanese democracy has not helped Japan to deal rationally with its war past. The Japanese government has tried hard to hide the war atrocities. Worse still, its leaders honor war criminals at the Yasukuni Shrine. All this naturally causes anger among Japan's neighbors.

So, today's Japan is very different from Germany still. Since World War II, the German government has been willingly condemning the Nazi crimes, but with regard to Japanese war crimes, the Japanese government has done just the opposite. It has taken six decades for Japan to offer some apologetic words. Why do the Japanese leaders continue to honor convicted war criminals even today?

Such acts irritate the victimized nations. How can any civilized nation forget these kinds of atrocities? It has been said that wrongs done to a single man are wrongs done to all men. Imperial Japan was responsible for the killing of 20 million people in China alone. Who has the right to forget this? Above all, condemning the wrongs is the only way leading to peace in the future.

What is most troublesome is this: On one day, the Japanese leaders offer some comforting words, but on the next day they backtrack. This is what happened when Japanese Prime Minister Junichiro Koizumi made a public apology on April 22, 2005. His speech, delivered at the opening ceremony of the Asia-Africa Summit in Jakarta, was attended by many world leaders.

He said, "In the past, Japan, through its colonial rule and aggression, caused tremendous damage and suffering for the people of many countries, particularly those of Asian nations."

He went on, "Japan squarely faces these facts of history in a spirit of humility . . . with feelings of deep remorse and heartfelt apology always engraved in mind, Japan has resolutely maintained, consistently since the end of World War II, [the policy of] never turning into a military power but [rather] an economic power, its principle of resolving all matters by peaceful means, without recourse [to] the use of force."

This speech was well received; the world seemed to feel that a sad chapter was closed. But afterward, the prime minister and many other Japanese ministers continued to honor the convicted warlords as usual. Apart from the offensiveness of these acts, they violate the Japanese constitution, which prohibits combining religion and the state.[7]

According to the post-World War II International Military Tribunal for the Far East, there are three types of war crimes: Class A, crimes against peace; Class B, conventional war crimes; and Class C, crimes against humanity.

Under the tribunal, more than 300,000 Japanese were charged with Class B and C war crimes. Twenty-five military and political leaders were convicted of Class A crimes. Of those, 12 warlords, including wartime prime minister General Hideki Tojo, General Seishiro Itagaki, General Iwane Matsui (the leader of the Nanking Massacre), and four others sentenced to death by the tribunal, are enshrined at Yasukuni. Two others, also enshrined at Yasukuni, were charged with Class A crimes but died before their trials were completed.

The Class A indictment accused the convicts of promoting a scheme of conquest that "contemplated and carried out . . . murdering, maiming and ill-treating prisoners of war [and] civilian internees . . . plundering public and private property, wantonly destroying cities, towns and villages beyond any justification of military necessity; [perpetrating] mass murder, rape, pillage, brigandage, torture and other barbaric cruelties upon the helpless civilian population of the overrun countries." The victim nations cover most Asian countries as well as the United States, United Kingdom, and Australia, among others.

More Irritations

Many Asians believe that the Japanese government has aimed to alter history, perhaps in order to rebuild the old Japanese ideology. Acts along these lines are common today. For example, some senior Japanese politicians, such as Japan's Chief Cabinet Secretary Shinzo Abe (the newly elected prime minister) and Japanese Foreign Minister Taro Aso, have claimed that the Japanese Class A war criminals are not actually criminals according to Japanese law. Therefore, worshiping these "war criminals" is the right thing for the Japanese government to do.[7] Taro Aso even suggests that the Japanese emperor should pay respect to these war criminals by visiting the shrine.

Such intention to alter history has taken on a new passion. The Japanese officials just mentioned claim that Japanese aggressions have produced many good things for the victim nations. On this, a *New York*

Times editorial included the following comment:[8]

"Japan's new foreign minister, Taro Aso . . . has been neither honest nor wise in the inflammatory statements he has been making about Japan's disastrous era of militarism, colonialism and war crimes that culminated in World War II. . . . Yet public discourse in Japan and modern history lessons in its schools have never properly come to terms with Japan's responsibility for such terrible events as the mass kidnapping and sexual enslavement of young Korean women, the biological warfare experiments carried out on helpless prisoners of war, and the sadistic slaughter of hundreds of thousands of Chinese civilians in the city of Nanjing. . . ."

The editorial went further: "That is why so many Asians have been angered by a string of appalling remarks Aso has made since being named foreign minister last autumn. Two of the most recent were his suggestion that Japan's emperor ought to visit the Yasukuni Shrine, where 14 Japanese war criminals are among those honored, and his claim that Taiwan owes its high educational standards to enlightened Japanese policies during the 50-year occupation that began when Tokyo grabbed the island as war booty from China in 1895. . . ."

One wonders why these Japanese politicians wish to honor the executed warlords today. Perhaps they hope that this is a way to regain political assertiveness. This in turn may call for a restoration of the old national ideology.

But the Japanese government seems to have a bigger purpose. In particular, confronting a fast-developing China, the Japanese government may hope to find ways to contain it. On this issue, an international journalist told me, "The Japanese are very emotional over China's quick development."

But is it not a basic reality that Japan is one of the biggest beneficiaries of China's development? The same journalist noted, "Not really. Some Japanese feel that they must do things to contain a rising China."

Another opinion on the latest Japanese gestures in relation to China is that Japan may hope to get more international help toward containing China's development. On this issue, an international businessman noted, "The Japanese government is fearful about China's growth, hence it must find all possible ways to reach out for this end."

Larger Events

This effort on the part of the Japanese government to alter history has affected Japanese society in no small way. For one thing, Japanese youth have a difficult environment in which to learn about history as it actually happened, which impedes their ability to learn to deal properly with the world—not a good thing.

An Australian man told me that a group of Japanese students stated to him that there had never been a war between Japan and Australia. Evidently they had no idea that only six decades ago, Australia was bombed by the Japanese.

Japan's closed society is not helping its government to become more rational. Even inside Japan, more and more Japanese citizens feel the need for Japan to become more open and more rational. One high-profile Japanese is Tsuneo Watanabe, 79 years old, chairman of the Yomiuri Shimbun group, the biggest Japanese newspaper company. He talks about the need for Japan to move into a new direction.

Watanabe said, "Ever since I was in university, I always argued against war. In the last war, several million people died in the name of the emperor. I was drafted and made to work like a slave as a buck private. . . . During the war, I truly felt that no nation should be allowed to do such things. Especially in the name of the emperor. . . . It is wrong for the prime minister to visit such a place [the Yasukuni Shrine]."[9]

Some Japanese citizens have taken the Japanese government to court to demand a separation of government and religion. But unfortunately, such claims have been denied in court. The action of these Japanese citizens required tremendous boldness, which is rather unusual in the Japanese society, where the collective interest is placed above all.

Outward Expansion vs. a Closed Society

Since World War II, Japan's military expansion has stopped; instead the nation has pursued an outward economic expansion. At the same time, however, Japan's society and market have been very much closed. Reluctance to admit past crimes coexists with a closed Japanese society even today.

Indeed, many international trading partners feel that doing business with Japan is very troublesome. The Japanese government has created countless barriers to the entrance of foreign parties. Entering the Japanese market takes more than pricing, quality, and competitiveness. For example, there are several hundred technical tests required if one wants to sell beef to Japan, which is one of the ways for the Japanese government to stop free trade.

Yet Japan Inc. now faces huge challenges at home, which has partly happened for lack of foreign "wolves." This is so simply because a closed network prohibits competition and thus dynamics and progress.

One traditional practice within the Japanese business formations is to allow group members to sell uncompetitive components at uncompetitive prices to other group members. Naturally, this has done harm on the Japanese competitiveness, not to mention other things.

The closed character of Japan has backfired in this era. What is really behind it? Japan lacks of outside competition. As such, the Japanese economy has lost much of its competitive edge. This is shown in the stock market and real estate crashes as well as the general distress of a vast number of Japanese companies and banks.

This depressed condition cannot really be altered under a closed society—as the Japanese public is beginning to realize, though painfully.

The closed Japanese system is based on ancient tribal culture rather than modern management, which runs opposite of what Francis Fukuyama says.[10] Modern Japanese businesses are still organized like ancient Japanese tribes. Naturally, this has led to all sorts of abnormal conduct.

For now, under internal pressures, Japan's market is beginning to open up, though slowly and painstakingly. Harsh realities have forced some to take this new attitude. Opening up to foreign talent, ideas, and capital has become a necessity for Japan in order to regain growth. This is a healthy development both for Japan and for the outside world.

Companies are beginning to hire foreign managers for senior Japanese posts. For example, Sony recently selected a foreigner to serve as the new Sony CEO. Why?

Sony has been doing badly, and its profits have been reduced to a small fraction of those only five years ago. In general, very painfully, more and more Japanese companies are embarking on a more open path, but slowly and on a small scale.

More Internal Woes

Greater openness for Japan is all needed if the nation wishes to become a truly modern, progressive society. Under the old closed environment, Japan has vast weaknesses. But hiding problems causes even more harm.

In particular, individual citizens are still weak in relation to institutions and organizations. As one example, the tradition of employees working for one organization for life is still strong. This creates a unique Japanese behavior: *The collective will far stands above that of all individuals.* As such, it is very difficult for typical Japanese to speak out openly about what is in their mind.

Furthermore, individuals' concerns can be easily swept away by organizations and institutions. To many educated Japanese, unwanted international tensions are caused by an irresponsible government, but there is very little they can do about it.

Organizations and institutions dominate citizens' life in ways that are nonexistent in the West. But these organizations and institutions face enormous difficulties in becoming more open even if the traditional practices do them more harm than good.

In this environment, naturally, rational handling of Japan's war past is very difficult, to say the least. On the contrary, pretending that problems do not exist is still common. Undemocratic measures are taken.

For example, Iris Chang's book, *Rape of Nanking*, has still not been published in the Japanese language. A few years ago, a Japanese publisher tried to do just that and received nasty threats. So the company had to abandon the project, although copies of the book in Japanese had already been printed.

Some former Japanese soldiers have dared to speak up about their war experiences and the atrocities committed back then, but their voices are often criticized by main street in today's Japan. Some of them have even received personal threats. They have been called traitors. Some Japanese citizens feel that the popular denial of past war crimes is "Japan's national shame."[11]

Today, Japan's closed society remains the major weakness standing in the way of Japan's joining the global community in spirit and practice. All this directly contradicts the spirit of democracy. Again, today's Japan is very different from Germany although both nations have democratic institutions. In daily life, Japanese citizens still have a very weak role in the society, and this has created a weakness in Japanese life as a whole.

On this issue, an international businessman noted, "On the surface, the Japanese society is open to foreigners. But deep inside, it is still difficult for the Japanese to walk out of their inclusiveness. They still face enormous problems in integrating into a truly open life in spirit as of now."

For Japan to become a truly modern, open society, the road ahead will hardly be smooth. Help will be required from the entire world. Even then, making progress will take a very long time and will be a painful process. But there is no alternative and no shortcut. Nevertheless, once Japan becomes more open, the biggest beneficiary will be the Japanese people.

Notes

Chapter 1

1. *Xinhua News,* May 2, 2006.
2. For information on rural migrants, see, for example, George Zhibin Gu, *China's Global Reach: Markets, Multinationals, and Globalization,* revised edition, Fultus, 2006; Hao Zaijin, *80 Million Migrants,* Beijing: China Social Publisher, 1996; Chen Guidi and Chun Tao, *An Investigation on China's Farmers,* Beijing: People's Literature Publisher, 2004; Liu Huailian, *The Issues of China's Rural Migrant Workers,* Beijing: People's Publisher, 2005; and China's State Council Special Research Team (editor), *Investigation Reports of China's Migrant Workers,* Beijing: China Yanshi Publisher, 2006.
3. China State Travel Bureau Statistics.

Chapter 2

1. For further information, see note 2 of Chapter 1; Li Qiang, *Urban Migran Workers and Social Stratification in China,* Beijing: Social Science Academic Press, 2004; and Wu Si, *The Bloody Payment Law: Surviving Games of China's History,* Beijing: China Workers' Publisher, 2003; Xia Geng, *A Study of the Transformation of the Dual Economic Structure in China's Urban and Rural Areas,* Beijing: Peking University, 2005.
2. For more information, see, for example, George Zhibin Gu, *Made in China: National and Business Players and Challengers in the 21st Century,* Portuguese edition, Centro Atlantico, 2005 (English version will be forthcoming in 2007).
3. For more information, see, for example, George Zhibin Gu, *China's Global Reach: Markets, Multinationals, and Globalization,* revised edition, Fultus, 2006; Guo Wanda and Zhu Wenhui, *Made in China: World Factory Is Turning to China,* Jiangsu People's Publisher, 2003; and Liu Zhebiu et al., *Made in China in the Yangzi Delta,* Beijing: China Renmin University Press, 2006.

Chapter 4

1. *China's Government Annual Report,* 2005.
2. Robert Skye, *Globalization and European Welfare States,* Macmillan, 2001.
3. Chalmers Johnson, *The Sorrows of Empire: Militarism, Secrecy, and the End of the Republic,* Owl Books, 2005; William Bonner and Addison Wiggin, *Empire of Debt: The Rise of an Epic Financial Crisis,* Wiley, 2005; Addison Wiggin, *The Demise of the Dollar . . . And Why It's Great for Your Investments,* Wiley, 2005.

Chapter 6

1. *Shenzhen Special Zone Daily,* September 12, 2006.

Chapter 8

1. "An Interview with McDonald's China CEO," *Sunshine Daily,* June 26, 2006, p. B9.
2. *Win Weekly,* April 7, 2006.
3. Alain Peyrefitte, L'empire Immobile ou Le Choc des Mondes, Fayard, 1989.

Chapter 10

1. *Shenzhen Government Annual Report,* 2006.
2. "New Methods of Dealing with Court Execution Problems," *Shenzhen Special Zone Daily,* May 10, 2006, p. A7.
3. *Sunshine Daily,* April 12, 2006.
4. George Zhibin Gu, China's Global Reach: Markets, Multinationals, and Globalization, Fultus, 2006.
5. *Sunshine Daily,* July 12, 2006, p. A2.

Chapter 12

1. Chen Guidi and Chun Tao, *An Investigation on China's Farmers,* Beijing: People's Literature Publisher, 2004.
2. China Statistics.
3. "Court Corruption of Wuhan," *China Newsweek,* no. 176, April 19, 2004, pp. 22-30.

Chapter 13

1. Lao Zi, *The Tao Principle,* Shaanxi Travel Publisher, 2004, Chapter 17.
2. For more information, see, for example, Guo Zhishen et al. (editors), *Chinese Historical Chronicles,* 11 volumes, Shanghai: Century Group Publisher and Shanghai People's Publisher, 2004; Chen Pai et al. (editors), *China's General History,* 32 volumes, Beijing: Economic Daily Publisher, 1999; Li Guozhang and Zhao Changping (editors), *New Edition of 25 Historical Dynasties,* Shanghai: Shanghai Ancient Books Publisher, 1998.
3. Li Guozhang and Zhao Changping (editors) in note 2.
4. Guo Zhishen et al. (editors) in note 2.
5. This point was one issue in the great intellectual debate and the consequent government purge in the so-called Anti-Rightist Movement of 1957. See, for example, Niu Han and Deng Jiuoing (editors), *Grass on Plains: Remembering Anti-Rightist Movement,* Beijing: Economics Publisher, 1998, pp. 125-127.
6. Given by Ren Yuling, a government official, in "Two National Conferences Pay Attention to Civil Servants: Member of Political Consultancy Conference Demands Government Reductions," *Xinhua News,* March 8, 2005.
   http://news.xinhuanet.com/newscenter/2005-03/08/content_2666994.htm.

7. Given by Zhou Tianyong, in "Experts Claiming the Ratio of Civil Servants over Citizens 1:18 and Demanding Reductions," *Legal Daily* (via *South Daily*), June 14, 2005.
    http://southcn.com.cn/law/fzxw/200506140007.htm.

8. For background information, see, for example, Xin Xiangyang, *Decisions Inside Red Wall – the Reasons for China's Government Structural Reform*, Beijing: China Economics Publisher, 1998; Wang Jinnian, *China's Government Trimming: The Realities and Thoughts on the 4th Institutional Reform*, Jinan Publisher, 1998.

9. These numbers first appear in Survey Project Research Team (editor), *Analysis on China's 3rd Population Survey*, Beijing: China Fiscal Economics Publisher, 1987. For further information, see Xin Xiangyang, *Decisions Inside Red Wall – the Reasons for China's Government Structural Reform*, Beijing: China Economics Publisher, 1998; Wang Jinnian, *China's Government Trimming: The Realities and Thoughts on the 4th Institutional Reform*, Jinan Publisher, 1998; and Chen Guidi and Chun Tao, *An Investigation on China's Farmers*, Beijing: People's Literature Publisher, 2004, pp. 166-176.

10. See note 2; Sun Wenliang, *Emperor Zhu Yuanzhang*, Jilin History Archive Publisher, 1996; and Wu Si, *The Bloody Payment Law: Surviving Games of China's History*, Beijing: China Workers' Publisher, 2003.

11. Joseph Needham, *Science and Civilization*, multi-volumes, Cambridge University Press, 1956 on; Andre Gunder Frank, *ReOrient: Global Economy in the Asian Age*, University of California Press, 1998; and also Frank's afterword in George Zhibin Gu, *China's Global Reach: Markets, Multinationals, and Globalization*, revised edition, Fultus, 2006.

Chapter 14

1. Wang Meng, *My First Half Life*, Flower City Publisher, 2006.

2. Li Rui, Collected Works of Li Rui, volume 1: Truth of the Lushan Conference; volume 2: The Tragedies of Mao Zedong in His Late Years; volume 3: First-hand Experience of the Great Leap Forward, South Publisher, 1999; Luo Pinghan, History of Rural People's Commune, Fujian People's Publisher, 2003.

3. See Li Rui, volume 1, in note 2.

4. See Li Rui, volume 1, in note 2.

5. Chen Guidi and Chun Tao, *An Investigation on China's Farmers*, Beijing: People's Literature Publisher, 2004.

6. For various discussions, see, for example, Shao Daosheng, *The Diseases of the Nation: Reflections on China's Ongoing Corruption*, Beijing: Hualing Publisher, 2000; Zhang Shuguang, *The Natural Road to Prosperity*, Guangdong Economic Publisher, 1999; He Qinglian, *Traps of Modernization*, Beijing: Today's China Publisher, 1998; Li Bin, *Overdrafted Power: A Deeper Observation of Misinvestment by the Local Governments*, Hubei People's Publisher, 2003; CCTV Economy Half-Hour Team, *China's Experiments*, Beijing: China Water and Power Publisher, 2005; Su Xin, *New China's*

Economic History, CCP Central Party School Publisher, 1999; and Chen Guidi and Chun Tao, *An Investigation on China's Farmers,* Beijing: People's Literature Publisher, 2004.

7. A Beijing reader, "On the Market Movement and the Changing Function of Government," *Caijing,* pp. 19-20, no. 3, February 6, 2006.

8. For more information, see, for example, references in note 4; Long Xicheng (editor), *Macro China,* Beijing: China Machine Press, 2003.

9. For various discussions see references in notes 4 and 6; George Zhibin Gu, *Made in China: Players and Challengers in the 21st Century,* Portuguese edition, Centro Atlantico, 2005 (English edition will be forthcoming in 2007).

10. George Zhibin Gu, China's Global Reach: Markets, Multinationals, and Globalization, revised, Fultus, 2006.

11. *South Metro Daily,* April 9, 2006, p. A11.

12. *Sunshine Daily,* June 13, 2006, p. B4.

Chapter 15

1. *Win Weekly,* March 17, 2006, p. 33.

2. Shenzhen Special Zone Daily, May 27, 2006, p. A3.

Chapter 16

1. For various discussions on central plan, see for examples, Su Xin, *New China's Economic History,* Beijing: CCP Central School Publisher, 1999; Wang Junwei, *Struggles: From Great Leap Forward and Western Imported Leap Forward to Soft Landing,* Beijing: Jin Cheng Publisher, 1998; Zhibin Gu, *China Beyond Deng: Reform in the PRC,* McFarland, 1991.

2. Xinhua News, August 1, 2006.

3. For further discussions on Japan's banking reform, see for example, George Zhibin Gu, *China's Global Reach: Markets, Multinationals, and Globalization,* revised, Fultus, 2006.

Chapter 17

1. Dai Po (editor), *Sell-Buy War under Control,* Beijing: China Machine Press, 2003.

2. These cases are widely reported in the Chinese media, for example, *Jingji Magazine,* no. 4, 2004, and *Caijing,* no. 5, March 21, 2005.

3. *Xinhua News,* April 29, 2006; "The End of the De Long Myth," *Caijing,* no. 8, April 20, 2004.

Chapter 18

1. *Fortune,* July, 2006.

Chapter 19

1. William Ratliff, "Pragmatism over Ideology: China's Relations with

Venezuela," *China Brief, Jamestown Foundation,* volume 6, issue 6, March 15, 2006; "Red Dragon, Black Gold," *Hoover Digest,* no. 2, Spring 2005. Also see Kerry Dambaugh and Mark P. Sullivan, "China's Growing Interest in Latin America," *CRS Report to Congress,* April 20, 2005, *http://fpc.state.gov/documents/organization/45464.pdf;* "China and Latin America: Magic or Realism," *Economist,* December 29, 2004, www.economist.com/World/la/displayStory.cfm?story_id=3521240.

2. *Clyde Prestowitz, Three Billion New Capitalists: The Great Shift of Wealth and Power to the East,* New York: Basic Books, 2005.
3. Tu Dongxiao, "TCL Faces Uncertain Future," *Xin Caijing,* no. 1, 2005, p. 49.
4. John G. Spooner, "Lenovo, It's Time to Grow Up," eWeek, http://www.eweek.com/article2/0,1895,1952608,00.asp.
5. *Asia Times,* April 5, 2006.
6. *China Daily,* May 26, 2006.
7. For further discussions, see, for example, George Zhibin Gu, *China's Global Reach: Markets, Multinationals, and Globalization,* Fultus, 2006.

Chapter 20

1. *Win Weekly,* May 12, 2006, pp. 17-18.
2. Xiang Noung, "A Chinese Chipmaker that Attracts Attention for Global Giants," *IT Times Weekly,* pp. 40-49, January 20, 2006.
3. Shenzhen Special Zone Daily, May 19, 2006, p. A42.

Chapter 21

1. "China's Hu Jintao Offers Taiwan Negotiations on 'Equal Basis'," *Bloomberg,* April 16, 2006.
2. Some thoughts on a Chinese federation in a broader context are presented in Zhibin Gu, *China Beyond Deng: Reform in the PRC,* McFarland, 1991.

Chapter 22

1. For more information on Taiwanese business in mainland China, see, George Zhibin Gu, *China's Global Reach,* Trafford, 2005; and also references in note 3 below.
2. Richard Chang, "Taiwan's Silicon Invasion," *Business Week,* December 9, 2002. For additional information on Taiwan Inc. in the mainland, see references in note 3 below.
3. Huang Wanhua, "Trust-Mart's Potential Selling and Its Impacts," *Win Weekly,* May 12, 2006, p. 15.
4. Ting-I Tsai, "Forced to Choose, China or Taiwan," *Asia Times,* December 14, 2005; Guy de Jonquieres, "Taiwan's Troubles," *Financial Times,* May 29, 2006; Craig Meer, "The Politics of Cross-strait Business," *Asia Times,* March 9, 2006; Sam Ng, "Taiwanese Gold Rush to China," *Asia Times,* June 30, 2004; Mac Williams Bishop, "Taiwan High-tech Jobs to China: Fact vs. Fiction," *Asia Times,* August 10, 2004; and Jason Dean, "Collateral Damage," *Far East Economic Review,* July 24, 2004.

5. Craig Meer, "Diminishing Status of Taiwan's Status Quo," *Asia Times,* March 1, 2006; Kathrin Hille, "New Challenges for Taiwanese Investors," *Financial Times,* April 5, 2006.

Chapter 23

1. For various discussions, see, for example, Edward Friedman and Bruce Gilley (editors), *Asia's Giants: Comparing China and India,* Palgrave, 2005; Jairam Ramesh, *Making Sense of Chindia: Reflections on China and India,* India Research Press, 2006; Pallavi Aiyar, "China-India IT Cooperation: One 'Pagoda' Short," *Asia Times,* March 23, 2006, and, "Chindia: Not Quite a Juggernaut Yet," *Asia Times,* September 16, 2006; Anna Greenspan, "China's Hardware, India's Software," February 8, 2006; Indrajit Basu, "China Wily, India Shy," *Asia Times,* April 14, 2005; "China and India: The Challenge," *Business Week,* August 22, 2005, http://www.businessweek.com/magazine/content/05_34/b3948401.htm; and Jing-dong Yuan, "Promises and Problems," *Asia Times,* April 9, 2005.
2. Amartya Sen, *Development as Freedom,* First Anchor Books, 2005.
3. For more information on this issue, see George Zhibin Gu, *China's Global Reach: Markets, Multinationals, and Globalization,* revised edition, Fultus, 2006; and Jagdish Bhagwati, *In Defence of Globalization,* Oxford University Press, 2005.

Chapter 24

1. T.N. Srinivasan and Suresh D. Tendulkar, *Reintegrating India with World Economy,* Institute of International Economics, 2003.
2. Gurcharan Das, India Unbound: The Social and Economic Revolution from Independence to the Global Information Age, p. 3, Knopf, 2001.
3. Mao Zengyu (editor), Searching for the Rootcause of Corruption: Will China Become a Rent-seeking Society?, Beijing: China Economics Publisher, 1999.
4. Lu Lei, "Breaking Down the Heilongjiang Chains of Selling Government Posts," May 2, 2005, no. 9, pp. 24-35.
5. Lu Lei, "Breaking Down the Heilongjiang Chains of Selling Government Posts," May 2, 2005, no. 9, p. 26.

Chapter 25

1. George Zhibin Gu, *China's Global Reach: Markets, Multinationals, and Globalization,* revised, Fultus, 2006.
2. Henny Sender, "Japan Inc—a Rude Wakening," *Far East Economic Review, www.feer.com,* September 3, 2003.

Chapter 26

1. Ray Huang, *1587: A Year of No Significance,* Yale University Press, 1981; Frederick Mote and Denis C. Twitchett et al. (editors), *The Cambridge History of China, The Ming Dynasty, 1368-1644,* volumes 7 and 8, Cambridge

University Press, 1998; John Whitney Hall et al. (serial editors), *The Cambridge History of Japan*, volumes 3 and 4, Cambridge University Press, 1999.

2. Ray Huang in note 1.

3. Ray Huang in note 1.

4. References in note 1; Ki-Baik Lee, *A New History of Korea*, Harvard University Press, 2005; Carter Eckert et al., *Korea Old and New: A History*, Harvard Korea Institute, 1991.

5. John Rabe and Erwin Wickert, *Good Man of Nanking: The Dairies of John Rabe*, Knopf, 2000; Iris Chang, *The Rape of Nanking: The Forgotten Holocaust of World War II*, Penguin, 1998; Yuki Tanaka and Tushiyuki Tanaka, *Hidden Horrors: Japanese War Crimes in World War II*, Westview Press, 1998; Yuki Tanaka, *Japan's Comfort Women: The Military and Involuntary Prostitution During War and Occupancy*, Routledge, 2001.

6. Daniel Barenblatt, *A Plague Upon Humanity: The Hidden History of Japan's Biological Warfare Program*, Harper Collins, 2004; also, Sheldon H. Harris, *Factory of Death: Japanese Biological Warfare, 1932-45 and the American Cover-Up*, Taylor and Francis, 2002; Hal Gold, *Unit 731 Testimony: Japan's War Time Human Experimentation Program*, Tuttle Publisher, 2004; Lawrence Rees, *Horror in the East: Japan and the Atrocities in the East*, Da Capo, 2002; Peter Li and International Citizens' Forum on War Crimes and Redress (editors), *Japanese War Crimes*, Transaction Publishers, 2003; Barbara J. Brooks, *Japan's Imperial Diplomacy: Consuls, Treaty Ports, and War in China, 1895-1938*, University of Hawaii Press, 2000; Steve I. Levine and James C. Hsiung (editors), *China's Bitter Victory: The War with Japan 1937-45*, M. E. Sharpe, 2003.

7. Christopher Reed, "Emperor's New Clothes," *New Statesman*, November 21, 2005; Robert Marquand, "Tokyo Teacher Embattled Over War History: City Official Said Japan Never Invaded Korea," *Christian Science Monitor*, November 22, 2005;

8. "Japan's Offensive Minister," *New York Times*, February 13, 2006.

9. Yomiuri, "Asahi Editorial Chiefs Call for a National Memorial," February 8, 2006, Asahi,
http://www.asahi.com/english/Herald-asahi/TKY200602080515.html.

10. Francis Fukuyama, *Trust: Human Nature and the Reconstitution of Social Order*, New York: Free Press, 1996.

11. Katsuichi Honda and others, *The Nanjing Massacre: A Japanese Journalist Confronts Japan's National Shame*, East Gate Books, 1999.

About the Author

George Zhibin Gu, a native of Xian in central China, is a journalist/consultant based in Guangdong, China. He obtained his education at Nanjing University in China and Vanderbilt University and the University of Michigan in the United States. He holds two MS degrees and a PhD from the University of Michigan.

For the past two decades, he has been an investment banker and business consultant with an emphasis on China. His work focuses on helping international multinationals to invest in China and helping Chinese companies to expand overseas. He has worked for Prudential Securities, Lazard, and State Street Bank, among others. He generally covers mergers and acquisitions, venture capital, business expansion, and restructuring.

The author is also a journalist on China and its relations with the world. His articles or columns have appeared in *Asia Times, Beijing Review, The Seoul Times, Financial Sense, Gurus Online, Money Week, Online Opinion, Asia Venture Capital Journal,* and *Sinomania,* among others. He has written three other books, *China's Global Reach: Markets, Multinationals, and Globalization* (revised edition, Fultus, 2006), *Made in China: National and Business Players and Challengers in the 21st Century* (English edition forthcoming, Fall 2007; Portuguese edition, Centro Atlantico, 2005); and *China Beyond Deng: Reforms in the PRC* (McFarland, 1991). He is a member of the World Association of International Studies hosted by Stanford University.

Printed in the United States
71171LV00002B/154-165